REVOLUTIONARY DIPLOMACY

Revolutionary Diplomacy

CHINESE FOREIGN POLICY AND THE
UNITED FRONT DOCTRINE

J. D. Armstrong

UNIVERSITY OF CALIFORNIA PRESS
Berkeley · Los Angeles · London

University of California Press
Berkeley and Los Angeles, California

University of California Press, Ltd.
London, England

Copyright © 1977 by
The Regents of the University of California

ISBN 0-520-03251-9
Library of Congress Catalog Card Number: 76-14315
Printed in the United States of America
Designed by Dave Pauly

1- 09- 79

Contents

Preface

An intrinsic logical conundrum has bedevilled attempts to weigh the influence of ideology in the foreign policies of Communist states. On the one hand, it is relatively easy to demonstrate that any specific international act by a Communist state may be explained by factors other than ideology, such as strategic interests or economic advantage. Hence, it is difficult in any single instance to point confidently to ideological causation. On the other hand, Marxism-Leninism has so many facets and is so flexible in its role as a guide to action that it is equally difficult to maintain that it was not a factor in the making of a particular foreign policy decision.

Such circularity is inseparable from the normal analytical approach, that of commencing with observable behaviour (such as a foreign policy decision) and proceeding to seek an explanation of it. This study has, as it were, reversed the normal approach by starting with explanation, or more accurately explanatory paradigm, and then proceeding to observable behaviour. No momentous breakthrough is claimed as a consequence of this cunning strategem, but I believe that it has produced some fresh insights into China's foreign policy and that it may offer some opportunities for further research and refinement.

My thanks are due to a number of individuals who have provided considerable help at various stages in the writing of this book. Coral Bell of Sussex University and Michael Leifer of the London School of Economics gave me much early support. I should like also to express my thanks, in their due proportions, to Ian Adie, Carsten Holbraad, Geoffrey Jukes, and Fred Teiwes, who shared in the supervision of this work in its previous incarnation as a Ph.D. thesis at the Australian National University. I am deeply indebted to Geoffrey Warner of Hull University for his unfailing encouragement and friendship. Most of all, my gratitude goes to Maggie for her patience and support throughout a sometimes difficult period.

Introduction

The principal question that is posed in this study is, what has been the influence of Mao's united front doctrine on China's foreign policy? A related but secondary question is also considered: In what ways, if any, has China's participation in the international system caused Peking to revise its conception of a united front in world politics?

Insofar as Mao's thoughts about united fronts are part of the total array of theories and operational principles that make up the Chinese Communist "ideology," this essay considers one aspect of the relationship between ideology and foreign policy. Since this question has long been the subject of a mostly inconclusive and often circular academic debate, I shall state briefly my reasons for returning to it here. The first is that the problem is no less important because it admits of no easy solution. Indeed, with the breakdown in the twentieth century of even the limited consensus over norms and values that permitted a great power concert to exist for part of the nineteenth, the question is clearly one of major significance in contemporary international relations. Since China has become in many ways a symbol of the postwar ideological challenge to the established order in world politics, the question is particularly relevant in a study of China's foreign policy. Finally, by combining a strictly limited focus of enquiry with a systematic approach to the problem it may be possible to overcome some of the analytical difficulties that surround the larger issue of the relation of ideas to social practice. This point is argued more fully in the following pages.

IDEOLOGY AND "REALISM"

The Concise Oxford Dictionary defines "ideology" as follows: "Science of ideas; visionary speculation; manner of thinking characteristic of a class or individual; ideas at the basis of some economic or political theory or system."[1] The considerable differences of meaning among these four definitions are easily explained, for the dictionary has simply provided, in chronological order, a compressed history of the principal meanings attached to the word since it first became popular in the nineteenth century.[2] Here "ideology" will be taken to mean the "ideas at the basis of some economic or political theory or system." However, the definition of ideology has *evolved* and not simply *changed* so that it has not completely lost the normative connotations of the first three dictionary meanings. As this in turn has influenced the academic debate about ideology, it is necessary to look more closely at the history of the word.

The notion of ideology as "visionary speculation" may be attributed to Napoleon's contempt for a French philosophical school known as the "ideologists," who themselves saw ideology as the "science of ideas."[3] The word was used in a derogatory sense by Napoleon, being intended to imply a distinction between the idle dreamer and the pragmatic, realistic man of action, in which role Napoleon cast himself. In this way Napoleon framed one of the two formulations of a dichotomy between "ideology" and "realism" that have most affected subsequent discussions of ideology. "Realism" in this context denoted such qualities as an awareness of the importance of power in political relations, a constant regard for *raison d'état,* and an ability to balance the desirable against the practical.[4] The "ideologist," in contrast, was supposedly dogmatic, doctrinaire, and idealistic.

When Marx defined ideology as the "false consciousness" of particular social classes—the origin of the third dictionary definition—he too was employing a distinction between "ideology" and "realism."[5] Here "realism" had a philosophical meaning signifying awareness of the true state of things beneath their appearance, which could only be comprehended by means of

1. *The Concise Oxford Dictionary* (London, 1960), p. 589.

2. For the history of the concept, see K. Mannheim, *Ideology and Utopia* (London, 1946), pp. 53–62, and J. Plamenatz, *Ideology* (London, 1970), pp. 15–58.

3. Plamenatz, p. 15.

4. For example, Realism is thought that "takes into consideration the implications for political life of those security and power factors which are inherent in human society." J. H. Herz, *Political Realism and Political Idealism* (Chicago, 1951), p. 18.

5. This was not the only sense in which Marx used the word. For a discussion of the various Marxist uses of "ideology," see J. Plamenatz, *Man and Society* (London, 1963), vol. 2, pp. 323–327.

"true consciousness." However, the same objections could be raised against dialectical materialism—Marx's version of "true consciousness"—as Marx himself had asserted against "bourgeois" ideology, to the extent that the meaning of "ideology" as "false consciousness" or distorted view of reality has as often been applied to Marxism as to any other "world view."[6]

The dichotomy between "realism" (of either kind) and "ideology" is a popular starting point for discussions about the influence of ideas on social action. In international relations it underlies the debate that has been conducted at least since the establishment of Soviet Russia about the relative influences of "ideology" and "national interest" on foreign policy.[7]

"National interest" has two closely related meanings. It denotes the interests of the whole community that supposedly transcend those of groups within that community. It also refers to the particular interests of one nation state as against those of another. "National interest" is thought by some to provide an objective basis for a state's foreign policy: one, that is, founded upon "reality" rather than a subjective perception of reality. Attention to the "national interest" is also thought to signify "realism" (in the sense of pragmatism) on the part of the administrators of a country's foreign policy. The concept of "national interest" has been used both as description and prescription: It has been advanced as the yardstick by which states actually *do* manage their affairs as well as the standard by which they *should*.[8] Ideology has been depicted as a "disguise" that conceals a state's true, interest-motivated objectives, or as performing a "rationalising" function by presenting a state's self-interested behaviour in terms of the prevailing values of its citizens.[9]

6. Most notably by K. R. Popper. See his *The Open Society and its Enemies* (London, 1963), vol. 2, pp. 212–223.

7. Many of the more significant contributions to this debate are included in V. V. Aspaturian (ed.), *Process and Power in Soviet Foreign Policy* (Boston, 1971); E. P. Hoffman and F. J. Fleron (eds.), *The Conduct of Soviet Foreign Policy*, (Chicago, 1971); "Ideology and Power Politics: A Symposium," *Problems of Communism*, March–April, 1958.

8. Or sometimes as both. See H. J. Morgenthau, *In Defense of the National Interest* (New York, 1951), for a normative view of "national interest" and the same author's *Politics among Nations* (New York, 1966), p. 5, for one of the most positive claims about the actual role of "national interest" in international relations.

9. Morgenthau, *Politics among Nations*, pp. 83–86; W. Levi, "Ideology, Interests, and Foreign Policy," *International Studies Quarterly*, vol. 14, no. 1 (March 1970), p. 8.

If this conception of national interest were acceptable, the national interest-ideology dichotomy would offer a useful means of ordering a
discussion of the influence of ideology on foreign policy. There are three
reasons why it will not be employed here:
  1. "National interest" is a vague and ambiguous term without objectively
determinable content.
  2. The "national interest-ideology" dichotomy is a false one.
  3. The dichotomy is particularly inapplicable when the ideology under
consideration is Marxism-Leninism.
  That states seek advantage for themselves is not a startling proposition.
However, the notion that in particular situations there is a single course of
action to which states are unerringly guided by consultation of their "national interest"—the fundamental assumption of those who postulate an
"objective" national interest—is untenable. A choice of policies is always
available to decision-makers, even with regard to such goals as national
survival, and what they choose may depend on many factors, including their
ideology.[10] Many other problems with the concept are apparent: the
ambiguous nature of the "nation" and the difficulty of specifying whose
interests it encompasses,[11] the near impossibility of conceiving of a "self
acting against its own interests" (which reduces the concept to a truism),[12]
and the nature of "power" as a goal that is generally contingent upon some
other goal.[13] The subjectivist attempt to retain the concept by defining it as
"what the decision-maker decides it is" merely makes it redundant.[14]
George Kennan's call for analysts and statesmen to have "the modesty to

  10. Faced with the threat of an imperialist invasion by a powerful state, the
leaders of a small state could decide not to resist it, thus preserving the lives of
their "nationals" at the cost of the "nation." Similarly, states can and do choose
to join larger federations, thus voluntarily relinquishing their own sovereign
status.
  11. J. N. Rosenau, "National Interest," in D. L. Sills (ed.), *International
Encyclopaedia of the Social Sciences* (New York, 1968), p. 36.
  12. W. R. Schilling, "The Clarification of Ends or Which Interest Is the National," *World Politics*, July 1956, p. 576.
  13. Morgenthau's "signpost" for the student of international politics is "the
concept of interest defined in terms of power" (*Politics among Nations*, p. 5). For
the view that power as such is usually subordinate to some other goal, see R.
Aron, *Peace and War* (London, 1966), pp. 89–90.
  14. For the "subjectivist" and "objectivist" views of "national interest," see
Rosenau, *International Encyclopaedia*, p. 35, and J. Frankel, *National Interest*
(London, 1970) pp. 16–17.

admit that our own national interest is all that we are really capable of knowing and understanding" was clearly more ambitious than he imagined.[15]

If the "national interest" is not an objective and abiding reality but is merely the changing perceptions of decision-makers—perceptions which may derive in part from ideology—then clearly there is no dichotomy between an "ideological" foreign policy and one based on pursuit of the "national interest." It may also be noted that the concept of "national interest" was itself part of a revolutionary ideology when it was first advanced in opposition to the prevailing doctrine of "dynastic interest."[16]

Apart from these general problems there are special difficulties in determining the relative importance of "national interest" and "ideology" in the foreign policies of Communist countries. The first derives from Stalin's familiar definition of an "internationalist" as one who was prepared to work for the defence of the Soviet Union.[17] The logic here was that the furtherance of world revolution depended on the survival of the Soviet state, so that the two goals were inseparable: The "national interest" of the Soviet Union was world revolution; the essential precondition of world revolution was the security of the Soviet Union. An additional problem arises from the assumption that the "national interest" represents "realism" and "ideology" represents "idealism," where "realism" means an emphasis on limited and short-term goals or on flexible and subtle means of attaining goals, whereas "idealism" denotes long-term, utopian, or revolutionary goals and/or impractical, naive methods of attaining goals. The difficulty in the case of Communist countries stems from the fact that the Leninist component of their official ideology as well as Mao Tse-tung's additions to the "treasury of Marxism-Leninism" are concerned as much with the practical techniques of winning and maintaining power as with ultimate purposes. Moreover, their emphasis is consistently on the necessity of employing "realistic" means in the sense discussed here. When Litvinov said, with reference to the persecution of German Communists in the 1930s, "We are, of course, sensitive to the sufferings of our German comrades, but we Marx-

15. G. Kennan, *American Diplomacy* (Chicago, 1951), pp. 102–103, cited in R. C. Good, "The National Interest and Political Realism: Niebuhr's Debate with Morgenthau and Kennan," *Journal of Politics*, November 1960, p. 603.

16. H. S. Dinnerstein, "The Future of Ideology in Alliance Systems," *Journal of International Affairs*, vol. 25, no. 2 (1971), p. 239.

17. Cited in G. Stern, *Fifty Years of Communism* (London, 1967), p. 49.

ists are the last who can be reproached for permitting our feelings to dictate our policy,"[18] he was claiming, in effect, that Soviet policy was "realistic" *because* it was based on Marxism-Leninism.

IDEOLOGY AND THE INTERNATIONAL SYSTEM

The foregoing section suggests a basic dilemma in analysing the influence of ideology on foreign policy, especially in the case of Communist countries. This may be stated as follows: If the "national interest" and "ideological" components of foreign policy are analytically inseparable, and if foreign policy can be "realistic" without breaking any ideological canons,

1. How is it possible to distinguish meaningfully between a foreign policy that is "ideological"—concerned with achieving specific, ideologically de-rived goals—from one that is not?

2. How is it possible to determine the "ideological" content of an action which benefited the state performing it in some conventional way, such as by improving its power, prestige, or security?

One significant analytical approach to ideology has been suggested by the "functionalist" school which, briefly, points to the role that ideology can play in legitimising authority, integrating the community, rationalising or justifying policy decisions, assisting bureaucratic or elite-mass com-munications, and providing legitimate foci for popular emotions.[19] It is clear that ruling Communist parties derive their legitimacy—and indeed *raison d'être*—in part from an ideology which allocates them the pre-ordained role of leadership during a particular historical stage of unspecified duration. It is equally clear that this provides them with strong reasons for maintaining the importance of ideology in their societies and for finding ideological justifications for their policies. Ideology may also perform some of the social functions just listed without conscious manipulation. However, functionalism complicates rather than clarifies the problem of the possible predispositional effects of ideology on policy-making, for it avoids the ques-tion altogether by suggesting alternative ways of considering ideology. Moreover, by going directly to the functional consequences and effects of ideology it leaps over a vital intermediate stage: how and why people

18. Cited by H. L. Roberts, "Maxim Litvinov: Soviet Diplomacy 1930–1939," in Aspaturian (ed.), *Process and Power*, p. 162.

19. Ibid., pp. 194–195; F. Schurmann, *Ideology and Organization in Com-munist China* (Berkeley, 1970), pp. 58–73.

adopted an ideology in the first place.[20] If part of the answer to this is that they were persuaded of its validity, then one has to ask whether they ceased to be persuaded at the point in time when they were successful in establishing their ideology as the official state ideology. Finally, there is a similar problem to that which was raised in the discussion of "national interest": If ideology is not (as Communists claim) a "guide to action," then what is? By stressing the primacy of a system's needs as a total organism over the operation of its separate components, functionalism comes close to denying to the part any life independent from that of the whole. In the case of foreign policy this is akin to the argument that policy is "objectively" determined by some higher imperative regardless of the beliefs and preconceptions of policy-makers—the same notion that already has been discarded in the discussion of "national interest" theories.

The "system maintenance" functions of ideology do not, then, constitute a complete explanation of the role of ideology in society. Specifically, their existence does not exclude the possibility that ideology may also directly influence policy. Similarly, the currently fashionable "decision-making" approach to the analysis of foreign policy does not so much resolve the question of whether ideology is a "guide to action" in the foreign policies of Communist countries as provide us with an alternative set of problems. In the most sophisticated application to date of this approach, Graham Allison distinguishes three foreign policy models, each of which amounts to a different explanatory paradigm of foreign policy decision-making.[21] In the "rational policy model" decision-makers act "rationally" in the sense that, confronted with a problem, they attempt to find that decision which will result in the greatest advantage to their nation for the lowest acceptable cost. The "organizational process model" presents decisions as essentially the "output" of large and complex organizations which, over time, have developed a relatively inflexible set of "routines," armed with which they approach such problems as come their way. In Allison's own favoured approach, the "bureaucratic politics model," decisions are seen as the "outcomes" of a process of bargaining among different governmental factions, each with its own specific interests to defend.

The problem for this study is that those models have little to say about

20. On this point, see C. Geertz, "Ideology as a Cultural System," in D. E. Apter (ed.), *Ideology and Discontent* (Chicago, 1964), p. 56.
21. G. T. Allison, *Essence of Decision: Explaining the Cuban Missile Crisis* (Boston, 1971).

the relationship between ideology and foreign policy. "Rational" behaviour merely denotes behaviour that is consistent with an established set of interests, values, and norms but it does not specify in advance the content of the set. In other words, value-maximising behaviour consistent with an ideologically derived view of the universe is quite as rational as any other kind. Similarly, organizational "routines" do not develop in a vacuum but within an intellectual framework of assumptions, attitudes, and predispositions, which again could originate from a particular ideology. The "bureaucratic politics" approach does offer a partial escape from the ideology/foreign policy conundrum by focussing on the process of bargaining among groups and individuals that often may precede decision-making. Certainly, if much more were known about the conflicts within the Chinese foreign affairs bureaucracy and the extent to which foreign policy questions are involved in factional infighting among the Chinese leadership, a "bureaucratic politics" model of Chinese foreign policy decision-making might well provide some interesting insights. However, it would not make it possible for questions relating to the influence of China's ideology to be declared irrelevant, nor would it suggest convincing answers to such questions. The apparent requirement within China for policies to be ideologically defensible makes it impossible for any faction to avoid, at the very least, the necessity of framing its policies in ideological formulations. Even if, in the case of some factions, this amounted to little more than paying lipservice to the official ideology, the direct influence on policy of Mao himself needs to be considered. How good a Maoist *is* Mao? To what extent and in what ways has Mao's thought affected bureaucratic bargaining in the foreign affairs area, if indeed decisions there truly are a product of bureaucratic politics?

All this still leaves unanswered the questions that were raised at the beginning of this section. As the remainder of the book constitutes an attempt to come to grips with these questions, the next stage in the argument is to outline the analytical approach that will be employed.

IDEOLOGY VERSUS SECURITY: IDEAL TYPES

The approach that is adopted here involves the derivation of two inferential schemes from two "ideal type" models of foreign policy motivation. The first model assumes that ideology is the dominant influence on Chinese foreign policy and attempts to predict the pattern of behaviour that follows

from this assumption. The second places Peking's foreign policy in the context of China's situation in the international system and depicts it as
primarily a reaction to its security problems and assesses the implications of
this assumption. The principal developments in China's foreign policy—or
at least one aspect of it—as well as four case studies are then considered in
the light of these two models. Before proceeding to a more detailed outline, I
shall explain why this approach was chosen as well as the reasons for
selecting the two specific models that will be used.

Talcott Parsons, discussing Weber's study of the relation between
Protestantism and capitalism, has written,

> But Weber early became acutely aware, as many participants in the
> discussion still are not, that the problem of causation involved an
> *analytical* problem, one of the isolation of variables and the testing of
> their significance in situations where they could be shown to vary in-
> dependently of each other. The purely "historical" method . . . is
> inherently circular. It was only by establishing a methodological
> equivalent of experimental method, in which it is possible to hold certain
> factors constant, that even the beginnings of an escape from circularity
> was possible.[22]

Even "the beginnings of an escape from circularity" may be an overam-
bitious aim in a study of the relation of ideology to foreign policy. However,
the problem involved is essentially similar to that referred to by Parsons:
one of finding an analytical perspective for considering the question
systematically rather than searching for a complete explanation of an im-
possibly complex reality. To give meaning to the question "does ideology
influence foreign policy," one must first ask what one would expect to
observe if it did. That is what the first model attempts to do, not for the
whole of ideology or foreign policy but for one part of Maoist ideology and
one type of foreign policy decision.

The choice of specific models is in part arbitrary. There is no suggestion
that either ideology or the search for security in the international system
constitutes complete explanations of Chinese motivations or that, taken
together, they are the only influences on Chinese foreign policy making.
Nor are the two factors wholly separable except for analytical purposes, as
will be argued shortly. However, three reasons suggest themselves for using
just these two models. First, China's security problems and its ideology are
the two factors most commonly stressed in the literature on China's foreign
policy. The Chinese themselves assert that their foreign policy is derived

from their ideology, and this claim is in itself worthy of examination. Second, it is a truism that the domestic political (or "internal") and the world political (or "external") environments constitute the complete "setting" within which foreign policy is made and which both constrains and directs policy choices.[23] However, the truism may become a significant basis of enquiry if one asks what is the relative influence of "internal" and "external" factors and seeks to identify the important components of each type of environment. In this study one model postulates the dominance of the "internal" and the other of the "external" environment, while "ideology" and the "international system" are suggested as key aspects of each environment.[24] Third, the two models will be used to consider a specific *type* of decision, one involving a substantial and extensive commitment by China to aid another state. The type of decision suggests the choice of models. The united front doctrine provides an "ideological" interpretation of such a decision, whereas alternatively it may be seen as involving an "alliance" in response to external threats.

A so far unstated but obvious assumption underlying the use of two models to examine the same phenomena is that the models will explain the phenomena in different ways. However, it has already been argued that one of the difficulties in assessing the influence of Marxist-Leninist ideology on foreign policy is that the imperatives of national security are not excluded from the ideology and indeed are an important part of Lenin's and Mao's contributions to it. Why then will the two models yield different hypotheses?

The basis for this conclusion is to be found in the Leninist concept, much used by Mao, of "dual policy." In Lenin's work the notion of "dual policy" is part of his general conception of a "transitional period" during which temporary compromises have to be made because of the global dominance of the bourgeoisie.[25] What the term means when employed by Mao is that

22. T. Parson's Introduction to Max Weber, *The Sociology of Religion* (London, 1971), p. *xxi*.

23. S. Hoffman, *Gulliver's Troubles, or the Setting of American Foreign Policy* (New York, 1968), pp. *xiii–xix*.

24. It could be argued that the "international system" is not an "aspect" of the external environment but all of it. However, here the term "international system" is used in a more limited way, as defined in Chapter 2.

25. See, for example, Lenin, "Report on Foreign Policy," *Collected Works* (Moscow, 1961), vol. 31, p. 377, and J. Y. Calvez, *Droit International et Souveraineté en U.R.S.S.* (Libraire Armand Colin, 1953), pp. 100–104.

in planning policy a situation is to be viewed from two different perspectives and with two different time scales in mind. Every policy will thus have two aspects: It will meet the needs of the moment, but at the same time it will take account of the longer term goal of revolution. If the assumptions of dualism are made explicit, as they are in the united front model that is developed in Chapter 2, a "dual policy" does not simply concern itself with immediate exigencies but attempts to *integrate* short- and long-term requirements. As will be seen in Chapter 2, the integrative aspects of dual policies enable the development of an ideological model of foreign policy that is different in certain (but not all) important respects from the nonideological model.

Although the primary objective of this study is to ascertain the influence of an ideological concept on China's foreign policy, I recognise that in the real world ideology and the constraints of the international system are not independent but interacting factors. Ideological formulae may affect the way in which external events are perceived and the kinds of policies that are consequently adopted, even in highly threatening situations where the obvious course of action might seem quite clear.[26] Indeed the notion of "dual policy" implies that this will be the case. Moreover, ideological innovations may be made in response to a changing external situation, as when Khrushchev announced new doctrines on the question of war and peace in 1956. The second major question that this book considers asks whether a similar process has operated in the case of the united front doctrine.

Experience can work to reinforce or to weaken previously held views. This is not, however, a simple matter of incorrect ideas being modified or correct ideas being strengthened as evidence emerges to refute or confirm them. To use Kenneth Boulding's analogy, the Aztecs who offered human sacrifices to obtain good harvests would not necessarily have ceased to do this if one year's harvest were bad.[27] They might have increased the

26. Although Moscow clearly did perceive the threat from Hitler's Germany and did seek a rapprochement with Britain and France in response to this—the "obvious" policy—its ideologically based suspicion of "imperialism" was one of the factors that prevented an alliance being formed. Similarly Litvinov remarked in 1946 on the subject of the growing East-West tension, "As far as I am concerned, the root cause is the ideological conception prevailing here that conflict between the Communist and capitalist worlds is inevitable" (Aspaturian, ed., *Process and Power*, p. 174).

27. J. C. Farrell and A. P. Smith (eds.), *Image and Reality in World Politics* (New York, 1967).

numbers being sacrificed in the belief that the bad harvest "proved" that the gods were not satisfied with the existing offering. Similarly, if ideological tenets do not appear adequately to account for some event or to describe some situation, the ideologue could either *adapt* his doctrines to make them fit reality more closely or he could attempt to *reconcile* an apparent contradiction by depicting reality in such a way that it did fit the doctrine. In principle Marxist-Leninists are able to adapt ideology to changing circumstances, but the near-sacred quality that much of the doctrine has attained has tended to create problems whenever significant alterations have been made. This has meant in practice that "reconciliation" (or making the facts fit the ideology) has been the safer course, with "adaptation" rarer and therefore all the more significant when attempted.

The concept of "adaptation," in Darwinian terms, relates to the ability of living organisms to change physically in order to survive in a changing natural environment. In the present context, the "adaptation" of ideology may be seen as a part of the process of "socialization" whereby men consciously or unconsciously conform to the conventions of the society in which they live in order to function more effectively within it. As well as pointing to specific instances of "adaptation," the book also considers the question of evolution: whether such instances, taken together, add up to the "socialization" of China within the international system. It should be added that the term "socialization," as used here, does not carry any value connotations. It does not, for instance, bear the implication of "civilization" as a process involving movement from a lower to a higher order but simply denotes a process whereby an increasing entanglement within an existing structure of relationships brings about an increasing degree of adaptation to the normal behaviour patterns of that structure.

CHAPTER ONE

The United Front Doctrine in Historical Perspective

There would be little point in constructing an abstract model, however elegant, unless there were some a priori grounds for believing that the model might have some correspondence with reality. My a priori reasons for undertaking this study are, first, that the united front doctrine is a key aspect of Maoist ideology and, second, that concepts derived from the united front doctrine are frequently employed in Chinese discussions of international relations. Taken together, these two facts suggest the main question that is posed in this book: What has been the influence of the united front doctrine on China's foreign policy? The use of united front concepts in official Chinese pronouncements on international relations is illustrated in Chapter 3. In this chapter I intend not only to examine the content of the united front doctrine but also to demonstrate that it occupies an important place in Maoist ideology.

Three working definitions of terms that are employed throughout the book may appropriately be introduced at this point. A "united front" is a limited and temporary alignment between a Communist party or state and one or more non-Communist political units with the dual purpose, on the Communist side, of confronting a common enemy and furthering the revolutionary cause. The "united front doctrine" is, most broadly, all the theories and operational principles that relate to united fronts and, more narrowly, the specific ideas of Mao Tse-tung on this subject. A "dual policy" is a policy that attempts to integrate long-term revolutionary objectives with short-term requirements.

Good (and bad) advice about alliances and the tactics to be employed in dealing with powerful adversaries is not an exclusive possession of Lenin and Mao. In Chinese literature, for example, *The Art of War* urges the wise commander, "If the enemy is united, split him."[1] Similarly, the *Romance of the Three Kingdoms* "offers a host of strategies to be adopted by a state wishing to increase its power in an environment of ever-shifting and temporary alliances."[2] One could even suspect General Yang Hu, one of the characters of the *Three Kingdoms,* of being an early Maoist when he reflects at one point, "I shall not attack till there be trouble and confusion among our enemies. To be rash and not await the proper moment to attack is to invite defeat." And later he observes that "although fate is superior to man, yet success depends upon human efforts."[3]

It would be easy to discover ideas analogous to some parts of the united front doctrine in Western as well as Eastern thought, simply because the problems (of weakness and unreliable but necessary allies) to which the doctrine is addressed are basic to political life. However, the doctrine is not just a collection of useful hints about tactics. It is, as I argue further on, an integral part of Maoist ideology and follows *logically* from some of the central propositions of that ideology as well as being initially a *practical* consequence of the problems faced by the Bolsheviks in pre-1917 Russia and the CCP in revolutionary China. Indeed it is in part this "unity of thought and practice" embodied in the united front doctrine that has led to its continuing importance in the official ideology of the People's Republic of China.

LENIN'S DEVELOPMENT OF THE
INTERNATIONAL UNITED FRONT DOCTRINE

As the united front doctrine is an aspect of Marxist-Leninist ideology, it is not necessary to go back to early Chinese classics to trace its intellectual lineage. Most of its core ideas have their origin in the writings of Lenin and specifically in the answers that he gave to four questions:

1. Tang Zi-chang, *Principles of Conflict*, translation and recompilation of Sun Wu's *Art of War* (San Rafael, 1969).
2. S. M. Goldstein, "Chinese Communist Perspectives and International Affairs, 1937–1941" (Ph.D. thesis, Columbia University, 1972), p. 520.
3. *Romance of the Three Kingdoms,* trans. C. H. Brewitt-Taylor (Oxford, 1925), vol. 2, pp. 612, 614.

1. Why was it necessary for his party of professional revolutionaries to form alliances with other parties and political forces?

2. Who were the potential allies of the Bolsheviks?

3. What should be the party's tactics in such alliances?

4. What were the international applications of his ideas on political alliances?[4]

The necessity for united fronts

Lenin's argument that united fronts were not only necessary but inevitable followed naturally from his assertion in 1902 of the need for a new kind of revolutionary party.[5] According to him, "The history of all countries shows that the working class, exclusively by its own efforts, is able to develop only trade union consciousness."[6] Since a far higher level of "consciousness" was deemed necessary if the proletarian revolution was ever to take place, the proletariat required guidance from a "vanguard" party that was itself "guided by the most advanced theory."[7] The intellectually exclusive character of such a party, combined with the obligation to secrecy and efficient organisation that was imposed upon it by the internal conditions of Russia in 1902, meant inevitably that the party could not be a mass organisation. However, since the party's aims were revolutionary, not reformist, its range of activities could not be as exclusive as its membership. In order for it to have a real and hopefully decisive influence on the course of events, the party, therefore, had to form alliances with other forces in society that did have a popular base of support.

However logical Lenin's conclusion of the indispensability of alliances with groups that might not be fully committed to the proletarian revolution, it did not prevent his receiving criticism from other revolutionaries. He op-

4. Lenin himself cited Marx's *Critique of the Gotha Programme* in support of his claim that temporary alliances were permissible (Lenin, "What Is to be Done," *Collected Works*, Moscow, 1961, vol. 5, p. 369). However, Marx's intention in that work was to criticise an ally, not, as Lenin implies, to argue in favour of alliances in general. Hence Lenin must be regarded as the true originator of the united front concept.

5. The actual term "united front" was not used until the 1920s. However, Lenin's ideas about "temporary" or "limited" alliances were the forerunners of the united fronts of the 1920s and the term is used here for convenience.

6. Lenin, "What Is to be Done," p. 375.

7. Ibid., p. 370.

posed such attacks by arguing pragmatically that "a political alignment is determined not only by ultimate aims but also by immediate aims, not only by general views but also by the pressure of direct practical necessity."[8] He put forward the idea, with increasing elaboration over the years, that so long as the "vanguard" retained its independent identity and revolutionary consciousness it would be able to steer a correct course regardless of who its allies were, and he maintained that "only those who are not sure of themselves can fear to enter into temporary alliances, even with unreliable people; not a single political party could exist without such alliances."[9] The "temporary" nature of such alliances was to be a constant item in Lenin's writings on the subject.

The choice of allies

Lenin based his criteria for selecting allies on both theoretical and pragmatic grounds. The dialectical conception of history held that any historical period was characterised by a struggle between a dominant but declining economic class and an oppressed but rising class. The alliance policy of the Bolsheviks should thus, according to Lenin, derive in the first instance from their appraisal of the current historical epoch. Their purpose was to make history move more quickly than it otherwise would, and to achieve this they needed to align themselves with the main "progressive" tendency at any given point in time. In Russia of 1902 the chief struggle in Marxist terms was seen to be between the last vestiges of feudalism and emergent capitalism. Hence, although the bourgeoisie was destined by Marxist analysis to be the eventual enemy of the proletariat, the "direct or indirect, conscious or unconscious supporters of the bourgeoisie" could be "our temporary and partial allies in the struggle against the remnants of the serf-owning system."[10] As always, Lenin was contemptuous of critics from the Left who, he claimed, wished "to substitute noisy declarations for rapprochement with definite classes."[11] For example, he criticised the Menshevik conference in 1905 for setting too rigid conditions for alliance with the bourgeoisie. The Mensheviks had insisted that the bourgeois

8. Lenin, "Review of Home Affairs," *Collected Works*, vol. 5, p. 301.

9. "What Is to be Done," p. 362.

10. Lenin, "The Agrarian Programme of Russian Social Democracy," *Collected Works*, vol. 6, p. 125.

11. Lenin, "Revolutionary Adventurism," *Collected Works*, vol. 6, p. 186.

parties had to give "energetic and unequivocal" support to every action taken by the Socialist parties. Lenin felt that this was logically impossible because of the class nature of the bourgeoisie and contended that genuine commitment by the bourgeoisie to its own class interest, the struggle against tsarism, was sufficient.[12]

That doctrinal considerations, such as those about the nature of the historical era, did genuinely influence Lenin may be illustrated by two incidents. In 1902 he was far stricter in applying conditions for a possible alliance with the peasantry than he had been with the bourgeoisie on the ideologically based grounds that the peasantry could not possibly be a progressive force.[13] Second, in 1905 he insisted that the newly established Soviet of Workers' Deputies should *not* attach itself to a single party, even his own, since the revolution in Russia was perceived to be only in its democratic stage and not yet the proletarian stage which would be the party's task to lead.[14] However, Lenin was flexible enough to amend dogma when it was contradicted by actual events. Hence, he was quick to change his assessment of the revolutionary potential of the peasantry after it had shown itself in 1905 to be far more capable of violent action than he had thought possible. Indeed he was sufficiently impressed to go to the lengths of "adapting" ideology by inventing a new formulation to account for the proletariat-peasantry alliance that he now urged: ". . . a coalition of the proletariat and the peasantry, winning victory in a bourgeois revolution, happens to be nothing else than the revolutionary democratic dictatorship of the proletariat and the peasantry."[15]

United front tactics

According to Lenin, revolution had to be seen as a process, not as a single momentous event: " . . . the revolution itself must not be regarded as a single act . . . but as a series of more or less powerful outbreaks rapidly alternating with periods of more or less complete calm."[16] Given this, an important at-

12. Lenin, "The Two Tactics of Social Democracy in the Democratic Revolution," *Collected Works,* vol. 9, pp. 91–92.

13. Lenin, "The Agrarian Programme," pp. 114–116.

14. Lenin, "Our Tasks and the Soviet of Workers' Deputies," *Collected Works,* vol. 10, p. 23.

15. Lenin, "The Assessment of the Russian Revolution," *Collected Works,* vol. 15, p. 57.

16. "What Is to be Done," p. 514.

tribute of his new party needed to be an "ability to adapt itself immediately to the most diverse and rapidly changing conditions of struggle."[17] Specifically it had to be "sufficiently flexible to be able, on the one hand, to avoid an open battle against an overwhelming enemy, when the enemy has concentrated all his forces on the one spot, and yet, on the other, to take advantage of his unwieldiness and to attack him when and where he least expects it."[18]

The party's alliance policy, Lenin believed, should take account of both the nature of the revolutionary process and the need for flexibility: ". . . the immediate task of our party is not to summon all available forces to the attack right now, but to call for the formation of a revolutionary organisation capable of uniting all forces and guiding the movement in actual practice and not in name alone."[19]

Permanent alliances with any party were unnecessary (as well as forbidden, as we shall see), since different stages of the revolutionary process would bring to the fore different forces to which Lenin's party might need to attach itself. However, the party also needed to be in constant readiness to take advantage of the ebb and flow of revolution, and for this reason a key aspect of its alliance policy was what was later to be called "the united front from below."[20] That is, it required a network of contacts and positions of influence at levels below that of the leadership of existing organisations in order to be able to mobilise "the masses" when the time was "ripe."

However, the most important reason for building up a "united front from below" was that the party's long-term aims were not the same as those of its allies. Indeed, the "dialectical" view of history implied not only that any alliance would inevitably collapse at some point but that an ally of Lenin's party in one historical stage could become its principal enemy in another. Hence the party needed to build up its popular strength by means of a "united front from below" in order to prepare for the ultimate split. Further tactical conclusions that Lenin drew from this analysis were that his party must retain its separate identity and aims and also maintain vigilance over its allies:

17. Ibid., p. 513.
18. Lenin, "Where To Begin," *Collected Works*, vol. 5, p. 23.
19. Ibid., p. 20.
20. Lenin did the fact distinguish between "struggle from below" and "action from above" in "The Two Tactics," pp. 29–30.

A social democrat must never for a moment forget that the proletariat will inevitably have to wage a class struggle for socialism even against the most democratic and republican bourgeoisie and petty bourgeoisie. This is beyond doubt. Hence the absolute necessity of a separate, independent, strictly class party of Social Democracy. Hence the temporary nature of our tactics of "striking a joint blow" with the bourgeoisie and the duty of keeping a strict watch *"over our ally as over our enemy"* [emphasis added].[21]

Lenin was here introducing an idea that was to be considerably developed by Mao Tse-tung: that united fronts should be characterised by "struggle" as well as unity. In Mao's case a tactical necessity was turned into a positive virtue, for he argued that united fronts were not just temporary expedients but offered a means of revolutionising certain components of the allied party through struggle against right-wing elements in the ally's leadership. However, the germ of this notion originated with Lenin, who argued that the party's role in the 1905 revolution was to conduct "struggle" within the revolutionary movement to guide it to a higher level of "consciousness."[22] A similar point was made in Lenin's post-1905 writings on the subject of a proletariat-peasantry alliance, in which he urged his party to avoid "not only fusion but any prolonged agreement" with peasant parties, for

Only if it pursues an unquestionably independent policy as the vanguard of the revolution will the proletariat be able to split the peasantry away from the liberals, rid it of their influence, rally the peasantry behind it in the struggle and thus bring about an "alliance" *de facto*—one that emerges and becomes effective when and to the extent that the peasantry are conducting a revolutionary fight.[23]

Finally, Lenin's general formula for Communist tactics should be noted, both because of its similarities to Mao's later ideas and because of certain significant differences. In "Left-Wing Communism" Lenin wrote that before the "final and decisive battle" was joined, it was necessary to determine

... whether the historically effective forces of all classes—positively of all classes in a given society without exception—are arrayed in such a way that: (1) all the classes hostile to us have become sufficiently entangled,

21. Ibid., pp. 91–92.
22. Ibid., p. 30.
23. "The Assessment of the Russian Revolution," p. 58.

are sufficiently at loggerheads with each other, have sufficiently weakened themselves in a struggle which is beyond their strength; (2) all the vacillating and unstable intermediate elements . . . have sufficiently exposed themselves in the eyes of the people, have sufficiently disgraced themselves through their practical bankruptcy; and (3) among the proletariat a mass sentiment favouring the most determined, bold, and dedicated revolutionary action against the bourgeoisie has emerged and begun to grow vigorously.[24]

Lenin, as Mao was to do later, insisted upon the importance of careful analysis of the relative strengths and weaknesses of all social classes before making any decisive move. The image both had of revolution was as a process in which the final, violent stage would be preceded by a long period of preparing, mobilising potentially revolutionary forces, and manipulating the other forces until, overall, society was so orchestrated that the success of the final *coup de grace* was inevitable. Both employed a three-way division of society as the basis of their analysis, but at this point they part ways. For Lenin the proletariat still retained its ultimate importance; middle forces merely had to be neutralised. For Mao, although proletarian (or simply "advanced") consciousness was a vital leadership attribute, emphasis was placed on mobilising an overwhelming majority, including the middle forces and even some of those in the enemy camp, in order to isolate the principal enemy.

The international applications of the united front

Lenin regarded social classes as international rather than national entities and assumed that his victory in 1917 was the first blow in a *global* class struggle. Hence, many of the images, concepts, and policies that originally had been designed to meet the exigencies of the Communist party in tsarist Russia were simply transplanted from the national to the international sphere, with the whole of Soviet Russia now assuming for the world the "vanguard" mantle that Lenin's party had held in Russia. Since Soviet Russia was the vanguard of an international *class,* Lenin could declare after 1917 that "economic interests and the economic position of the classes which rule our state lie at the root of both our home and foreign policy."[25]

24. Lenin, "Left-Wing Communism, an Infantile Disorder," *Collected Works,* vol. 31, p. 94.
25. Lenin, "Report on Foreign Policy," *Collected Works,* vol. 27, p. 365.

Just as Lenin had been able to urge his party to form alliances as a tactical necessity *inside* Russia, so the same principle applied to Soviet Russia's *international* relations:

> To carry on a war for the overthrow of the international bourgeoisie, a war which is a hundred times more difficult, protracted, and complex than the most stubborn of ordinary wars between states, and to renounce in advance any change of tack, or any utilisation of a conflict of interests (even if temporary) among one's enemies, *or any conciliation or compromise with possible allies (even if they are temporary, unstable, vacillating, or conditional allies)* —is that not ridiculous in the extreme? [emphasis added].[26]

It should be noted that Lenin referred to the utilisation of conflicts of interest among enemies, on the one hand, and alliance policy, on the other, as two distinct tactics. Mao's united front doctrine tended to combine the two into a single policy.

In 1917 Lenin declared that Soviet Russia's foreign policy was to be based on "alliance with all the revolutionaries of the advanced countries and with all the oppressed nations against all and any imperialists."[27] Although alliance with revolutionaries in the capitalist world was clearly acceptable by any ideological criterion, the notion of an alliance with "oppressed nations" posed some problems in terms of the validity of the idea that a whole nation, rather than one or more classes within it, could be "oppressed." Here the integrating device of the "dual policy" was employed to explain to the more orthodox the pragmatic *and* revolutionary bases of Soviet foreign policy. On the one hand, the proposed alliance with "oppressed nations" offered a means of distracting Britain and the other imperialist powers away from any designs they might have against the new government of Russia. On the other, since imperialism was "the highest stage of capitalism" and the means by which capitalism had been able to postpone its inevitable doom, alliance with anti-imperialists was also the ideologically correct policy for the current historical era.[28]

Lenin's insistence at the Second Comintern Congress in 1920 that the Asian Communist parties ally with "bourgeois nationalists" may be seen as

26. "Left-Wing Communism," p. 70.
27. Lenin, "The Foreign Policy of the Russian Revolution," *Collected Works*, vol. 25, p. 87.
28. Lenin, *Imperialism, the Highest Stage of Capitalism* (Peking Foreign Languages Press), pp. 148–155.

an attempt to integrate both long- and short-term perspectives into the same "dual policy." Had his sole aim been to embroil the imperialist powers in wasteful military activities in their colonies, this might have been better achieved by urging the Asian Communist parties to embark upon a campaign of sabotage and insurrection—which was the clear preference of some of them.[29] However, Lenin's policy was also intended to accommodate the long-term purpose of achieving Communist victories in Asia and the perceived historical necessity for Asian countries to pass through a "bourgeois" stage. Moreover, Lenin's united front proposals for the colonial and semicolonial countries were not simply an attempt to curry favour with the nationalists there since he set exactly the same restrictions on Asian Communists as had been imposed earlier on the Bolsheviks: "The Communist International must enter into a temporary alliance with bourgeois democracy in the colonial and backward countries *but should not merge with it,* and should under all circumstances uphold the independence of the proletarian movement even if it is in its most embryonic form" [emphasis added].[30]

THE DEVELOPMENT OF THE
UNITED FRONT DOCTRINE AFTER LENIN

The Comintern and European Social Democracy

The actual term "united front" first gained wide currency in the 1920s, when it was employed by the Comintern with reference to Communist collaboration with Social Democrat parties in Europe and the "national bourgeoisie" in the colonies and semicolonies. The expression served two purposes, according to the audience toward whom it was directed: It was a propaganda slogan aimed at rallying potential allies, while at the same time it carried a deeper significance to Communists, implying, as it did, a summation of Lenin's alliance theories. Just as Lenin had turned to alliances as a short-term expedient to be used in conditions in which the chances of mak-

29. As emerged during the debate on the "national and colonial question" in 1920. *The Second Congress of the Communist International* (Washington, D.C., 1920).

30. Lenin, "Preliminary Draft Theses on the National and Colonial Questions," *Collected Works,* vol. 31, p. 150.

ing a successful revolution seemed slight, so too did the Comintern. Trotsky made this clear in a speech he gave on 20 October 1922:

> If we consider that the party is on the eve of the conquest of power, and the working class will follow it, then the question of the united front does not arise. But . . . if we become convinced that a certain interval must elapse, perhaps several years, before the conquest of power . . . it is necessary to consider what will happen in the interim to the working class.[31]

The Comintern set the same kind of restrictions on Communist participation in united fronts as Lenin had earlier imposed on his own party: They should not sacrifice their independence, or compromise on principles; they should struggle against their allies; alliances were always to be viewed as a temporary tactic. As the Fifth Comintern Congress put it,

> United front tactics were and remain a method of revolution, not of peaceful evolution. They are the tactics of a revolutionary strategic manoeuvre of the Communist vanguard, surrounded by enemies, in its struggle against the treacherous leaders of counter-revolutionary social democracy. . . . United front tactics were and are a means of gradually drawing over to our side the Social Democratic and the best non-party workers; they should in no circumstances be degraded to the tactics of lowering our ideals to the level of understanding reached by these workers.[32]

However, it was one thing to reiterate Lenin's general tactical principles in this way, but quite another matter to put them into practice in the immeasurably more complex environment that faced Comintern in the 1920s, a difficulty that the Comintern recognised: "It is obvious that the united front tactic is to be applied in different ways in different countries, according to the actual conditions prevailing there."[33]

In general, the Comintern distinguished three possible types of united front in Europe. A "united front from below" was necessary "always and everywhere,"[34] for it was through this agency that the party worked towards its long-term ends of splitting workers away from their allegiance to Social

31. In J. Degras, *The Communist International* (London, 1965), vol. 1, p. 316.
32. Ibid., vol. 2, p. 152. See also F. Borkenau, *The Communist International* (London, 1938), p. 224.
33. Degras, *Communist International*, vol. 1, p. 425.
34. Ibid., p. 395.

Democracy. In situations where a Social Democratic party was a political force of some significance, the local Communist party was permitted to form a limited alliance with it at the leadership level in what was termed "a united front from above and below." However, a united front *only* from above was not permitted. From 18 December 1921, when the Comintern executive adopted the "Directives On the United Front," until the Comintern's leftward swing in 1928, a policy (in theory at least) of united front from above and below was followed by the Comintern in its relations with Social Democracy.[35] In practice the Communists were so openly intent on splitting the Social Democrat leadership and winning workers for their own party, that a genuine political alliance with Social Democracy stood little chance of developing. Faced with frank statements by Zinoviev to the effect that the united front policy was a way of fighting Social Democracy "by roundabout means," or by Radek that the united front was not designed to enable Communists to merge with Social Democrats but to "stifle them in our embrace," the Social Democrats were to be forgiven for treating Communist approaches with a certain amount of suspicion.[36]

However, even when the united front with Social Democracy was formally abandoned in 1928, Bukharin insisted that "the adoption of sharper methods of struggle against the Social Democratic parties is not in any way identical with the abandonment of united front tactics."[37] The united front *concept* had by now clearly attained too much significance to be discarded upon the failure of a *specific* united front.

State-to-state relations

Apart from its role in the advice given by the Comintern to European and Asian Communist parties, the terminology associated with the united front was also used by Moscow in explanations of its relations with other states. In one case, that of Kemalist Turkey after 1920, Moscow's attempt to establish close relations could be ideologically justified to some extent on the grounds that Turkey's government was "bourgeois nationalist" and anti-imperialist

35. A brief account of this period is contained in J. Degras's contribution "United Front Tactics in the Comintern, 1921–1928," in D. Footman (ed.) *International Communism*, London, 1960, pp. 9–22.

36. Quotes from ibid., pp. 10–11.

37. X. J. Eudin and R. M. Slusser, *Soviet Foreign Policy 1928–1934* (Stanford, 1965), vol. 1, p. 118.

in character.[38] A more doubtful case was that of Germany, with whom Moscow signed the Treaty of Rapallo in 1922—a treaty described by the Comintern as a "treaty of alliance."[39]

Rapallo raises some of the problems that will be encountered later in this study with reference to China's relations with Indonesia and others. In short, was it an "alliance" or a "united front"? It should be noted that an attempt was made to justify Rapallo by implying that it was in fact the *interstate* equivalent of a united front. For example, Radek asserted that Germany temporarily belonged to the same camp as the Asian semicolonies because of its treatment at the hands of the Allies at Versailles.[40] Similarly the Comintern described the treaty as a temporary alliance with a "bourgeois-Menshevik" government that would itself inevitably be overthrown.[41]

However, these comments appear to have been rationalisations of Moscow's main interest in Germany, which was a desire to intensify the conflict between Germany and France. This was clearly demonstrated during 1923. The German economic crisis of that year offered some prospect of developing into a revolutionary situation, particularly if the leftist parties there had been able to present a united front. But the German Social Democrat and Communist parties proved unable to unite their forces, largely because the Communists, following the Comintern line, opposed the Social Democrat policy of seeking a peaceful settlement with France. Indeed at one point in 1923 the Comintern proposed a united front between the Communists and the Nazis, the most anti-French party, and for two months such a front did exist until it was ended by the Nazis on August 15. Moreover, the German Communists opposed the general strike which broke out in August, and only when the new Stresemann government attempted to reach an understanding with Britain and France did it adopt a revolutionary line—by which time the situation had eased considerably.[42] In this

38. J. Degras (ed.), *Soviet Documents on Foreign Policy* (London, 1961), vol. 1, pp. 187–188; J. Harris, "Communist Strategy towards the National Bourgeoisie in Asia and the Middle East 1945–1961" (Columbia University, Ph.D. thesis, 1966), pp. 17–30.

39. Degras, *Communist International*, vol. 1, p. 347.

40. D. Boersner, *The Bolsheviks and the National and Colonial Question* (Geneva, 1957), pp. 136–137.

41. Degras, *Communist International*, vol. 1, p. 347.

42. J. Braunthal, *History of the International 1914–1943* (London, 1967), vol. 2, pp. 271–281; G. Hilger and A. G. Meyer, *The Incompatible Allies* (New York,

case it seems clear that Moscow was more concerned about the foreign policy of the German government than any revolutionary prospects in Germany. Its use of united front concepts to explain its policy may thus be regarded as an attempt to "reconcile" theory with practice rather than as an accurate statement of Soviet objectives.

By 1935 the threat to Russia from Nazi Germany had caused an "adaptation" of the Soviet line on united fronts together with a further extension of the doctrine into the area of interstate relations. No attempt was now made to justify the Soviet Union's alliance policy in terms of the "oppressed" nature of its prospective allies against Germany. As Manuilsky made clear in his report to the Seventh Comintern Congress in July 1935, *any* potential anti-German forces were to be sought as allies: "It is the duty of the proletariat to extend the front of all possible allies in the struggle against fascism and war to include such social groups, classes, and nations which are neither supporters of the social revolution nor supporters of the proletarian dictatorship."[43] The previously stressed revolutionary objective of united fronts was also played down with the main emphasis placed upon the defensive requirements of the Soviet Union. This imperative overrode the domestic class struggle where that struggle weakened governments which might share with the Soviet Union a common interest in containing fascism:

> Today the interests of the defence of the Soviet Union determine the main policy of the world proletariat towards war, whilst in 1914, the best proletarian revolutionary elements adopted the standpoint of defeatism, the defeat of their own imperialist governments. . . . In the struggle for peace today it is necessary that we should adopt a much more concrete attitude towards the various countries in accordance with the realignment which has taken place in the camp of the capitalist states.[44]

A third change of some significance was that the tactic of exploiting "contradictions among the imperialists," which had hitherto been distin-

---

1953), pp. 84–208; and G. Nollau, *International Communism and World Revolution* (London, 1961), pp. 79–86, were the principal works consulted for this section.

43. *International Press Correspondence (Inprecor)*, vol. 15, no. 6, 9 February 1935.

44. *Inprecor*, vol. 15, no. 69, 17 December 1935.

guished from the united front policy, was now to some extent amalgamated with it:

> Today the world proletariat, with the support of the Soviet Union and by utilising the contradictions and antagonisms between the capitalist states, has the possibility of creating a broad people's front against war, a front for which it can win not only other classes but also weak nations and peoples whose independence would be threatened by war. Thanks to the peace policy of the Soviet Union the international proletariat is now in a position to utilise in its struggle against war the attitude of those great powers which for various reasons do not want and even fear war.[45]

The significance of this "adaptation" is twofold. First, the suggestion that it was possible to find allies in one side of the "contradictions" among the imperialists was a considerable advance from the earlier Leninist position which had simply seen in the "contradictions" a potential advantage to Soviet Russia. Neither side had been considered by Lenin to be inherently preferable to the other; now the clear implication was that some imperialists were objectively more "peace-loving" than others. Second, the ideological basis of the united front doctrine had been the dialectical conception of history and specifically the notion that Communist parties should align themselves with whatever was perceived to be the "progressive" tendency of a particular historical period. According to this conception the united front was a means of carrying on a revolutionary *offensive* by indirect means. However the "united front against fascism" that was initiated in 1935 was clearly a *defensive* venture. Admittedly it was directed against an enemy who was a threat to both Soviet Russia and communism in general but the possibility of an alliance with *any* force, even for defensive purposes, had not been contemplated by Lenin and necessitated an "adaptation" of the original doctrine. This process reached its logical conclusion when Stalin described the wartime alliance with the U.S.A. and Britain as a "united front."[46]

The united front in the Chinese revolution

From an early stage in the history of the Chinese Communist party the united front, both as a concept and a policy, assumed considerable im-

45. Ibid.
46. Degras, *Communist International*, vol. 3, p. 476.

portance for the development of the Chinese revolution. It is not my intention to trace in detail the history of the united front in China, for one
such history already exists,[47] but merely to point to some of the special
factors which influenced Mao's united front doctrine.

At the first congress of the CCP in July 1921, the party adopted an ex-
clusivist stand toward all other parties: "Towards the existing political
parties, an attitude of independence, aggression and exclusion should be
adopted. . . . Our party should stand up in behalf of the proletariat and
should allow no relationship with the other parties or groups."[48]

The manifesto adopted by the CCP one year later is a far more Leninist
document in both its proposals and language, evidence of a rapid learning
process by the party during the year, and especially at the Congress of
Toilers of the East in January and February 1922. The manifesto declared
that China had reached a stage of national revolution in which the immediate tasks facing the whole Chinese people were to overthrow the
warlords, unite the country, and oppose foreign imperialism. In such
circumstances, the manifesto continued, "there is only one way to make the
real nationalistic revolution come about speedily—that is the cooperation of
the proletarian revolutionary forces and the national revolutionary."[49] In
other words, in the given historical situation in which China found itself, it
was possible for the CCP to form a united front with nationalist forces,
specifically the KMT, in order jointly to oppose imperialism and militarism.
The usual Leninist reservations were made: The alliance was to be considered only as a short-term expedient pending a nationalist victory, after
which the party and the KMT would find themselves in opposition to each
other. Moreover, even while the alliance was in operation,

> . . . the workers should take care not to be the tool of the petty
> bourgeoisie in the nationalists' joint battlefield, and at the same time
> they must be bold to struggle for our own class privileges. . . . All workers
> should always remember that they are the independent class, should
> discipline themselves to prepare for organisation and fighting, should
> prepare the peasants to unite and organise the soviet in order to reach
> complete emancipation.[50]

47. L. P. Van Slyke, *Enemies and Friends: The United Front in Chinese Communist History* (Stanford, 1967).

48. Ch'en Kung-po, *The Communist Movement in China* (Columbia
University East Asian Institute Series, no. 7, 1960), p. 109.

49. Ibid., p. 120.

50. Ibid., p. 122.

The distinctive Leninist note in these pronouncements recurred in CCP statements throughout the period of the first united front. This was particularly so after Voitinsky replaced Maring as chief Comintern agent in China, and urged the CCP to distinguish three groups within the KMT—left, right, and centre. The party, according to Voitinsky, should ally with the left, win over and seek occasional support from the centre, and oppose the right.[51] Voitinsky also supported Chang Kuo-t'ao's proposal not to share control of left-wing trade unions with the KMT. However, although these tactical considerations were spelt out as early as 1922, it was not until after Sun Yat-sen's death in 1925 that any serious effort was made to capitalise on splits in the KMT. By this time the policy was becoming one of desperation rather than a clearly worked out strategy, although even as late as July 1926 the party could still sound as if it were fully in control of the situation:

> We unite with the Left and force the Center to attack the reactionary Right. At the same time, we guard against the rise of the Center and force it to turn left against the Right. The victory of the National Revolution will be assured if our tactics of united front are successfully carried out.[52]

This July meeting came at a time when the Communists were being forced out of high-ranking positions in the KMT and the party did recognise, belatedly, that its unsophisticated comprehension of united front tactics was partly responsible for the crisis in which it found itself:

> One of the chief reasons the KMT Right and even the KMT Center were able to attack us easily and demand that we withdraw from the KMT is the incorrect formula we previously employed in directing the KMT. Under that formula, the Left was not able to participate in party activities and in the fight against the Right. We ourselves created the situation of a KMT-CCP struggle which overshadows what is actually a struggle between the Left and Right.[53]

However, the party may have been somewhat harsh on itself in accepting all the blame for the difficulties it had encountered. At least part of the responsibility for the specific course taken by the first united front lay with

51. C. M. Wilbur and J. L. Howe, *Documents on Communism, Nationalism, and Soviet Advisers in China 1918–1927* (New York, 1956), p. 89.

52. Ibid., p. 275.

53. Ibid., p. 278.

the Comintern agent Maring, who had a considerable role in the formation
of the front, and also with Stalin, who played a part in its subsequent
misdirection. Three unusual aspects of the front may be partly attributed to
Maring's influence:

1. The assertion that the KMT did not represent a single class interest,
but constituted a bloc of various classes—listed by Maring as intellectuals,
overseas Chinese capitalists, soldiers and workers, and redefined in a more
orthodox way by the Comintern as intelligentsia, liberal democratic
bourgeoisie, petty bourgeoisie, and the workers;

2. The notion of a "bloc within," whereby individual Communists joined
the KMT while retaining their membership in the CCP;

3. The acceptance of the KMT as the leading force in both the national
revolution and the united front.[54]

Stalin contributed an additional element of confusion, as well as confirming Maring's emphasis on working with the KMT. In a speech in 1925
he attempted to distinguish three categories of colonial countries according
to their stage of development and argued that each category called for a
different united front policy. In countries "like Egypt and China," he argued
that "Communists must pass from the policy of a united national front to
the policy of a revolutionary bloc of the workers and petty bourgeoisie,"
and added that this bloc could assume the form of a single party.[55] Exactly
what the CCP made of this cryptic remark is not known. However, that
Stalin did not have in mind a break with the KMT but continuation of the
policy of working with it became apparent when he urged this more directly
some months later.[56] Even after Chiang Kai-shek's coup in 1927, he continued to stress the "value and significance" of the CCP's misguided attempts to win over the "Left KMT."[57]

54. Maring's account of his role was given in an interview with Harold Isaacs
on 19 August 1935, published as "Documents on the Comintern and the Revolution in China" in *China Quarterly*, no. 45, January–March 1971. It is also
discussed in H. Isaacs, *The Tragedy of the Chinese Revolution*, 2nd rev. ed.
(Stanford, 1966), pp. 58–59, with further detail in D. Bing, "Sneevliet and the
Early Years of the CCP," *China Quarterly*, no. 48, October–December 1971,
especially pp. 685–686.

55. J. Stalin, "The Political Tasks of the University of the Peoples of the
East," *Collected Works* (Moscow 1954), vol. 7, p. 149.

56. J. Stalin, "The Prospects of the Revolution in China," *Collected Works*,
vol. 8, p. 383.

57. J. Stalin, "Questions of the Chinese Revolution," *Collected Works*, vol. 9,
p. 23.

One of the effects of Maring's and Stalin's advice to the CCP had been for the latter to obtain the impression that the KMT was to be regarded as a party containing several classes and not as the representative of one. Stalin was later to deny that he had ever said this and maintained—in a remarkable example of hair-splitting—that his position had been that the KMT was merely the party of a bloc of several classes.[58] However, so far as the evolution of the united front doctrine is concerned, the Comintern's advice reinforced a tendency on the part of some CCP leaders to view events in China in terms of a national rather than a class struggle and to draw less sharp distinctions between the Communist party and its allies than had been the case in Lenin's united front writings. In Mao's united front doctrine there is also a universalist tendency to concentrate on the "contradiction" between a numerically very small enemy and an overwhelming majority and to downgrade conflict among different sections within the majority, so this point deserves further elaboration.

If some of the Chinese Communists were inclined to view events in China in terms of a national rather than a class struggle, an additional and more important reason may have been that they had been nationalists before they were Communists. In certain cases, notably that of Li Ta-chao, co-founder of the Chinese Communist Party, this perception of events was reinforced by a populist tendency to regard "the people" as a single entity possessed of a collective will.[59] Interestingly, an official CCP history of the united front describes an essentially populist article written by Mao in 1919 (before he became a Communist) calling for a "great union of the popular masses" as one of the forerunners of the united front.[60]

Li Ta-chao retained an unorthodox approach to the analysis of Chinese society long after his conversion to Marxism. In 1924 he even went so far as to suggest that racial conflict occupied essentially the same position as class struggle in the determination of world events:

The white peoples [see themselves] as the pioneers of culture in the world; they place themselves in a superior position and look down on

58. J. Stalin, "Talk with Students of the Sun Yat-sen University," *Collected Works*, vol. 9, p. 246.

59. On Li Ta-chao's populism, see M. Meisner, *Li Ta-chao and the Origins of Chinese Marxism* (Cambridge, Mass., 1967), especially pp. 73–97, 217–223, as well as the same author's article "Leninism and Maoism—Some Populist Perspectives," *China Quarterly*, no. 45, January–March 1971, pp. 2–36.

60. Li Wei-han, "The United Front Leads the Chinese People to Victory," *Red Flag*, no. 11, June 1960.

other races as inferior. Because of this the race question has become a class question and the races on a world scale have come to confront each other as classes. . . . The struggle between the white and coloured races will occur simultaneously with the class struggle. . . . Thus it can be seen that the class struggle between the lower-class coloured races and the up-per-class white race is already in embryonic form and its forward move-ment has not yet stopped.[61]

Li also held the related opinion that because of its inferior status vis-à-vis the rich, white countries, China could be considered a "proletarian nation." This was a considerable distortion of the Comintern distinction between "oppressed" and "oppressor" nations, implying, as it did, the absence of class conflict within China, not to speak of the possible superiority of such "proletarian nations" over other states, including the Soviet Union. Indeed this was a point of view that had been specifically criticised by the Comintern when, in the 1920s, it was advanced by Sultan Galiev with reference to the Muslim countries. Galiev in fact had gone one step further than Li Ta-chao by arguing that the Western proletariat would retain a colo-nialist attitude even after it had won victory in the revolution, in which case the only solution would be to reverse Marxism and impose a dictatorship of the "proletarian nations" of the East over the former colonial powers of the West.[62]

MAO'S UNITED FRONT DOCTRINE

Although the second united front between the KMT and the Communists was never quite the orderly, planned, and controlled affair that the CCP was later to claim, it was sufficiently successful for it to be the model for what became, after the revolution, a "united front doctrine." When Mao wrote his various articles, he was usually considering some specific problem of the time and often his emphasis would vary according to the problem or sometimes the particular audience to whom his remarks were addressed—an obvious case being articles aimed at winning support among the KMT. However, there are enough common themes running through his writings on united fronts to justify the use of the word *doctrine* here. Mao's united

61. Meisner, *Li Ta-chao*, pp. 190–191.
62. H. C. d'Encausse and S. R. Schram, *Marxism and Asia* (London, 1969), pp. 35–36.

front doctrine may be conveniently divided into three sections: theory, strategy, and tactics, each of which will be considered in turn.

Theory

The practical importance of the CCP-KMT united front for the Chinese revolution—indicated by its position alongside the CCP and the PLA as one of the three "magic weapons" of the revolution[63]—is matched by the ideological significance that Mao attached to the united front as a concept. The united front to Mao was not simply a useful tactic but something that approached the status of an historical law. This emerges most clearly from the way in which Mao integrated the concept into the total ideology of Marxism-Leninism in his principal essay on dialectics, "On Contradiction."

Mao, in "On Contradiction," follows Engels's formulation of dialectical laws. His starting point is the Marxist theory of history and nature: Nothing is static; all things are involved in a continual process of motion and change. True comprehension of a particular thing, therefore, consists of understanding it in its dynamic aspect—as something that is "becoming" rather than something that "is." Thus it is necessary to understand the basic law governing change, which for Marxists is found in the notion of "contradiction": "The fundamental cause of the development of a thing is not external, but internal; it lies in the contradictoriness within the thing. There is internal contradiction in every single thing, hence its motion and development."[64]

Mao proceeds to examine four specific aspects of contradictions theory, each of which has important practical implications, especially with regard to Mao's approach to united fronts. The first of these Mao terms "the particularity of contradiction." In this section of his article, Mao attempts to combat what he terms "dogmatism"—dialectical analysis which takes no account of the specific circumstances of each "concrete" situation. His main concern is to counter critics of the second united front with the KMT by placing this within a dialectical framework. His arguments are, first, that it is necessary to distinguish among different kinds of contradictions: "Every form of motion contains within itself its own particular contradiction. This particular contradiction constitutes the particular essence which distin-

63. Li Wei-han, "United Front."
64. Mao Tse-tung, "On Contradiction," *Selected Works* (Peking, 1969), vol. 1, p. 313.

guishes one thing from another. . . . Every form of society, every form of
ideology, has its own particular contradiction and particular essence."[65]

"Qualitatively different contradictions," states Mao, "can only be resolved by qualitatively different methods." This seemingly innocent comment
marks the intellectual starting point of Mao's "sinification" of Marxism in
its implication, later spelt out by Mao, that revolutionary situations differ
from place to place, and that revolution does not need to follow a single
path. The "dogmatists," Mao states, "do not observe this principle. . . . On
the contrary they invariably adopt what they imagine to be an unalterable
formula and arbitrarily apply it everywhere, which only causes setbacks to
the revolution, or makes a sorry mess of what was originally well done."[66]

Mao moves even further toward flexibility in the application of dialectics
by his assertion that, although the form of any fundamental contradiction
will not change until it is resolved, the conditions under which it develops
will differ at different stages in time. In addition,

> Among the numerous major and minor contradictions which are
> determined or influenced by the fundamental contradiction, some
> become intensified, some are temporarily or partially resolved or
> mitigated, and some new ones emerge; hence the process is marked by
> stages. If people do not pay attention to the stages in the development of
> a thing, they cannot deal with its contradictions properly.[67]

Mao then broaches the political point that is the purpose of the
article—that the united front between the KMT and the CCP can be justified
by "Marxist-Leninist dialectics." He defines the KMT and the CCP as the
two sides or "aspects" of a contradiction, and argues that the relationship
between the two, while remaining one of underlying antagonism, has
not been the same at different stages of time as a result of each "aspect"
being involved in contradictions with other forces at different periods.
Specifically, when both have been opposed to imperialism this has given rise
to a situation where, in one contradiction, that between China and imperialism, the KMT and the CCP have been part of the same "aspect,"
whereas in another, that between the KMT and the "people," they have
been opposing aspects. These circumstances, Mao states, "have resulted
now in alliance between the two parties and now in struggle between them,

65. Ibid., p. 320.
66. Ibid., p. 322.
67. Ibid., p. 325.

and even during the periods of alliance there has been a complicated state of simultaneous alliance and struggle."[68]

The next section of Mao's article, headed "The Principal Contradiction and the Principal Aspect of a Contradiction," develops an idea which was to have a continuing importance in Chinese Communist analyses of both domestic and world politics. On the notion of a "principal contradiction," Mao writes as follows: "There are many contradictions in the process of development of a complex thing, and one of them is necessarily the principal contradiction whose existence and development determines or influences the existence and development of the other contradictions."[69] This leads to a further justification of the united front, and an elaboration of his earlier argument about the existence of many different contradictions. Mao asserts that

When imperialism launches a war of aggression against [a semicolonial country], all its various classes, except for some traitors, can temporarily unite in a national war against imperialism. At such a time the contradiction between imperialism and the country concerned becomes the principal contradiction, while all the contradictions among the various classes within the country . . . are temporarily relegated to a secondary and subordinate position.[70]

The last two sections of Mao's article, entitled "The Identity and Struggle of the Aspects of a Contradiction" and "The Place of Antagonism in Contradiction," are also attempts to place the united front policy in a dialectical context. Mao states that the two aspects of a contradiction exist in a relationship with each other of both identity (or unity) and struggle. There is identity because, "first, the existence of each of the two aspects of a contradiction in the process of the development of a thing presupposes the existence of the other aspect, and both aspects coexist in a single entity; second, in given conditions, each of the two contradictory aspects transforms itself into its opposite."[71]

On the other hand, struggle is the basic form of development for two aspects of a contradiction in the process of transforming themselves into each other. What Mao is trying to imply is that the "unity" between the CCP and the KMT can be considered in a dialectical light as a normal but

68. Ibid., p. 328.
69. Ibid., p. 331.
70. Ibid.
71. Ibid., p. 337.

temporary development. The key passage in this section is a quotation from Lenin: "The unity (coincidence, identity, and equal action) of opposites is conditional, temporary, transitory, relative. The struggle of mutually exclusive opposites is absolute, just as development and motion are absolute."[72] Mao elaborates on this argument by a further use of Engels's theory that there are nodal points at which a quantitative addition produces a qualitative change.[73]

Although Mao had the specific purpose in "On Contradiction" of arguing the case for the CCP-KMT united front, he could have achieved the same end by confining himself, like Lenin, mainly to pragmatic reasoning. That he chose instead to write a major theoretical essay may have been in part due to a desire to establish himself as a theoretician. However, it also reflected Mao's conviction of the significance of the united front concept. Mao's argument may be reduced to a few basic points: In any period of history one "contradiction" (and therefore one enemy) will be more important than the rest; as all other contradictions are secondary to this "principal contradiction," the objective possibility exists of uniting all other forces against the "principal enemy"; the historical role of the Communist party is to perceive the "principal contradiction" and turn the objective possibility of a united front into a reality; a particular united front is always temporary, for once its purpose is accomplished a new "principal contradiction" will emerge and the process will be repeated. The "concrete" message of "On Contradiction" is that the end product of a Communist's dialectical analysis of any situation will *always* be one form or another of united front. In an earlier article, also attacking "dogmatism," Mao spells this out even more clearly:

> Our chief method of investigation must be to dissect the different social classes, the ultimate purpose being to understand their interrelations, to arrive at a correct appraisal of class forces, and then to formulate the correct tactics for the struggle, defining which classes constitute the main force in the revolutionary struggle, which classes are to be won over as allies, and which classes are to be overthrown. *This is our sole purpose* [emphasis added].[74]

72. Quoted in ibid., pp. 341–342.
73. Ibid., p. 342.
74. Mao Tse-tung, *Oppose Book Worship* (originally published May 1930; Peking Foreign Languages Press, 1966).

Strategy

The united front strategy is defined most succinctly by Mao in his essay "On Policy." It is "to make use of contradictions, win over the many, oppose the few, and crush our enemies one by one."[75] "Making use of contradictions" implies several things which have already been discussed in the previous section: The principal contradiction must be distinguished from secondary contradictions; contradictions between the main enemy and other forces as well as "contradictions within the enemy camp" must be exploited.

The aim is to "win over the many." Mao's belief that it was possible to "win over" the overwhelming majority (sometimes said to amount to 90 percent of the people of China) to a united front may in part reflect the universalist aspects of the united front doctrine as it developed in China in the 1920s. It was also regarded by Mao as following logically from a correct dialectical analysis of a particular situation. Dialectics to Mao was essentially a matter of making distinctions, or "splitting one into two." In appraising the "balance of forces" in order to ascertain who are "enemies" and who are "friends," one first distinguishes one contradiction from another (the "particularity of contradiction") or, in other words, one analyses society in terms of the different contending forces within it: landlords-peasants, proletariat-bourgeoisie, and so forth. This will result in a balance sheet with a range of enemies on one side and on the other the historically "progressive" forces, all of whom may be considered temporary allies. Next one distinguishes principal from secondary contradictions. This immediately enables a whole batch of "enemies" to be moved across to the friendly side of the balance sheet. Finally one considers "contradictions within the enemy camp" and makes the necessary adjustments. The end product is likely to be what Mao claims—a united front of 90 percent or more of all social elements involved, and a "handful" of enemies.

Several points emerge from this. First, it is possible to distinguish three categories of "temporary allies" of the party according to their place in the overall framework of contradictions. First are those like workers and peasants who might be termed "close allies." Next are the "secondary enemies"—allies of today who are likely to be tomorrow's enemies. Third, there is a category which does not really consist of allies at all but which can

75. Mao Tse-tung, "On Policy," *Selected Works*, vol. 2, p. 289.

be counted as a favourable factor only by virtue of conflicts within the enemy camp. These give rise to what might be termed "unwitting allies." Finally, to work out by the "revolutionary algebra" of dialectics such a distribution of forces and to obtain in practice the "overwhelming majority" as members of a united front are clearly two different matters. For this reason the united front should be seen from three different perspectives: as an actual alliance of the Communist party with other parties; as a general policy directive instructing Communists to be alert to the many possibilities of securing allies; and as an expression of a belief that the dynamics of dialectics will inevitably produce allies.

Enemies will be defeated "one by one." Once a united front has achieved its purpose by isolating and defeating one enemy, another front will emerge, this time directed against an erstwhile ally. Each defeated enemy constitutes a successful stage in the revolutionary process. For this reason the united front strategy is essentially a *revolutionary* policy or, more correctly, "dual policy." As Mao explains,

> . . . for the whole period of the anti-Japanese war the party has a single integral policy—the national united front policy [a dual policy] which integrates the two aspects, unity and struggle—towards all those in the upper and middle strata who are still resisting Japan. . . . United front policy *is* class policy and the two are inseparable; whoever is unclear on this will be unclear on many other problems.[76]

United front tactics

If Mao's united front strategy can be summed up by a single sentence, the same cannot be said of his tactics. Tactical advice is scattered throughout Mao's work, and any attempt to organise this runs the risk of making his thoughts on tactics appear more orderly and systematic than they may in fact be. Moreover, the bulk of his work relates to the domestic political situation facing the Communists during the period of the Japanese war and is not always universally applicable. An additional problem is presented by Mao's constant reiteration of the need for flexibility in tactics in order to be able to meet all possible situations. However, certain tactical principles recur in many of Mao's writings with such consistency that they may be regarded

76. Mao Tse-tung, "Conclusions on the Repulse of the Second Anti-Communist Onslaught," *Selected Works*, vol. 2, pp. 466–467.

as essential to any united front operations, and it is these that this section will consider.

In accordance with his usual practice of "making distinctions," Mao asserts that different kinds of allies call for different tactics. Thus, the first requirement in planning tactics is some system of classification of enemies and friends. Mao is an obsessive categoriser, as the nineteen subdivisions in his article "Analysis of the Classes in Chinese Society" indicate.[77] However, in the original version of this article he distinguished among three broad social categories (upper, middle, and lower), which were further divided into five classes, defined essentially according to their attitude toward the revolution: complete opposition, partial opposition, neutrality, participation, and being the principal force. With some later elaborations to fit the altered circumstances, this remained the basis of subsequent attempts to differentiate among social groups by reference to their attitude toward the anti-Japanese war. In later articles Mao worked toward a tighter system of classification. For instance, in one article the peasantry was termed a "firm ally," whereas the petty bourgeoisie was a "reliable ally." The national bourgeoisie (essentially the KMT) was a vacillating ally which would join a united front "at certain times and to a certain extent because foreign oppression is the greatest oppression to which China is subjected." The "comprador big bourgeoisie" (local capitalists working for foreign enterprises) could be used only because different groups within this class worked for different imperialist powers, so that "when contradictions among these powers become sharper and when the edge of the revolution is narrowly directed against a particular power, the big bourgeois groups dependent upon the other powers may join the struggle against that particular imperialist power to a certain extent and for a certain time."[78] This group would continue to be antagonistic toward the Communists even when it was involved in a united front with them, and for this reason was the most suspect ally.

In one of his most important articles on united front tactics, Mao defines the three basic social groups within the united front as progressive, middle,

77. *Selected Works*, vol. 1, pp. 13–19. Original article translated in S. R. Schram, *The Political Thought of Mao Tse-tung* (Harmondsworth, 1969), pp. 210–214.

78. Mao Tse-tung, "Introducing the Communist," *Selected Works*, vol. 2, p. 289. See also "The Chinese Revolution and the Chinese Communist Party," *Selected Works*, vol. 2, p. 320.

and diehard.[79] The tactics to be employed with each group are summarised by the slogan "develop the progressive forces, win over the middle forces, and combat the diehard forces." From this (and many other references) it is clear that the purpose of a united front is not simply to oppose a common enemy but to bring about changes in the distribution of forces within the united front itself.

This is also the implication of one of Mao's central united front concepts, unity and struggle—the notion that, although unity against the principal enemy is the chief objective of a united front, this does not preclude the possibility of "struggle" (variously defined by Mao as education, criticism, or armed conflict) within the front. Indeed struggle is for Mao an essential requirement both for achieving the right kind of unity and for the purpose of altering the balance of forces in the front in favour of the "progressives." On the general relationship between unity and struggle, Mao states,

> . . . the means to unite all the anti-Japanese forces is struggle. In the period of the anti-Japanese united front, struggle is the means to unity and unity is the aim of struggle. If unity is sought through struggle, it will live; if unity is sought through yielding, it will perish. This truth is gradually being grasped by party comrades. However, there are still many who do not understand it; some think that struggle will split the united front or that struggle can be employed without restraint, and others use wrong tactics towards the middle forces or have mistaken notions about the diehard forces. All this must be corrected.[80]

Thus the first purpose of "struggle" was to achieve a solidly based unity. The second purpose was to "develop the progressive forces," which in the context of the time meant expanding the Communist armies, establishing base areas, and building up mass organisations. All this could be achieved only through struggle: "Within our own party and army, persistence in the struggle against the diehards is the only way to heighten our fighting spirit, give full play to our courage, unite our cadres, increase our strength, and consolidate our army and party."[81]

The third purpose of struggle related to the policy of "winning over the middle forces." This was thought by Mao to be "an extremely important task" and therefore one to be approached with the greatest care. There was a

79. Mao Tse-tung, "Current Problems of Tactics in the Anti-Japanese United Front," *Selected Works*, vol. 2, p. 422.

80. Ibid.

81. Mao Tse-tung, "Freely Expand the Anti-Japanese Forces and Resist the Onslaught of the Anti-Communist Diehards," *Selected Works*, vol. 2, p. 433.

wide range of groups and attitudes among the ranks of "middle forces": Some would join the Communists in struggling against the diehards, others might observe a benevolent neutrality, and still others a "rather reluctant neutrality." However, the characteristic possessed by all middle forces was their tendency to vacillate: "On the one hand they dislike imperialism, and on the other they fear thorough revolution, and they vacillate between the two."[82] This meant that the middle forces themselves would be the objects of education and criticism. Winning over the middle forces could be achieved only given certain conditions: "(*i*) that we have ample strength; (*ii*) that we respect their interests; and (*iii*) that we are resolute in our struggle against the diehards and steadily win victories."[83] The middle forces would thus be forced to take sides between the Communists and the diehards as a result of the struggle between the two and also would be encouraged to do so because of "material benefits" offered by the CCP.[84]

The "diehards" were of course the principal target of struggle within the united front. Because of their "counter-revolutionary dual policy" of opposing both the Japanese and the Communists, the party would pursue a "revolutionary dual policy" of unity and struggle against them. The struggle was to take ideological, political, and military form, and certain tactical principles were to be observed during the course of it:

> First, the principle of self-defence. We will not attack unless we are attacked; if we are attacked, we will certainly counter-attack. . . . Herein lies the defensive nature of our struggle. . . . Second, the principle of victory. We will not fight unless we are sure of victory. . . . We must know how to exploit the contradictions among the diehards and must not take on too many of them at a single time, but must direct our blows at the most reactionary of them first. Herein lies the limited nature of the struggle. Third, the principle of truce. After repulsing one diehard attack, we should know when to stop and bring that particular fight to a close before another attack is made on us. A truce should be made in the interval. . . . On no account should we fight on day after day without cease or be carried away by success. Herein lies the temporary nature of each struggle.[85]

82. Mao Tse-tung, "On Tactics against Japanese Imperialism," *Selected Works*, vol. 1, p. 155.
83. "Current Problems of Tactics," pp. 424–425.
84. Mao Tse-tung, "On Some Important Problems of the Party's Present Policy," *Selected Works*, vol. 4, p. 188.
85. "Current Problems of Tactics," pp. 426–427.

The slogan most commonly used to summarise these three principles was that struggle should take place "on just grounds," "to our advantage," and "with restraint."

Another important principle to be observed in united front operations, in Mao's view, was that the Communist party must secure the leadership of the front: The party must "criticise its allies, unmask the fake revolutionaries, and gain the leadership."[86] "Leadership" implied more to Mao than simply Communist control and direction of the united front, which explains the apparent contradiction in Mao's simultaneous call for all groups in the front to preserve their "ideological, political, and organizational" independence.[87] "Gaining the leadership" meant that the Communist party should set an example of model behaviour in united front organs of political power in order to win over wavering elements:

> Leadership is neither a slogan to be shouted from morning till night nor an arrogant demand for obedience; it consists rather in using the party's correct policies and the example we set by our own work to convince and educate people outside the party so that they willingly accept our proposals.[88]

The "independence" of different groups in the united front was, according to Mao, to be relative and not absolute, but he insisted that all should have a degree of independence. Mao did not spell out in any more detail this particular principle, but it would appear to relate to his concept of struggle within the united front, especially as the areas of autonomy that he lists (ideological, political, and organizational) are similar to his envisaged areas of struggle.

Two further points made by Mao in relation to united front tactics are worth noting. The first concerns what Mao calls "united front work" or "friendly armies work," while the second is on the necessity for all parties in the united front to have a common programme. "Friendly armies work" in

86. "On Tactics," p. 158. Mao was not entirely consistent on this point, even going so far as to declare in 1938 that the KMT "occupies the position of leader and framework of the united front" (cited in Schram, *Political Thought of Mao*, p. 299. Such references are, however, rare, as Schram points out.

87. Mao Tse-tung, "The Role of the Chinese Communist Party in the National War," *Selected Works*, vol. 2, p. 200.

88. Mao Tse-tung, "On the Question of Political Power in the Anti-Japanese Base Areas," *Selected Works*, vol. 2, p. 418.

the context of the time meant Communist operations in KMT-controlled areas. On this subject Mao wrote,

> Our policy in the KMT areas is different from that in the war zones and the areas behind the enemy lines. In the Kuomintang areas our policy is to have well-selected cadres working underground for a long period, to accumulate strength and bide our time, and to avoid rashness and exposure. In conformity with the principle of waging struggles on just grounds, to our advantage, and with restraint, our tactics in combatting the diehards are to wage steady and sure struggles and to build up our strength by utilising all Kuomintang laws and decrees that can serve our purpose as well as everything permitted by social custom. . . . [Party members] should develop extensive united front work, i.e., make friends in the Central Army. . . .[89]

This is a clear statement of the longer term function performed by a united front in undermining an ally by operating a united front "from below" as well as "from above."

On the need for a common programme, Mao writes, "Resistance to Japan requires a consolidated united front, and this calls for a common programme. The common programme will be the united front's guide to action and will serve also as the tie which, like a cord, closely binds together all the organisations and individuals in the united front."[90] As well as assisting "unity," a common programme would also have the effect of committing the KMT to a set of principles and policies, which, as the governing party, it would have the responsibility of putting into practice. In fact, Mao makes it clear that the main policy concessions in the programme would have to come from the KMT.[91]

CONCLUSION

There is much that Lenin and Mao have in common in their writings on united fronts. Both saw united fronts as "dual policies" and urged Communists to "struggle against" as well as "unite with" their allies. Both were at pains to point out to "dogmatists" the practical necessity for united

89. "Freely Expand," p. 435.
90. Mao Tse-tung, "Urgent Tasks Following the Establishment of Kuomintang-Communist Cooperation," *Selected Works*, vol. 2, p. 40.
91. Ibid., pp. 41-45.

fronts. Both based their advice about Communist policy in united fronts on a distinction among three broad categories of social forces. However, for Lenin united fronts were "transitional" policies, temporary expedients to be employed only during periods of Communist weakness. For Mao they were an intrinsic and essential part of the revolutionary process, necessary even after a Communist victory because contradictions would continue to exist, even "among the people," and united fronts were one means of resolving contradictions.

This difference between Mao and Lenin—essentially one of emphasis—is primarily responsible for such other, lesser differences as may be discerned. Mao's united front doctrine is more comprehensive and systematic than Lenin's, as well as being more fully integrated into an overall ideology. Ideas that in Lenin's work are only embryonic are translated by Mao into substantial treatises on "unity and struggle," "united front work," and so on. In particular Mao's treatment of the problem of intramural "struggle" is more detailed and sophisticated than its Leninist equivalent, primarily because Lenin was less interested in "winning over" the middle forces than in having them reveal their inadequacies.

There are many reasons for these differences, some of which have already been touched upon, such as the nationalist-populist ideas which influenced the early Chinese Marxists. Of primary importance, however, was the different revolutionary experience of the two men. To Mao "struggle" was not simply an intellectual concept but was for many years a normal part of existence. If his party were not to degenerate into just another warlord's army, its struggle needed to be placed clearly into the context of a longer term vision and a total ideology. "Struggle" had to be seen as both good in itself because of its "consciousness-raising" side effects and as a necessary part of a protracted revolutionary process. Similarly, the united front meant for Mao not just the party's alliance with the KMT and its short-term purpose of joint opposition to Japan but a grand strategic design involving the party's relations with the entire Chinese people and a continual, step-by-step revolutionary progression. This distinction between the broad applicability of the united front to "grand strategy" and its narrower role in influencing goals and tactics in relations with individual parties (or states) is further developed in the next chapter.

It was observed in this chapter that Lenin tended to keep the exploitation of "contradictions among imperialists" and the policy of forming united fronts with "vacillating allies" in separate analytical categories, whereas to Mao the existence of any "contradiction" implied the possibility of allies. It was further noted that the Comintern also combined the two tactics when it urged the formation of an anti-Fascist alliance in 1935. In this case the united front doctrine had been "adapted" to reflect the interests of the Soviet Union as a geopolitical rather than a class or revolutionary entity and also the emergence of a single enemy that was considerably more threatening than any of the other capitalist states. China too faced a single enemy but Mao, as a not yet victorious revolutionary leader, had constantly to bear in mind that the chief obstacle to his particular aims was not the Japanese but the incumbent Chinese leadership. For this reason, Mao did not, like the Comintern, simply assert that China needed all the allies it could get against Japan but saw the united front as a "revolutionary dual policy"—a means of advancing the CCP cause against two different enemies. Similarly, whereas "united front work" within a "united front from below" was effectively suspended by the British and American Communist parties after the USSR entered the Second World War, this was far from the case in China during the period of the second united front. There the CCP was able gradually to build up its strength for an eventual confrontation with its own "principal enemy" at the same time as and partly *in consequence of* its cooperation in a united front against China's enemy. Thus Mao's united front doctrine, although superficially similar to that of the Comintern in 1935, managed to retain the original "dual policy" function of the united front in integrating short- and long-term ends.

The tendency in the Soviet Union for the revolutionary objectives of united fronts to become more distant and less clearly integrated into the policies that went under the "united front" label should not simply be ascribed to "revisionism" or a decline in revolutionary fervour. The crucial difference between the CCP and the Soviet Union was that the one was a political party whereas the other was a state encountering the familiar security problems of states. The Soviet Union's experience demonstrated that, for itself at least, the theories, strategies, and tactics which had sufficed the Bolsheviks in their struggle for power were not wholly appropriate or applicable to the international sphere. Indeed, in its first actions as a state the Soviet Republic had been obliged to conform to certain customary international practices in signing the Treaty of Brest-Litovsk at the same time as it continued to assert its rejection of the traditional laws and conventions of international relations. From that point a process of "socialization" was observable in the Soviet Union's relations with other states to the extent that it adapted both its practice and ideology to the prevailing norms of the international society to which it now belonged. The changes in its perspective on united fronts were a small part of this process. One of the principal questions that is considered in this book is whether a similar process took place in China after 1949.

CHAPTER TWO

United Front or Alliance: Two Models of Chinese Foreign Policy

If the united front doctrine was a major influence on the formation and conduct of China's foreign policy, how might one expect this to be reflected in China's international behaviour? That in brief is the first question posed in this chapter. It is answered by considering in turn each stage of the Chinese foreign policy making process and asking how it might be affected by the united front doctrine. For greater clarity the conclusions at each point in the discussion are presented formally as numbered axioms or propositions, with the propositions taken together constituting a "united front model."

The purpose of models when used as scholarly devices is to reduce the real world to manageable proportions by focusing on a limited range of variables and holding other factors constant. Any analytical study has to do this to some extent; models merely aspire to be more rigorous, systematic, and explicit. In this case the model will also serve a more limited purpose: It will provide a convenient checklist of points to be referred back to in subsequent chapters which attempt to consider the actual influence of the doctrine on China's foreign policy.

It should be stressed at the outset that the following discussion is not intended to be a description of how Chinese foreign policy makers *actually* behave. Indeed it is unlikely that Chinese foreign policy making could ever function in quite such a precise and systematic way as depicted in the united front model. However, it is hoped that the model may provide a means of assessing the degree to which there is an ideological component in China's foreign policy by measuring its actual conduct against an "ideal type" situ-

ation in which ideology is a dominant factor. The model essentially offers a
set of interrelated predictions about China's international behaviour. It
suggests that given a number of alternative courses of action, one course is
more likely to be taken than the rest if the assumption is made that Mao's
thought in general and the united front doctrine in particular provide the
key "guides to action" for Chinese foreign policy makers.

THE UNITED FRONT MODEL

The same classification system as used in the discussion of Mao's writings in
Chapter 1 is employed in outlining the model. Hence, the discussion is
ordered under three broad headings: world view, strategy, and tactics.

World view

The Maoist world view includes a set of basic axioms about the nature of
political reality and in particular about the nature of change and development, the criteria for successful political action, and the roles and objectives
of non-Communist actors. It also incorporates a number of fundamental
goals and values. Taken together these comprise a system of core beliefs
which, if wholly accepted and acted upon, would establish the cognitive and
conceptual framework within which Chinese policy-makers operate and
would shape and set limits to China's international behaviour. The world
view revolves around the notion of "contradiction."

   Mao's version of contradictions theory has already been discussed in
Chapter 1. The facets of it that are relevant here include, first, the belief that
there are objective social laws ascertainable only by those possessing
the correct "consciousness"—an understanding of Marxism-Leninism. Second, history is seen as a set of processes working towards objectively
determinable ends rather than as a series of random, unpredictable events.
Third, the motive force of history is the contradiction thought to be
inherent in all social relationships. Fourth, all contradictions involve a relationship of conflict between a dominant but declining force and an inferior
but rising one, with a large, vacillating middle group. Fifth, social stability is
always regarded as a temporary condition since, when present, it always
masks underlying contradictions which must be resolved. Sixth, one contradiction will always be the principal contradiction whose existence and

development, as Mao puts it, "determine and influence the existence and development of other contradictions." Finally, economic factors are assumed to be at the root of social contradictions, which are thus seen ultimately as conflicts between social classes.

These are all notions about reality presented in Mao's writings as applicable in any time or place: They are general "scientific" laws. In practice a second set of world view axioms has been put forward as the concrete application of these abstractions to the actual world situation. Since Lenin's time, these axioms have included the notion that the chief characteristic of the current era is imperialism and various corollaries to this, such as the assumption that frequent conflicts among imperialist powers and also between imperialists and "oppressed nations" will occur until the defeat of imperialism. More generally, such axioms suggest that political actors—enemies, middle forces, and friends—will tend to behave according to one of a relatively limited number of recurring patterns: They will act according to type. This in turn implies that it is possible to generalise about and predict the course and outcome of many geographically separated situations. This is qualified in Mao's writings by his assertion of the need to take account of particular circumstances but, in their fundamental aspects, phenomena such as national liberation and imperialist wars or national bourgeois regimes are still seen to be obedient to the specific "scientific laws" which govern their behaviour in each case.

It should be noted that these more specific axioms are not seen by Mao as abstract principles but often have been derived from Mao's reflections on the Chinese revolution. They represent "thought" (*szuhsiang*) rather than "theory" (*lilun*).[1] Hence it is appropriate to describe as a third aspect of the Chinese world view the belief that the Chinese revolution offers useful analogies for comprehending other situations, including world politics.

Finally, the Chinese world view encompasses a set of ultimate goals and values. These include a belief in the value of struggle, particularly armed struggle, and the goal of world revolution via struggle against imperialism and capitalism. Such goals and values are thought to be "objective" in the sense that they merely reflect an appreciation of inevitabilities.

To the extent that Chinese policy-makers accept this belief system, the following inferences can be made about their basic conception of world politics:

1. Schurmann, *Ideology and Organization*, p. 24.

Proposition One: They assume that world politics are characterised by a set of unfolding relationships among necessarily conflicting forces.

Proposition Two: They believe that only Marxist-Leninists are capable of correctly understanding the nature of world politics and hence of arriving at correct policy decisions. Such decisions, in their view, must be based on a comprehensive analysis of a situation that includes an appraisal of all the contradictions involved in it—including internal social contradictions.

Proposition Three: In their view, correct policy-making must also involve an understanding of *process* as well as *situation*. That is, it must take account of the fact that underlying any political situation is a changing relationship among forces, and it must accurately perceive the *direction* of the change as well as the point in a situation's dialectical evolution that has been reached at a particular time. This implies that policy will be made with reference to a long-term assessment of the probable future outcome of a situation and that short-term considerations may at times be discounted.

Proposition Four: Long-term projections will generally tend to concentrate on the revolutionary prospects of a particular situation.

Perception and evaluation. The world view of policy-makers will influence the way they perceive and evaluate specific events. It acts as a kind of filtering process through which information passes and as a system for organising information into comprehensible and acceptable categories. Since the same event may be perceived differently according to different world views, the way in which policy-makers perceive events—the first stage in any policy-making process—can influence the remaining stages and hence the eventual decision. Two aspects of perception are considered here: the identification of incoming data and the receptivity of policy-makers to different kinds of data.

Since all phenomena in the political universe are, in the Chinese view, characterised by contradictions, all political data may be classified in terms of their relation to one or more contradictions. Hence the task of identifying information, at least in an "ideal type" Chinese foreign affairs bureaucracy, will consist essentially of establishing its place in an overall schema of global contradictions. It would be possible to hypothesize a somewhat absurd situation in which policy-makers constantly redrew their map of world contradictions in the light of fresh information. More plausibly, they could be expected to relate information to an existing framework of basic contradictions which some higher ideological authority had set out as a guide to action for a particular period. This not only appeals to reason but is bolstered by the fact that the ruling Communist parties in both China and the Soviet Union have on many occasions issued broad formulations setting down the major contradictions thought to exist at any one time. The assumption made here is that such formulations are actually used by foreign policy bureaucracies.

All foreign policy makers are confronted with more information than they can possibly employ in making decisions. Hence, they need to select information according to some criteria of relevance or importance. It may be, as some have argued, that policy-makers consciously or subconsciously work to avoid "cognitive dissonance"—they exclude information that does not agree with their previous conceptions or reinterpret it so that it does ("reconciliation" in the terminology employed here).[2] This question is considered elsewhere. At present the problem is whether there is anything in this basic Chinese belief system that might predispose policy-makers to be more receptive to certain kinds of information than to others.

An ideologically programmed computer might be able to sift out only certain kinds of data and exclude everything else. Human beings do not behave so mechanically, so it is possible to speak only of a tendency on the part of policy-makers to select certain information. With this qualification, it may be argued that Chinese policy-makers could be expected to be most receptive to information which

1. Indicates revolutionary prospects in a country or region;

2. Points to an existing imbalance or the means to create an imbalance of world (or state or regional) forces, rather than suggests the possibility of a balance;

3. Indicates the underlying weakness or isolation of an enemy;

4. Suggests the similarities between social units thought to be part of the same "aspect" of a contradiction (for example, "semicolonies," "national bourgeoisies," "imperialists");

5. In general confirms the Chinese world view or could be related to the CCP's revolutionary experience.

The preceding analysis also suggests how Chinese policy-makers might evaluate information in terms of its relation to their world view and goals, for the selection of data is itself a form of initial evaluation. In addition Mao's theory of contradictions provides a more precise framework for

2. See K. Brodin, "Belief Systems, Doctrines, and Foreign Policy," *Cooperation and Conflict*, vol. 7, no. 2 (1972), p. 99.

evaluating the significance of particular events. All information may be fitted into the categories of principal or secondary contradictions. This suggests a hierarchy of importance with events relating to the principal contradiction at the top and information which implies a strengthening of the lesser (or revolutionary) aspect of the principal contradiction most important of all.

The foregoing discussion may be presented in the following manner:

Proposition Five: Chinese policy-makers classify and evaluate information in terms of Mao's theory of contradictions.

Proposition Six: They are inclined to select information which accords with their world view and revolutionary goals.

Strategy

Two propositions need to be introduced immediately, for they advance the fundamental assumptions on which this section is based:

Proposition Seven: There is such a thing as a Chinese foreign-policy strategy. That is, Chinese policy-makers attempt to relate individual policies to a set of long-range goals and to a general strategy for the attainment of those goals.

Proposition Eight: Although the details of China's foreign-policy strategy will change from time to time, it will always be conceived of as a united front strategy.

At the broadest level, any united front strategy would have four characteristics. It would be aimed against a single enemy; it would attempt to align many diverse forces against that enemy; it would distinguish among "progressive," "middle," and "diehard" components of such a broad united front; it would operate a "unity and struggle" strategy within the united front with the aims of "developing the progressive forces" and radicalising other elements in the front.

In the international context these general principles would take the form of a foreign-policy strategy derived in the first instance from a conception of the nature of the principal contradiction, which would be defined as the conflict between the major obstacle to world revolution and the chief force opposing it. The aim of the strategy would be to assist the resolution of this contradiction by uniting all possible forces against its principal "aspect." As, in Mao's view, the revolutionary process consists of precisely such resolving of contradictions, the purpose of the strategy would be seen as the promotion of world revolution. This is not to say that such a strategy might not also have a defensive aspect. Indeed it could be argued that a policy of uniting all possible forces against an enemy points to an essentially defensive purpose. However, a genuine united front strategy would have one fundamental distinguishing feature: It would be a "dual policy" with the aims not only of opposing an enemy but also of revolutionising allies.

In pursuit of this second aim, Chinese leaders would have to translate into concrete terms the two general principles referred to earlier: distinguishing different categories within the united front and conducting a "unity and struggle" strategy. L. P. Van Slyke has commented on the difficulties which might be involved for Peking in an attempt to apply the united front doctrine to its international relations:

> In so complex an arena the analysis is hard to make and even harder to apply. The inducements and threats that are so much a part of the united front are difficult for China to exercise internationally; perhaps more important there is as yet no world wide common goal to which the Chinese Communists can claim exclusive rights, as they once succeeded in doing with nationalism inside China.[3]

Whether Peking actually has employed an international front strategy, how (if it has) it translated the united front doctrine into specific formulations suitable for the international arena and whether it met with problems of the kind referred to by Van Slyke are all questions considered in the next chapter. Here it needs simply to be noted that while the united front doctrine does broadly indicate the characteristics that would be present in any united front strategy, including an international one, it does not give clear guidelines for the conduct of an international united front strategy. Mao, for example, in one article merely outlined the main facets of his *domestic* united front strategy, and asserted "We deal with imperialism in the same way."[4]

A number of further propositions may now be added to the united front model:

> *Proposition Nine*: The main target and "core allies" of an international united front strategy would be determined by a conception of what constituted the "principal contradiction" at any time.

3. Van Slyke, *Enemies and Friends*, p. 4.
4. "On Policy," p. 291.

Proposition Ten: An international united front strategy would have the dual purpose of isolating and defeating a principal enemy and shifting leftward the balance of forces within the united front.

Tactics

Mao is at pains to point out the need for tactical flexibility in many of his writings, so it would be wrong, even in an "ideal type" model, to assert that a united front policy *must* employ specific tactics. Nevertheless, it may be argued that the Chinese leadership might be predisposed to use certain tactics simply because they were familiar and had been successful in other circumstances. Hence,

Proposition Eleven: Some or all of the following tactics would be likely to be employed by Peking in an international united front:

a. Isolating the diehards. Peking would seek ways of containing and eventually destroying the influence of the most anti-Communist elements in an international united front. Mao suggests various tactics towards this end, including "direct blows at the most reactionary of them first," "wage steady and sure struggles," and "use all laws and decrees that can serve our purpose as well as everything permitted by social custom."

b. Winning over the middle forces. A united front strategy succeeds to the extent that it is able to create a bandwaggon effect in the desired "progressive" direction. It aims to achieve this by both carrot and stick (or unity and struggle) as well as subtler forms of pressure. In the international arena "material benefits" (such as trade or aid agreements) might be offered as inducements to "middle force" governments to adopt positions closer to those of China on international issues. International forums of "middle force" countries might be encouraged by Chinese representatives to adopt a series of "common programmes," each one more "progressive" than the last. "Vacillating" elements might either feel obliged to go along with the tide or be subjected to "struggle"—most probably of the "education and criticism" variety. Peking might have dealings not only with the official leaderships of "middle force" countries but with radical groups inside such countries, thus operating a "united front from above and below."

c. Developing the progressive forces. The "principal contradiction" would define not only the main target of a united front but also the chief force seen to be in antagonism with it. In a domestic united front an alliance between this force and the Communist party (for example, peasantry-CCP in revolutionary China) would represent the core alliance within the united front, with the two together making up the "progressive forces" whose "development" would be a major Communist objective. By this analogy, one sector of an international united front would be seen by Peking as having the most important role in combating the principal enemy, whereas other sectors would be regarded as having supporting roles.

Specific united fronts

It has been argued here that the united front doctrine might have an application to China's foreign-policy strategy, or to what might be termed the "general line" of China's foreign policy. It might also provide a model for China's relations with individual non-Communist countries. If it is assumed that this is in fact the case, then a number of implications may be inferred about Peking's objectives in situations where it establishes a close relationship with a non-Communist government. The chief of these may be stated as follows:

Proposition Twelve: When China develops a close relationship with a non-Communist state, Peking's objective is to pursue a "dual policy" towards that state of encouraging revolutionary tendencies within it at the same time as and partly by means of an alignment with it against an external enemy.

The implication of this is clear enough: Peking's objective in forming what may be termed a "specific united front" is the same as that of the CCP in its united front with the KMT. Given this, a number of additional inferences may be made:

Proposition Thirteen: The criteria that Peking will use in selecting a state for membership of a "specific united front" will include the local revolutionary possibilities in the state concerned as well as the line taken by its government on international issues.

Proposition Fourteen: As well as working with the government of its "specific united front" partner, Peking will also establish a "united front from below" with local leftist forces.

Proposition Fifteen: Peking will encourage the government of its "specific united front" partner to adopt a radical line on international issues as part of its "broad united front" strategy but also as a means of enhancing the position of local "progressive forces" and isolating local "diehards."

Proposition Sixteen: The same tactics that Peking might use as part of a "broad united front" strategy might also be employed in a "specific united front."

AN ALTERNATIVE APPROACH TO CHINA'S FOREIGN POLICY

Three of the key facets of the united front model are, first, its depiction of China's foreign policy as a long-term strategy aimed at the promotion of world revolution; second, that foreign policy is seen by the model as *internally* determined—derived from factors peculiar to China, namely, the united front doctrine and the CCP's revolutionary experience; third, its portrayal of China as primarily an *active* initiator of events rather than as simply reacting to them. This is not to claim that policy-making in China is a one-way process, with a flow of decisions from Peking that are influenced only by ideology and take no account of external developments (although China's foreign policy did sometimes have this appearance during the Cultural Revolution). Rather, it suggests that any changes in China's foreign policy that might take place in response to external developments would be conceived of by Peking as merely tactical adjustments to exploit fresh opportunities or take account of new circumstances, with no alteration of long-term strategic aims. Furthermore, even the range of tactical options open to China might be circumscribed by the tactical principles that are also a part of the united front doctrine, with ideology thus shaping *both* "action" and "reaction."

Of the many other possible interpretations of China's foreign policy, one is particularly interesting in the present context for its basic premises stand directly opposed to those of the united front model, that is, it sees China's foreign policy as concerned with short-term problems, externally determined, and reactive. This is the view which, emphasising China's weakness and vulnerability, points to the threat to China from several powerful adversaries and sees a concern for security as the dominant theme of China's foreign policy.[5] This conception tends to see Chinese objectives as limited and short term[6] and China's international behaviour as consisting primarily

5. "A highly realistic judgement of China's multiple weaknesses would appear to be the most consistently held view of her policymakers." A. Huck, *The Security of China* (London, 1970), p. 35.

6. For example, C. P. Fitzgerald, "The Directions of China's Foreign Policy," *Bulletin of the Atomic Scientists*, June 1966, pp. 65–70.

of reactions to the moves of others.[7] Peking's policy in the Korean and Sino-Indian wars as well as its support for "people's wars" in Southeast Asia and its conflict with the Soviet Union have all been explained by some analysts as primarily reactions to perceived security threats.[8] This approach, while not wholly discounting ideological considerations, tends to downgrade them on the grounds that Maoist ideology is so flexible that it allows and can justify whatever policy moves Peking cares to make.[9]

There is enough *prima facie* evidence to suggest that this approach might provide valuable insights into China's foreign policy objectives. China is unique among states since 1949 in having had its army exchange fire with both Soviet and American troops, and it is weak compared with its major adversaries. For this reason and because the approach is different in certain basic respects from the united front perspective, I propose to spell out its implications more formally by presenting them as an alternative model of China's foreign policy. The united front model attempted to explain China's foreign policy at both the general and specific levels: It hypothesised a single basic determinant of foreign policy as a whole and of a particular decision to establish a close relationship with an individual state. This latter aspect suggests both a name and a focus for the second model. Instead of being seen as a "united front," a close relationship between China and another state might be more conventionally regarded as an "alliance," with the equally conventional aim of enhancing China's security. Hence the term *alliance model* will be used to refer to this second approach to China's foreign policy, although, as with the first model, it attempts to explain not only China's bilateral relationships but the broader aspects of China's foreign policy aims and imperatives.

The use of the word *alliance* in this context needs to be defended—briefly—since it normally denotes a formal pact in which two or more states pledge to give each other military support in the event of their in-

7. For a detailed discussion of this view, and of the related notion that Chinese domestic politics have been affected by international developments, see M. B. Yahuda, "Chinese Foreign Policy: A Process of Interaction," in I. Wilson (ed.), *China and the World Community* (Sydney, 1973), pp. 41–66.

8. Korea: A. S. Whiting, *China Crosses the Yalu* (New York, 1960); the Sino-Indian conflict: N. G. A. Maxwell, *India's China War* (London, 1970); Southeast Asia: P. van Ness, *Revolution and China's Foreign Policy* (Berkeley, 1970); U.S.S.R.: O. E. Clubb, *China and Russia: The "Great Game"* (New York, 1971).

9. For example, J. Gittings, "The Great Power Triangle and Chinese Foreign Policy," *China Quarterly*, July–September 1969.

volvement in a war.[10] China has signed only one such pact, with the Soviet Union, so that clearly, if this definition of alliance were accepted here, it would be possible to consider only a single aspect of China's foreign policy. For this reason an alliance is defined here as a commitment by one state to another to render assistance in the event of a threat from a third state. The distinguishing features of an alliance are thus seen to be an act of commitment and a concern with security problems. By this definition, an alliance may be formal or informal, and the type of commitment embodied in the alliance is left unspecified.

This definition is employed partly because it enables three of the four case studies (China's relations with Cambodia, Indonesia, and Pakistan) to be analysed from the perspectives of both the "united front" and "alliance" models. However, the definition is also defensible on the grounds that it accords with contemporary international practice. For example, the Soviet Union is allied with China, while the United States has had no formal treaty with Israel or South Vietnam. Yet few would deny that the American *commitment* to Israel and South Vietnam in the 1960s was, to say the least, considerably stronger than that of the Soviet Union to its "ally." In fact, comprehensive formal alliances such as NATO have been the exceptions rather than the rule in international relations. The pattern before the 1870s was for formal treaty commitments to be entered into either just before or during a war, so that the treaty of alliance merely formalised an already existing alignment of states.[11] Since 1945 informal alliances (such as that between the Soviet Union and Egypt or the U.S.A. and Israel) often have been more significant than their formal counterparts and the latter, with a few exceptions, have tended to become vaguer and more loosely defined than earlier alliances.[12] Finally, although the dispatch of troops in the event of war is the usual kind of alliance commitment, this is not always, or necessarily, the case.[13]

10. See the discussion in O. R. Holsti, P. T. Hopmann, and J. D. Sullivan, *Unity and Disintegration in International Alliances* (New York, 1973), pp. 3–4.

11. W. L. Langer, *European Alliances and Alignments 1871–1890* (New York, 1950), pp. 5–6.

12. For example, where the North Atlantic Treaty states unequivocally that an attack on one signatory would be considered an attack on all, SEATO and the ANZUS pact refer only to the requirement for each party to "act to meet the common danger in accordance with its constitutional processes."

13. A. Wolfers, "Alliances," in Sills (ed.), *International Encyclopaedia of the Social Sciences*, p. 269.

Before outlining the alliance model, I may need to state that the intention of this chapter is not to present a "Cold War" view of China in the united front model and a "revisionist" view in the alliance model. The first model certainly depicts a China out to change the world and prepared to this end to interfere in the domestic politics of other states. However, this is not the same as portraying an aggressive, expansionist China. It would be quite improper to take seriously in a model one facet of Maoist ideology—the united front doctrine—and not the rest of it, which, among other things, envisages not a world in which one state is dominant but a free association of national Communist societies[14] and eventually the disappearance of the state altogether. Conversely, a concern for security does not necessarily imply a defensive posture. The initiators of many, if not most, wars have used the pretext, sometimes justly, that their security was threatened. The crucial question concerns the means available to a state to provide for its security. As some of the recent critiques of American foreign policy have pointed out, a state's "defensive" perimeters can, if it has the power, grow to include the whole world. In China's case, lack of power has precluded an attempt to provide for security by global or even regional domination, although if China had the necessary power, the "alliance model" would point to China's attempting to set up at least a sphere of influence in Asia.

In any case, the dichotomy proposed in this chapter does not depend only upon a distinction between "ideological" and "security" motivations. Goals such as survival and security are likely—if not certain—to be part of the value system of any social entity, including a revolutionary one. Rather, the two models derive from contrasting assumptions about the relationship between states and the international system of which they are part. The first model depicts a China in command of events and able to exploit them for her own long-term ends. The second stems from a more general assumption that the foreign policies of all states, including China, are shaped by the nature of the international system and their geopolitical location in it. By the "nature of the international system" is meant simply the condition of mutual conflict and competition that, according to some, is forced upon states by the anarchic character of international relations.[15] This, it is assumed

14. See Mao's interview with Edgar Snow in *Red Star over China* (London, 1968), pp. 102–103.

15. This view is referred to by one writer as the "traditional paradigm" of international relations theory. A. Lijphart, "The Structure of the Theoretical Revolution in International Relations," *International Studies Quarterly*, vol. 18, no. 1 (March 1974), p. 42.

here, creates its own imperatives and systemic patterns which tend to impose a conformity of behaviour upon the component parts of the international system. The phrase "geopolitical location" denotes the combined effect of a state's geographical situation vis-à-vis other states and its position in the political hierarchy of states—the factors which are assumed here to determine the specific impact of the international system upon an individual state.

In assessing China's geopolitical location five factors need to be emphasised. First, China is surrounded by powerful states, notably the USSR, Japan, and India, as well as the forces of the U.S.A. in Taiwan, Korea, and elsewhere. Second, China, as the world's third most powerful state, forms one side of a great power triangle, with its own inner dynamics and patterns of behaviour. Third, adjoining China are several small and often unstable Southeast Asian states with their own rivalries and conflicts. Fourth, China is an important member of the Communist world, which again has its own individual concerns and behavioural characteristics. Finally, China has an identity also as a member of the Afro-Asian "Third World" of developing states.

The principal assumption, therefore, of the alliance model is that China's foreign policy should be interpreted as a search for security in the context of an international system which shapes and limits the available options. This immediately suggests the first propositions of the alliance model, which concern the basic conceptions about the nature of world politics that will be held by Chinese decision-makers and the framework of assumptions which underlies their perception and evaluation of events:

> *Proposition One*: Chinese policy-makers see world politics as comprising a system of states competing for advantage over one another. In the existing system, China's position relative to her rivals is weak and, in the perception of her leaders, China faces a greater number of immediate and direct threats.
> *Proposition Two*: Chinese policy-makers perceive and evaluate international events in terms of their effect upon the security of China. Events will be ranked in importance according to the extent to which they involve an immediate and direct threat to China or offer some means of countering such a threat.

The main thrust of China's foreign policy, given such a perceptual framework, may be outlined in this fashion:

Proposition Three: Chinese diplomacy will be aimed at obtaining the most favourable global and regional balances of power, that is, balances in which threats to China are neutralised as far as possible by the countervailing force of other states.

It will be noted that these first three propositions are concerned primarily with security factors and situations involving threats to China and do not incorporate any suggestion that Chinese policy-makers might be motivated by stronger ambitions than the desire to ward off threats and hence survive. In other words, they do not postulate a China that is a very *active* competitor with the major powers. This is because the alliance model consists, much more than the united front model, of a "here and now" set of axioms derived from a central hypothesis that, given its *present* position of weakness, Peking has been obliged to adopt a defensive posture in which the keynotes are pragmatism and flexibility. A further proposition may be advanced on the basis of this assumption:

Proposition Four: There is no such thing as a long-term Chinese foreign policy strategy, merely a series of adjustments to external developments with the objective of maximising security.

In the united front model, Chinese policy-makers tended to act as if the only significant constraints upon them were the inexorable laws of history, their superior understanding of which, in any case, accorded them a greater capacity to control and influence events. Such freedom and initiative would be much less apparent in the alliance model's version of Chinese foreign policy since in most cases there would be a degree of inevitability about decisions, given both China's weakness and the pressures upon China that stem from her location in the international system. Hence,

Proposition Five: China's international behaviour will tend to be determined by imperatives and constraints arising out of China's geopolitical location in the international system.

As suggested earlier, the counterpart in this model to a "specific united front" is an alliance. Assuming that "specific alliances" are governed by the broad considerations outlined here, the following propositions may be added:

Proposition Six: China's primary objective in forming an alliance is to improve its military and diplomatic power vis-à-vis that of its adversary: The enemy, not the ally, is the object of the exercise. This means, *inter*

alia, that China would be unlikely to align itself for ideological or other reasons against a state which was not a direct threat to China.

Proposition Seven: The overriding criterion employed by China in selecting an ally is that the candidate for an alliance shares China's perception of a threat.

Proposition Eight: Although the possibility of interference by China in the internal affairs of its ally cannot be excluded from the alliance model, it is unlikely that China would interfere when its ally's international stance met its requirements.

Proposition Nine: The general pattern of China's alliance policy will be determined by regional and global balance-of-power considerations.

CONCLUSION

In the real world of policy-making in China or anywhere else, policy decisions are normally the result of a complex interplay among many different forces. This chapter has attempted, for analytical purposes, to isolate two of the possible forces which might affect Chinese foreign policy making—ideology and the international system—and to make explicit the consequences which could be expected if either formed the dominant influence on China's foreign policy. To reiterate an earlier point, this is not to claim that Chinese foreign policy does or could conform completely to either model. The following chapters, which assess the models against China's actual international conduct, do not ignore the many other forces that have affected China's behaviour, or the interplay among them.

It should be noted that the two models are not wholly dichotomous in all respects: There is some overlapping between certain of their propositions. This is inevitable given that both revolve around questions concerning the amity and enmity between states. For instance, there is only a thin dividing line between the Marxist notion of the inevitability of conflict and the "condition of mutual conflict and competition" between states that was postulated in the second model. In addition, considerations of security play a part in both "united fronts" and "alliances." Moreover, the regional and global balance of power factors that, it was suggested, would have a major role in determining the general pattern of China's alliance policy, would also enter into the formation of a united front strategy, even if in the latter case they would be termed "contradictions."

Nonetheless, if the models are taken in their entirety rather than as a series of isolated propositions, they represent fundamentally different sets of predictions about the course of China's foreign policy. Some of the basic differences have already been mentioned (the distinctions drawn between short- and long-term, active and reactive, and internally and externally determined policies). In other respects, the united front model contains a number of propositions which simply have no counterpart at all in the alliance model—its developmental conception of world politics and its tactical principles, for example. However, the most crucial difference between the models centres upon the depiction of united fronts as essentially revolutionary strategies and alliances as pragmatic, ad hoc arrangements.

The united front doctrine derives from the CCP's experience in fighting a revolutionary war and, if it has been applied to international affairs, this would be in part because of its earlier success in the domestic arena. If, however, all of the problems and situations that might be encountered on the international stage could *not* be extrapolated from the CCP's revolutionary experience, then inadequacies would appear in the united front doctrine. As suggested in the Introduction, two possible responses to such an occurrence are "adapting" doctrine or attempting to "reconcile" apparent contradictions between doctrine and reality in such a way that reality would fit the doctrine. This is a major theme of the next chapter.

CHAPTER THREE

The United Front
and the General Line

The two models developed in the previous chapter advanced interpretations of China's foreign policy at the general as well as the specific level. It is with the former of these levels that this chapter is concerned. It considers, in the light of the two models, the changes in Peking's foreign policy and formulations on international affairs that have occurred since 1949. Specifically it seeks the answers to five questions:

1. Which states were designated by Peking as "friends" and which as "enemies" during this period, and what distinctions were drawn within each category?

2. What factors were responsible for these designations?

3. What factors caused Peking to change its assessment of enemies and friends?

4. Did Peking conduct a "unity and struggle" strategy with its friends?

5. Is there any evidence of an "adaptation" of ideology over this period?

THE "HARD LINE" OF 1949–1950

What was to be the first foreign policy stance of the People's Republic of China had been unequivocally stated by Mao in his 1949 article, "On the People's Democratic Dictatorship"[1]: China was to "lean to one side" and participate in an "international united front" based on an alliance among

1. Mao Tse-tung, "On the People's Democratic Dictatorship," *Selected Works*, vol. 4, p. 415.

China, the Soviet Union, and other Communist states and containing the "broad masses of people in all other countries" in order to spearhead the world revolutionary struggle. Not only was neutrality eschewed by China—"sitting on the fence will not do, nor is there a third road"—but Peking accepted the current Soviet position which denied the possibility of any state remaining neutral in the conflict between "imperialism" and the world's "peace-loving forces."[2] This meant in particular that the claims of the new "national bourgeois" governments of Asia to be able to pursue an independent foreign policy were rejected, and such governments were not regarded as suitable candidates for an international united front.[3]

Hence, during 1949–1950 Peking's foreign policy was officially based upon a conception of an international united front, albeit one "from below," which excluded all governments except those of Communist countries. Two questions arise: Was this actually a united front strategy of the kind outlined in the last chapter, and what factors led Peking to adopt this position?

There is very little in the "leaning to one side" policy that suggests a Maoist united front strategy. United fronts were intended to apply to relations between Communist and non-Communist forces, not to an alliance among Communist states. Furthermore, in the Chinese conception they were supposed to be based on a very broad, not an exclusive association of forces. In addition, there was in the 1949–50 policy no distinction among different factions within the united front nor any suggestion of a "unity and struggle" strategy—nor was there a notion of a "core alliance" between the Communists and the force thought to be most in conflict with the "principal enemy" of the era. In short, none of Propositions Seven to Eleven of the united front model (those concerned with an international united front strategy and tactics) appears to fit China's policy during this period.

It is worth noting that the policy in 1949 did not fully accord with pre-1949 formulations on international affairs, that there are certain consistent threads in these earlier formulations, and that they are closer to the "ideal type" united front strategy outlined in Chapter 2 than were China's actual policies in 1949–1950. For example, in his 1946 talk with Anna Louise Strong, Mao declared that a U.S. attack on the Soviet Union could not take

2. The Soviet position had been spelt out in an important speech by Zhukov in 1947, reprinted in d'Encausse and Schram, *Marxism and Asia*, p. 262.

3. A detailed account of Soviet strategies towards the "national bourgeoisie" is contained in J. Harris, "Communist Strategy." See also J. H. Brimmell, *Communism in South East Asia* (London, 1959), pp. 249–263.

place until the U.S. had "subjugated" all the countries in the "vast zone" that lay between the two—thus implying the possibility of a united front policy towards these intermediate countries.[4] An inner-party memorandum, written by Lu Ting-yi in January 1947, advanced a more elaborate version of this argument, referring to a large "neutral area" between the U.S. and the Soviet Union and claiming that this meant that the contradiction between the two great powers, although "basic," was neither "imminent" nor "dominant."[5] This implied that another contradiction was "dominant," which by united front logic suggested the existence of a "core ally" for an international united front. A year later, Liu Shao-ch'i continued to present a uniquely Chinese view of the international situation. For example, instead of arguing a "hard-line," antineutralist thesis—"all those not for us are against us"—he reversed this to argue, in effect, that "all those not against us must be for us":

> When these two camps are in sharp conflict, people line up with one side or the other. That is, if one is not in the imperialist camp, if one is not assisting American imperialism and its accomplices to enslave the world or one's own people, then one must be in the anti-imperialist camp.[6]

Moreover, Liu urged Communists in colonial and semicolonial countries to form united fronts with "that section of the national bourgeoisie which is still opposing imperialism," adding that failure to do so would be "a grave mistake."[7] It is true that Liu, in accepting the "two camps" thesis, had abandoned the earlier CCP formulations about a "neutral area," but he retained a relatively generous approach to the question of who qualified for membership of the "peace camp."

None of these analyses can be seen as a sophisticated application of the united front doctrine to international politics. However, they do appear to reflect the influence of certain facets of the doctrine. In particular, they suggest an assumption on the part of the CCP leadership that relationships of conflict are inherent in world politics (Proposition One of the united front model), a long-term conception of the process by which the major world

4. Mao Tse-tung, "Talk with the American Correspondent Anna Louise Strong," *Selected Works*, vol. 4, p. 99.

5. Lu Ting-yi, "Explanation of Several Basic Questions Concerning the Post War International Situation," in L. P. Van Slyke (ed.), *The China White Paper August 1949* (Stanford, 1967), vol. 2, pp. 713–714.

6. Liu Shao-ch'i, *Internationalism and Nationalism* (Peking, 1951), p. 32.

7. Ibid., p. 47.

contradictions were to be worked out (Proposition Three), an ultimate revolutionary objective (Proposition Four), an attempt to classify and evaluate information in terms of contradictions theory (Proposition Five), a tendency to relate international issues to the experience of the CCP's revolutionary war (Proposition Six), and the beginnings of a conception of an international united front strategy in which a "principal enemy" would be opposed by a vast conglomeration of other forces, one of which would have the major role (Propositions Seven to Nine). There was no clear formulation of a "unity and struggle" strategy within the united front, although it may be noted that in April 1945, when the Soviet Union was still refraining from criticising its allies, Mao had made it clear that he saw the anti-German alliance from the perspective of his long-term notion of "unity and struggle":

> . . . within the camp now fighting Fascist aggression there are forces which oppose democracy and oppress other nations, and they will continue to oppress the people in various countries. . . . Therefore, after international peace is established, there will still be numerous struggles over the greater part of the world—between the anti-Fascist masses and the remnants of fascism, between democracy and anti-democracy, between national liberation and national oppression.[8]

Why then, if the CCP before 1949 appeared to have a relatively sophisticated and flexible approach to international affairs, did it adopt the rigid position of "uniting with" only the Communist states and not, as the united front doctrine would suggest, of seeking a much broader basis from which to oppose the United States? Part of the answer may be expressed in terms of the alliance model. It could be argued, for instance, that China's desperate economic conditions and Peking's perceived need for protection against the U.S.A. necessitated an alliance with a great power, and the Soviet Union was the only possible choice—as well as the only possible source of aid and advice for the building of a socialist economy. Hence, the alliance had to be accepted on Soviet terms, and these included the adoption of Moscow's line on international issues.

If this were a complete explanation of China's policy, it could be maintained that China, like the Soviet Union at Brest-Litovsk, had in its first international action been compelled to veer from its preferred course because of the international realities it faced. However, the matter is more

8. Mao Tse-tung, "On Coalition Government," *Selected Works*, vol. 3, p. 207.

complicated, and it is difficult to dispose of ideological factors so easily. In 1949 Stalin's ideological infallibility was still widely accepted by Communists, so that following a Soviet line could easily be justified on ideological grounds as well as those of expediency. Furthermore, in 1949 there did appear to be some prospect of Communist successes in Asia and Europe, and in such circumstances a "united front from below" might have been seen as a more appropriate weapon than a more defensive and long-term "united front from above and below."

More crucial than these considerations is the question of whether an alliance with the Soviet Union was the best option open to Peking for advancing China's security interests. The CCP had many reasons for feeling unsure about the degree of Moscow's attachment to its cause: Stalin's advice to it after 1945 to dissolve its army and seek a *modus vivendi* with Chiang Kai-shek[9]—exactly the same advice as Washington had rendered,—the patent Soviet ambition of regaining the concessions in China that it had lost to Japan in 1904,[10] Moscow's refusal to grant some of the CCP's requests for military aid in 1948–1949,[11] and its activity in Manchuria and Sinkiang,[12] to name only some of the most recent manifestations of Soviet ambivalence toward the CCP. Indeed, Stalin had made it clear in his negotiations with Mao that he did not particularly *want* an alliance with China.[13]

One possible option open to Peking was to follow Tito's example by remaining nonaligned and seeking a *rapprochement* with the United States. There were, of course, good reasons why the CCP should feel antagonistic in 1949 towards the state which had done most to prop up the Chiang Kai-shek regime. Nonetheless, there had been two consistent threads in Washington's China policy which might have suggested to the CCP that the Titoist alternative was at least worth considering. The first was that Washington had, from the beginning of the Marshall mission to China in 1946, made it clear that U.S. support for the KMT would not "extend to

9. V. Dedijer, *Tito Speaks* (London, 1953), p. 331.

10. M. Beloff, *Soviet Policy in the Far East, 1944–1951* (London, 1953), pp. 25–37.

11. D. Floyd, *Mao against Khrushchev* (London, 1964), p. 338.

12. Beloff, *Soviet Policy*, pp. 37–49.

13. Mao Tse-tung, "Speech at the Tenth Plenum of the Eighth Central Committee," in S. Schram (ed.), *Mao Tse-tung Unrehearsed* (Harmondsworth, 1974), p. 191.

14. Tang Tsou, *America's Failure in China* (Chicago, 1963), p. 352.

United States military intervention in the course of any Chinese civil strife."[14] Second, Washington's primary concern was with containing Soviet influence in China, not with keeping Chiang in power, and if the CCP had towards the end of the civil war made any serious move to indicate that China under its rule would not automatically align itself with Moscow, it might have met with some response from the U.S. This is hinted in a National Security Council report in 1948, which concluded,

> For the foreseeable future, therefore, U.S. policy toward China should be (*a*) to continue to recognise the National Government as now constituted; (*b*) with the disappearance of the National Government as we know it, to make our decision concerning recognition in the light of circumstances at that time; (*c*) to prevent as far as possible China's becoming an adjunct of Soviet politico-military power.[15]

After Tito's rift with Moscow became public in June 1948, Washington immediately began to explore the possibility of a repeat performance by the CCP,[16] although this possibility had of course been mooted much earlier.[17] Even after the Communist victory in China and particularly during the subsequent Sino-Soviet negotiations, Washington continued in its efforts to bring about a split between the two. Moreover, until the outbreak of the Korean War it refused to undertake a commitment to protect the KMT government on Taiwan.[18]

All this is not to say that the alliance with Moscow was a wholly irrational move by Peking. As well as economic benefits, China did receive a guarantee of its security against a threat from Japan or a state allied with Japan. If, however, one asks whether, in view of the foregoing argument, China really *needed* this guarantee or whether, perhaps, its alliance actually *decreased* its security—the guarantee itself thus creating the need for the guarantee—this can only be answered by saying that Peking clearly *perceived* that it needed an alliance. If one then asks why it held this perception, one is drawn unavoidably into the kinds of preconceptions and images of the world that were held by the Chinese Communists in 1949 and hence into the influence of their ideology.

15. Cited in G. Warner, "*America, Russia, China and the Origins of the Cold War 1945–1950*" (seminar paper of the Contemporary China Centre, Australian National University, 1974), p. 4.
16. Ibid., p. 17.
17. Tang Tsou, *America's Failure*, pp. 195–219.
18. Warner, "America, Russia, China," pp. 19–20, 22.

If the united front doctrine did not have much influence on China's policy towards non-Communist "friends" in 1949, it may have affected Peking's view of "enemies." The doctrine asserts that *inevitably* one "principal enemy" will be replaced by another, which will in its turn seek to dominate the world. When Mao began, in 1947, to refer to the U.S. as having "taken the place" of Japan and Germany, this may have reflected as much a predisposition to see the U.S. in this light as the impact of American policies.

THE BANDUNG PERIOD

Towards the end of 1950, a new note began to appear in Chinese pronouncements on international affairs. Statements began for the first time to number some of the Asian "nations" as well as "peoples" among the "peace-loving" forces of the world.[19] A distinction was also drawn among different Asian governments along the lines of the united front division between "diehard" and "middle" forces. For example, one article saw significance in the U.N. General Assembly voting pattern on the Korean question:

> The overwhelming majority of the Arab-Asian nations oppose the U.S. policy in Asia. Despite U.S. pressure, no Asian country, apart from the bankrupt governments of the Philippines and Thailand, supported the "thief cries thief" resolution of the U.S. The peoples of Asia now rightly see American aggression against Korea as only the most unbridled aspect of an aggressive policy towards Asia as a whole that carries a direct threat to each one of them.[20]

The most important hint of a change in China's attitude towards the new states of Asia came in a speech by Mao Tse-tung in which he appeared to call for a united front between the socialist countries, and India and other "peace-loving" nations: "Today . . . we hope that the two nations, China and India, will continue to unite together to strive for peace. . . . India, China, the Soviet Union, and all other peace-loving countries and people unite together and strive for peace in the Far East and the whole world."[21] The

19. *People's China*, 5 January 1951.
20. "Imperialist America Wants War, not Peace," *People's China*, 16 February 1951.
21. Report of a reception given by Mao for the Indian Ambassador, *People's China*, 26 January 1951.

culmination of this new period in China's foreign policy came with the Bandung conference of Afro-Asian nations in 1955, at which Chou En-lai went to some lengths to project a new, conciliatory image of China.

Many factors relating to China's short-term diplomatic requirements clearly contributed to the shift in China's foreign policy after 1950. The independent outlook shown by several Asian states over the Korean issue may have come as a surprise to Peking, but only a completely rigid and dogmatic government could have refused to capitalise on it. In the early 1950s Indian good will was particularly important to Peking in the aftermath of China's invasion of Tibet, since India was in a position to give a degree of legitimacy to China's move.[22] Furthermore, Peking needed to break down the American wall of containment and obtain some of the basic essentials of statehood—diplomatic recognition, trade, and a seat in the United Nations.

Was there anything more to China's diplomacy than such short-term considerations? In particular, can China's behaviour be seen as a shift towards a Chinese-style united front strategy? The first step in any united front strategy must be that of "uniting the many." Can Peking's Bandung diplomacy be seen as an effort to find the lowest common denominator among "the many" in order to take this first step?

Certain aspects of Chinese policy during this period do suggest that the united front doctrine might have had some influence on Peking's approach to its international relations. The first was Peking's comprehensive approach towards winning friends in the Afro-Asian world. At Bandung Chou En-lai not only sought ties with nonaligned states but also offered concessions to the Asian members of the American alliance system. The Philippines was offered a nonaggression treaty, while Thailand was invited to inspect the "Thai Autonomous Zone" in Yunan in order to be assured of its peaceful purpose. The united front doctrine implies that it is preferable to "struggle against" secondary enemies—"diehards" and "middle forces"—from *within* a broad united front directed against a single enemy, and this notion may have played some part in Chinese thinking.

Second, Peking consistently tried to draw connections between "American imperialism" and the specific local issues that were the chief concern of some of the Bandung participants, such as the Indian claim to

22. After at first strongly opposing the Chinese move, the Indian government signed an agreement with China over the status of Tibet on 29 April 1954. Text in *People's China*, 2 May 1954.

Goa, Indonesia's claim to West Irian, and the Palestinian question.[23] Peking clearly had short-term political motives in doing this—for example, it also tried to link such issues as the West Irian question to China's claim to Taiwan in an obvious attempt to secure a *quid pro quo* in terms of diplomatic support.[24] However, these moves could also have been intended to serve the longer term purpose of focussing the attention of a united front upon its principal enemy. Certainly Chinese media comment throughout the Bandung period is full of references to the necessity for "educating" the Afro-Asian countries to recognise "who are their friends and who are their enemies," and this suggests a less limited aim than simply obtaining support for China's Taiwan case.

Third, Peking's claims in the early 1950s that China occupied a position of leadership in Asia bear some resemblance to Mao's conception of the nature and purpose of CCP leadership of the united front inside China:

> The Chinese people have elevated their nation to its rightful place as one of the leaders of the world, . . . we have set a new standard for the peoples of Asia and the Pacific. We have given them a new outlook on their own problems. [Peking] serves as the birthplace of the new unity of the Asian and Pacific peoples in their struggle for harmony among nations.[25]

This appears to suggest that China would "lead by example," much as Mao believed the CCP should in China's domestic united front.

On balance, however, it is difficult to reach any definite conclusion about the influence of the united front doctrine as distinct from that of the more limited and short-term considerations mentioned earlier. Several characteristic features of united fronts were absent from China's policy during this period: a clearly enunciated long-term strategy, a "dual policy" element

23. Peking sometimes stretched logic a little far in this endeavour. For instance, Goa was described as "in effect" a U.S. military base because of the 1951 U.S.–Portugal defence agreement (*People's China,* 8 May 1955).

24. Afro-Asian leaders did not always take the proferred bait. See Indonesian Premier Ali Sastroadmidjojo's careful statement in 1956: "Essentially and juridically the West Irian question is comparable to Taiwan in the sense that West Irian is juridically Indonesia's and Taiwan is juridically China's. However, from the international political point of view the two questions are different and need different settlement" (Survey of China Mainland Press [SCMP] 1077).

25. "For Peace in Asia, the Pacific Regions, and the World," *People's China,* 17 September 1952.

in China's relations with Asian states, intramural "struggle," and clear distinctions among different parts of the united front. India does appear to have been singled out for special attention by Peking, but this seems to have been due more to India's importance for the security of Tibet than, as the united front doctrine would require, India's position as the leading "middle" force. Finally, the basis for unity within a united front was, in the Chinese view, struggle against a common enemy. In the early 1950s, Soviet and Chinese propaganda revolved around the "peace" slogan, but this was not wholly suited to the strict requirements of a united front policy since it did not create the desired image of confrontation. However, it may be noted that this problem seems to have been appreciated by Peking, judging by the way the Chinese press attempted to define "peace" in terms which suggested a process of struggle:

> Peace is a concept with many aspects for the peoples of Asia and the Pacific. It means more than the absence of general war. [Because even without a general war, imperialism still threatens the existence of many Asian nations.] To Asian and Pacific peoples, therefore, *peace and national independence are so closely linked as to be indistinguishable* [emphasis added].[26]

The nonapplicability of the united front model here does not mean that the alliance model provides a complete explanation of China's policy. Peking was not so much concerned with security problems at Bandung as with obtaining certain basic prerequisites, such as diplomatic recognition, which were essential if China was to have any significant degree of interaction with the outside world—whether its objectives in such interaction were revolutionary or conventional. However, the initial impetus for the shift in Peking's policy may be seen as an attempt to counter American moves in Asia perceived as threatening to China's security, notably intervention in Korea and the establishment of an Asian alliance system. In addition, China's concentration on India was largely a function of geopolitical factors—India's closeness to some of the most sensitive and strategically important areas of China. Hence, to the extent that China's policy in this period was reactive, short term, and determined by geopolitical considerations, the alliance model offers a better perspective for interpreting it than the united front model.

26. Ibid.

STRUGGLE AND UNITY 1957–1959

After the Suez crisis Peking tended to lay less stress on "peace" as a basis for solidarity and to emphasise instead the "national independence movement" in Asia and Africa. However, until the end of 1957 the main thrust of Peking's policy was still "unity," with even Western European allies of the U.S. praised in 1956 for "demanding peaceful coexistence"[27] and Thailand and the Philippines earning favourable mention for asserting their independence.[28]

The stress on "unity" in Peking's general line changed after Mao decided in November 1957 that the prevalence of the "East Wind" over the "West Wind" enabled an intensification of struggle.[29] One of the apparent repercussions of this decision was a change in Peking's attitude towards the Afro-Asian countries. For the first time since the early 1950s the Chinese press began to criticise a number of Afro-Asian states and to take sides in some of their disputes. In November 1957 it took the side of Syria in a dispute with Turkey.[30] In March 1958 it praised the formation of the United Arab Republic, while remarking that the Iraqi-Jordan federation was "quite another matter."[31] In the same year it supported Indonesia's suppression of a U.S.-backed rebellion in Sumatra,[32] whereas, by contrast, it supported the rebel side in Lebanon and criticised the Lebanese government for filing a complaint against the U.A.R. at the Security Council.[33] It also gave strong backing to the Iraqi rebellion of July 1958 and later criticised the U.A.R.'s attitude to the rebellion as well as its suppression of its local Communist party.[34] The U.A.R. was also criticised for its policy of nonalignment on the

27. See "Western European Countries Demand Peaceful Coexistence," *Shih Chieh Chih Shih*, 6 June 1956.

28. "A Year of Rapid Development of the National Independence Movement in Asia and Africa," *Shih Chieh Chih Shih*, 20 December 1956.

29. *People's China*, 16 December 1957.

30. *People's China*, 18 November 1957.

31. *Peking Review*, 11 March 1958.

32. *Peking Review*, 18 March 1958.

33. *Peking Review*, 17 and 24 June 1958.

34. The exact wording of its commentary on Iraq is worth noting: "The victory of the Iraqi people has greatly changed the balance of power in the Middle East. A keystone of imperialist aggression has collapsed; a whole nation has turned its guns in a new direction and become a forefront of the anti-imperialist front" (*Peking Review*, 22 July 1958). The criticism of Egypt appeared in an

grounds that this could become "a step towards going over to the enemy," and Nasser was likened to Chiang Kai-shek during the period of the first united front in China.[35] In 1959 China also came into conflict with India, Pakistan, and Indonesia. Finally, the formulation approving Afro-Asian states' "defence of national independence" came in 1958-1959 to be increasingly displaced by a new slogan with more military and revolutionary undertones, supporting their "struggle for national liberation."

Although some of these incidents, notably China's quarrels with India and Indonesia, clearly related to traditional Chinese concerns (the border question and the status of the overseas Chinese), several overall trends are discernible. In disputes between states Peking consistently backed the more anti-U.S. side, it supported tendencies towards unity among states where these appeared to work against U.S. interests, and it supported leftist revolutions against pro-U.S. regimes. In addition, it displayed a strong interest in Middle Eastern developments.

Peking explained its new emphasis on both anti-U.S. "struggle" and on "struggle" against some of the states which it had wooed at Bandung in terms of united front logic. Indeed from 1958 onwards it began to refer to an "international united front" whose members were supposedly linked either "objectively" or concretely by common opposition to "U.S. imperialism."[36] Peking argued that the U.S. was overextended in the world and lacked the necessary strength to intervene simultaneously in several different areas and hence was "vulnerable at many points."[37] In view of this, "broadly based, just struggles" would succeed in weakening the U.S. at little risk of their sparking off a world war.[38] Significantly, Peking also asserted that anti-U.S. struggles would prepare the ground for ousting local "reactionary" leaders. This was because in war people would "quickly raise

article entitled "The True National Interests of the Arab Peoples," *Peking Review,* 24 March 1959.

35. "Imperialism Is the Sworn Enemy of Arab National Liberation," *Peking Review,* 7 April 1959. The general thrust of this article was to argue the inadequacies of a posture of neutralism in the current world situation.

36. See "A New Upsurge of National Revolution," *Peking Review,* 26 August 1958. This used the term *international united front* and also maintained that the national independence movement and the socialist camp "now form a common front against imperialism."

37. *Peking Review,* 19 August 1958.

38. *Peking Review,* 5 January 1960.

their level of political consciousness," and in particular Communists and other revolutionaries would "grow to maturity amid stresses and strains which *provide them with the opportunity of getting to know the laws of struggle against the reactionaries*" [emphasis added].[39]

Although by 1959 a new category of "reactionary" states, headed by India, had taken its place alongside "imperialism," support for India's position in the Sino-Indian dispute or for other "anti-Chinese" policies did not, in Peking's view, place a state in the "reactionary" camp and disqualify it from membership of the united front. This was still to be determined—as the united front doctrine would suggest that it should be—mainly by a state's attitude towards imperialism:

> It must be pointed out that the leaders of these [Afro-Asian] countries often, in varying degrees, align themselves with the reactionary clique in its anti-Chinese movement. Where they differ from the latter is that there still exist certain contradictions between them and the imperialists, and besides that they cherish the desire for peace and neutrality.[40]

The united front model clearly fits China's policy during this period more closely than it did China's Bandung diplomacy. First, Peking appeared to be basing its 1957–1959 policies on certain ideologically derived assumptions. Specifically, its statements and policies imply a long-term conception of world politics in terms of various unfolding relationships among conflicting forces, all of which were seen as contributing to a single revolutionary process which Peking believed it could comprehend and guide (Propositions One to Four of the united front model). Second, international developments were classified and evaluated according to their relation to a schema of "contradictions" (Proposition Five)—"contradictions" with China over the Sino-Indian issue were regarded as less crucial than "contradictions" with the U.S.A. Peking also focussed upon those events (mainly in the Middle East) which could most readily be related to the Maoist world view and revolutionary goals, regardless of their geographical distance from China's own region and China's relative lack of influence in the Middle East (Proposition Six). Moreover, Chinese formulations on international affairs included the four chief characteristics of a united front strategy: a single enemy, a broad united front, distinctions among its different components, and a "unity and struggle" strategy within it (Propositions Seven and Eight). Peking had also

39. *Peking Review*, 19 August 1958.
40. "Ten Years' Peaceful Foreign Policy," *Shih Chieh Chih Shih*, 5 October 1959.

indicated that the united front strategy was to have the dual purposes of isolating a principal enemy and eventually defeating local "reactionaries" (Proposition Ten). However, Peking had not yet defined a "principal contradiction," so that although the identity of the main target was clear enough, this was not the case of the "core allies" (Proposition Nine). Nor was there much evidence of a sophisticated application of united front tactics to the international arena, primarily because the united front at this stage had no tangible reality. The significance for this study of the period 1957–1959 is that it produced the first systematic attempt to *formulate* China's foreign policy in terms of Mao's united front doctrine. The united front in this period may be seen principally as an intellectual construct—a device for making international relations intelligible in terms of the CCP's revolutionary experience and ideology and for establishing guidelines for China's foreign policy.

1960–1965: TWO UNITED FRONT STRATEGIES

The period 1960–1965 witnessed not only many major developments in China's foreign relations but also, in the polemics with Moscow, the most comprehensive and systematic formulation to date of a uniquely Chinese position on international affairs. It would be impossible here to give more than a cursory account of either the events themselves or the vast Chinese literature which accompanied them. Hence, commentary on this period is confined to three salient aspects of it: Peking's international united front policy, the impact of the Sino-Soviet dispute on the united front doctrine, and the changes in Peking's attitude towards Western European countries in 1963–1964.

Until 1964, Peking's argumentation on the issue of an international united front continued along the lines that had begun to emerge in 1958–1959: an emphasis on both anti-U.S. and intra-united front "struggle," coupled with an increasingly confident assertion that the key components of the united front were to be found in liberation struggles in the Third World. The principal difference was that the thesis that China's revolution—including its united front experience—provided a model for comprehending world politics and a strategy for revolution was now more fully and insistently stated.

In April 1960, "Long Live Leninism," the first major Chinese salvo in the initially indirect polemics with the U.S.S.R., set out the main points of the Chinese position on united fronts. Apart from its reiteration of the principal arguments of the united front doctrine—such as the necessity for a "unity and struggle" strategy towards vacillating middle elements—its chief point of interest here is the following demand:

> The liberation movement of the proletariat in the capitalist countries should ally itself with the national liberation movement in the colonies and dependent countries; this alliance can smash the alliance of the imperialists with the feudal and comprador reactionary forces in the colonies and dependent countries.[41]

Not only was the target of the united front clearly defined as the imperialists *and* local "reactionaries" but the subsequent Chinese position that national liberation movements in the Third World were at the centre of world revolution was already being hinted in 1960. This argument was to feature in the open polemics between China and the U.S.S.R. in 1963, when Moscow denounced the "new theory" of the "Chinese comrades" that the "decisive force in the struggle against imperialism" was the national liberation movement.[42] Peking replied that these were not the words it had used, but its refutation of the Soviet attack made it clear that only a semantic quibble was involved, since it also claimed, "In a sense...the whole cause of the international proletarian revolution hinges on the outcome of the revolutionary struggles of the peoples in these areas [Third World countries]."[43] The Chinese line received its strongest statement in Lin Piao's famous "cities and rural areas" thesis in 1965[44] and in a number of articles the same year which asserted for the first time that "the contradiction between the oppressed nations of Asia, Africa, and Latin America and imperialism is the primary one in the world today."[45]

Although Peking in 1960 gave armed revolutionary struggle in the Third World the leading role in combatting U.S. imperialism, it continued to assert the need for a *broad* international united front comprising many elements other than revolutionaries and many other "forms of struggle."

41. "Long Live Leninism," *Peking Review*, 26 April 1960.

42. *Apologists of Neo-Colonialism* (Peking, 1963), pp. 16–17.

43. Ibid., p. 18.

44. Lin Piao, *Long Live the Victory of the People's War* (Peking, 1965), pp. 48–49.

45. Mao K'uang-sheng, "The Khrushchev Revisionists' Fear of Contradictions," *Red Flag*, 31 July 1965.

Indeed in May 1960, Mao himself, in the first of several such statements, declared, "To defeat the reactionary rule of imperialism, it is necessary to form a broad united front and unite all forces, excluding the enemy, that can be united with and continue to wage arduous struggles."[46]

Peking's "general line" on the international united front may be briefly stated as follows. First, since armed struggle was "dealing imperialism direct blows,"[47] it had a "front-line" position.[48] Those countries in which armed struggle was taking place were equated with the revolutionary base areas during the Chinese revolution.[49] Second, it was believed that all "struggles for peace, national independence, democracy, and socialism" were interconnected in the sense that all would meet with opposition from "U.S. imperialism."[50] Since, given this, different kinds of struggle all "objectively" supported one another, it was possible for the assorted "strugglers" to cooperate in a broad united front.[51] The "patriotic national bourgeoisie and even certain kings, princes, and aristocrats who are also patriotic" could all form part of such a united front.[52] However, since these elements invariably vacillated and given the dual aims—defeat of imperialism *and* advancement of revolution—of a united front, "contradictions within the united front" would inevitably emerge, and hence the policy towards the "national bourgeois" members of the united front should be one of "unity and struggle."[53] To this end, distinctions were to be drawn among left, middle, and right sections of the national bourgeoisie,[54] with Nehru occupying the leading "rightist" position.[55] The aim was, as

46. *Peking Review*, 17 May 1960.

47. *Apologists of Neo-Colonialism*, p. 17.

48. "Form a Broad United Front to Defeat Imperialism," *Peking Review*, 24 May 1960.

49. "A Basic Summation of Experience Gained in the Victory of the Chinese People's Revolution," *Peking Review*, 8 November 1960.

50. Li Wei-han, "The Characteristics of the Chinese People's Democratic United Front," *Red Flag*, nos. 12, 16, June 1961.

51. Wen Shih-jun, "Scientific Judgement and Foresight: Study of Chairman Mao Tse-tung's Theses on International Questions as Expounded in the Fourth Volume of Selected Works of Mao Tse-tung," *Red Flag*, 16 November 1960.

52. "A Proposal Concerning the General Line of the International Communist Movement," *Peking Review*, 21 June 1960.

53. "Dialectics Is the Algebra of Revolution," *Red Flag*, 1 November 1960.

54. Ibid.

55. "More on Nehru's Philosophy in the Light of the Sino-Indian Boundary Question," *Peking Review*, 2 November 1962.

always, to change the balance of forces within the united front, which was also one of the purposes of "persisting in struggle" against the U.S.[56]

During the period 1960–1963, China's foreign policy posture came closer to the "ideal type" united front policy sketched in Chapter 2 than at any time before or since. Considerable thought clearly had been given to the question of how the united front doctrine was to be applied to international affairs without compromising principles. The result may be judged by a point-by-point comparison of the united front model with Peking's general line in 1960–1963. First, Mao's theory of contradictions lay at the heart of Peking's perception and evaluation of international affairs. Events were interpreted in terms of their relation to various global contradictions, while the importance of an event was assessed by considering its relation to the contradiction between the U.S. and the national liberation movement. Peking's replacement of the "national independence movement" as the leading force in the united front had the effect of highlighting its revolutionary objective. The same purpose was apparent in Peking's use of the "unity and struggle" concept in discussing its relationship with "national bourgeois" governments as well as in its attempt to distinguish progressive, middle, and diehard (or reactionary) categories within this group.

China's general line at this time could be considered a "reconciliation" of its practice with its ideology only if its actual behaviour was significantly different from its declaratory posture. One problem in assessing this is that Peking's involvement in world politics was not great in the early 1960s, so that very often—for example, with reference to Latin American affairs—there was little more substance to China's policy than the declarations and advice that appeared in Chinese newspapers. Hence, there was no need for "reconciliation" since on many occasions there was nothing to be reconciled. An additional difficulty lies in the fact that the "reactionary" nature of Indian policy—either in domestic or foreign affairs—was clearly less responsible for the Sino-Indian rift than the more traditional border conflict between them. In this case Peking's characterisation of India as "reactionary" and the close relationship it developed with America's SEATO ally, Pakistan, may accurately be described as "reconciliations"—attempts to reconcile practice with ideology. However, certain aspects of China's actual diplomatic behaviour do suggest a conscious attempt to apply the strategic and tactical principles of the united front doctrine to specific policies as well as to policy *formulations*.

56. "Dialectics Is the Algebra."

The first is some of the states which were the main objects of China's attention during this period: Indonesia, Algeria, Ghana, Mali, Guinea, and the Congo. The leaders of all of these countries were noted for their strongly "anti-imperialist" positions on international issues, and all could be considered to be either revolutionary states or in a revolutionary situation. Second, China's use of people's diplomacy and patronage of organisations like the Afro-Asian Journalists' Association or the Afro-Asian People's Solidarity Organisation bears comparison with the CCP's "united front work" behind the KMT lines in the 1940s.[57] Third, Peking devoted considerable time to pressing for a Second Afro-Asian Conference which, it made clear, it expected to adopt a much firmer stance against U.S. imperialism than had the first.[58] Indeed had the conference materialised, it would have been the culmination of one phase in a united front strategy and a showpiece for united front tactics.

Perhaps most important, however, was the long-term "educational" task which Peking had set itself in these years. The same messages were constantly reiterated at all meetings between Chinese and Afro-Asian leaders: the necessity for unity among Afro-Asian countries, the need to recognise the real enemy, the importance of struggle, the central role of the national liberation movement. Whatever the actual effect of such advice on its recipients, its intention was clearly that of "consciousness raising"—bringing about over time a fundamental change in the way in which Afro-Asian leaders viewed their problems. Of course it is impossible to state definitely what went on in the minds of China's leaders during this period, but it is not unreasonable to suppose that they genuinely believed they were participating in a classic united front exercise, that is, one based on a long-term appraisal of the underlying processes at work in the world and in which the objective was, through "consciousness raising," to bring about an orchestration of world forces such that the United States would find itself isolated and compelled to retreat and at the same time the "world view" of the participants would be changed in a revolutionary direction.

A problem already discussed in relation to China's policy in 1957–1959

57. For an analysis of the objectives of "people's diplomacy," see H. Passin, *China's Cultural Diplomacy* (New York, 1962), and also C. Neuhauser, *Third World Politics: China and the Afro-Asian People's Solidarity Organization 1957–1967* (Cambridge, Mass., 1968).

58. This was a very clear objective of Chou En-lai's visit to several African and Asian countries in late 1963–early 1964. See his report on his tour, *Peking Review*, 3 April 1964.

also arises for the 1960–1963 period: Can a policy which sought to isolate the United States be more properly interpreted in terms of the alliance model? That is, was China's policy basically conditioned by security factors (Proposition Two, alliance model), the involvement of the U.S. on the Asian mainland (Propositions One and Five), the possibility of taking advantage of the anti-imperialist sentiments of many Afro-Asian leaders (Proposition Four), and the aim of neutralising the threat to China by utilising the countervailing force of other states (Proposition Three)? Such an interpretation may be bolstered with a quotation from a Chinese article in 1963, which argued that the national liberation movement and revolutionary struggles in Afro-Asian countries "constitute an extremely important force safeguarding the socialist countries from imperialist invasion."[59]

The refutation of this line of argument may best be given by another quotation from the same article:

> The proletariat has very many allies in the anti-imperialist struggle in these [Third World] regions. Therefore, in order *to lead the struggle step by step to victory* and to guarantee victory in each struggle, the proletariat and its vanguard in the countries of these regions must march in the van, hold high the banner of anti-imperialism and national independence, and *be skilful in organising their allies* in a broad anti-imperialist *and anti-feudal* united front, exposing every deception practised by the imperialists, the reactionaries, and the modern revisionists, and leading the struggle *in the correct direction* [emphasis added].[60]

In other words the international united front was conceived of as a long-term and comprehensive strategy in which the Communist party in each component country of the united front would organise its own local united front and lead it along a revolutionary path similar to that which had been charted by the CCP. Such a strategy would aid the security of the "socialist countries," but it was clearly seen as a *dual* policy in which struggle against the U.S. would also be the vehicle of revolution.

While the U.S. continued to support genuinely "reactionary" regimes and to demonstrate its readiness for counterrevolutionary intervention in all three Third World continents, and while (as in the early 1960s) "national liberation" revolutions appeared to be enjoying a boom, Peking could be

59. "More on the Differences between Comrade Togliatti and Us," *Peking Review*, 15 March 1963.
60. Ibid.

both satisfied with the ideological correctness of its foreign policy and pleased that the course of events seemed to validate its basic theses. The development that was most instrumental in throwing into confusion Peking's view of world politics was its growing enmity with Moscow. Although denunciations of "revisionists" and "renegades" had been commonplace in the Communist movement since before 1917, there was little in Marxism-Leninism which either intellectually prepared Communists for or provided an ideological explanation of a split between the world's two greatest Communist powers. This was a totally new situation, and one which could be met only by a "reconciliation" or an "adaptation" of ideology. How Peking attempted to make the united front doctrine cope with this new development is considered shortly. First, however, two lesser points concerning the impact on the united front doctrine of the Sino-Soviet dispute need to be made.

First, the different Soviet and Chinese approaches to the question of an international united front formed one of the many issues in the dispute itself. The trend in Soviet doctrine on the Afro-Asian countries since 1956 had been towards acknowledging the possibility of some of them making a "peaceful transition" towards socialism.[61] In 1960 this process reached its fruition with the announcement of a new concept, "national democracy," which was intended to describe those countries making peaceful progress towards socialism.[62] Peking had privately criticised the notion of "peaceful transition" since 1957.[63] Although it accepted the reference to "national democracy" in the 1960 Moscow Conference of Communist Parties,[64] it made no subsequent mention of "national democracy" as such but, perhaps as a token gesture, sometimes used the phrase "national democratic revolution" interchangeably with "national liberation movement." China's attitude toward the "national bourgeoisie" retained its "unity and struggle" character and, unlike Moscow, Peking made no concessions to the possibility that the *internal* policies of "national bourgeois"

61. Donald S. Zagoria, *The Sino-Soviet Conflict 1956–1961* (Princeton, 1962), p. 40.

62. Ibid., pp. 360–362.

63. See its "Outline of Views on the Question of Peaceful Transition" in *The Origin and Development of the Differences between the Leadership of the CPSU and Ourselves* (Peking, 1963), pp. 58–62.

64. G. F. Hudson, Richard Lowenthal, and Roderick MacFarquhar, *The Sino-Soviet Dispute* (published by the *China Quarterly*, 1961), pp. 194–195.

governments might be "progressive."[65] In addition, as has already been noted, Moscow objected to Peking's elevation of the national liberation movement to the leading position in the struggle against imperialism. In fact, Peking was later to reveal that three aspects of the Chinese international united front strategy had been matters of contention at the 1960 Moscow Conference of Communist Parties and had been written into the final statement of the conference only after Chinese pressure. These were, specifically, the theses in the 1960 statement, "on the formation of the most extensive united front against U.S. imperialism; on the national liberation movement as an important force in preventing world war; on the thoroughgoing completion by the newly independent countries of their national democratic revolutions."[66] The last of these "theses" expresses obliquely the Chinese "dual policy" approach to the international united front—the notion that a united front with "national bourgeois" governments is aimed not only at the destruction of a principal enemy but, in the long term, at "thoroughgoing revolution" in the new states.

Second, the dispute adds to the complexity of the task of assessing Peking's motivations in advancing from 1960 a comprehensive set of Maoist doctrines on contemporary problems of revolution. When it first did this on a smaller scale in the late 1940s it might have genuinely believed in the value of its experience and/or seen it as a way of enhancing its own status. Now—particularly since the rift was clearly the catalyst for the flood of Chinese literature that appeared in 1960–1963—a third possible motivation emerged. Peking was from 1960 in more or less open competition with Moscow for the allegiance of Communist parties, particularly in the Third World. To obtain that allegiance it needed to demonstrate that Peking was an alternative, if not the only, source of ideological truth.

To return to the impact of the rift on the united front doctrine itself, as the enmity between the two states became increasingly bitter and less and less related to ideological issues Peking was gradually forced to recognise in Moscow at least as great a threat to its national security as Washington. As the U.S. began to wind down its involvement in Vietnam, Moscow emerged as the greater threat, but this period is dealt with in a subsequent section. However, one problem for Peking was apparent enough in 1960–1965: how to reconcile its hostility towards a state which was neither counterrevolu-

65. See *Origin and Development*, pp. 59–61.
66. Ibid., p. 37.

tionary nor particularly imperialistic, by accepted Marxist standards, with its ideology.

Several stages in Peking's approach to this problem may be discerned. In 1963, when the open polemics began, China's stand was relatively mild compared with what was to come later. Peking argued that its broad united front line was ideologically correct for five reasons:

1. It enabled the "political consciousness of the people" to be "ceaselessly" raised and the "struggle for world peace" to be expanded "in the right direction."

2. It made it possible to expand the "forces for world peace."

3. It enabled a constant growth in revolution and the consequent "manacling" of imperialism.

4. It permitted the fullest possible use to be made of contradictions between the U.S. and "other imperialist powers."

5. It made it possible to "smash the nuclear blackmail practised by U.S. imperialism"—presumably because, as the Chinese believed, nuclear weapons were useless in "people's wars."[67]

It was argued that by seeking détente with the U.S., Moscow was in effect collaborating with Washington and working against the true interests of the "world's people." Peking claimed that Moscow's "line of action denies the united front against U.S. imperialism and its lackeys in defence of world peace." Specifically, Peking denounced Moscow's "nuclear blackmail" and asserted that its "intimidation" of America's allies prevented them from struggling against U.S. "control."[68] However, confidence was expressed that the Soviet people would not allow themselves to be "manipulated" by the imperialists and that "many people now holding wrong views" would change their minds as U.S. policy became increasingly aggressive.

By 1964, references to Moscow's "great power chauvinism" had begun to appear alongside "revisionism" and "splittism"[69] in CCP denunciations of the CPSU. This clearly reflected the fact that the dispute between the two was coming increasingly to revolve around more traditional sources of international tension, such as irrendentism, and indeed, throughout 1964,

67. *Two Different Lines on the Question of War and Peace* (Peking, 1963), p. 36.
68. Ibid., p. 37.
69. *The Leaders of the CPSU are the Greatest Splitters of Our Time* (Peking, 1964), p. 61.

charges and countercharges of interference and border violations became a common theme in the polemics. The most forceful Chinese contribution was Mao's interview in July with a group of Japanese socialists, in which he declared "There are too many places occupied by the Soviet Union," and pointedly observed in reference to Soviet possession of former Chinese territories, "We have not yet presented our account for this list."[70] Although America's increasing involvement in Vietnam ensured that it would not lose its position as "principal enemy" of the united front, the expanding area of conflict between Moscow and Peking now placed the Soviet Union in *China's* enemy camp alongside U.S. "imperialism" and Indian "reaction." The latter categories could be easily justified ideologically, although, as explained earlier, in at least the case of India Peking's stance was clearly a rationalisation of its border dispute with New Delhi.

There were two principal reasons why it was less easy to write the Sino-Soviet dispute into united front formulations. "Reaction" had been a valid secondary target of an international united front, since it emphasised the revolutionary objective of a united front dual policy and could easily be related to the "struggle against the diehards" in the united front with the KMT. Attacks on "revisionism" could not be justified in this way, since the avowed objective of a *broad* united front policy was not to unite only those who agreed with every facet of Peking's world view but all forces except the principal enemy. Moreover, by the criterion of a state which did not feel itself threatened by Moscow, the U.S.S.R. would belong to the "progressive" or at least to the "middle" section of the united front. Peking at first tried to explain the necessity of struggle against "Soviet revisionism" by arguing that this weakened international communism, which was the core of the united front. Therefore, struggle *within the Communist movement* was essential if the united front were to receive the correct guidance.[71] By February 1966, it had become a dogmatic assertion that struggle against Moscow virtually had priority *for all* over opposing the U.S.: "Only by drawing a clear-cut line of demarcation between oneself and the Khrushchev revisionists and by carrying the struggle against Khrushchev revisionism through to the end can one wage a successful struggle against U.S. imperialism."[72] Since Peking was now urging opposition to a triple-headed

70. D. J. Doolin, *Territorial Claims in the Sino-Soviet Dispute* (Stanford, 1965), pp. 20–21.

71. *A Comment on the March Moscow Meeting* (Peking, 1965), p. 31.

72. *Confession Concerning the Line of Soviet-U.S. Collaboration Pursued by the New Leaders of the CPSU* (Peking, 1966).

monster—"imperialism, revisionism, and reaction"—this tended to discredit its simultaneous appeal for the "broadest possible" united front.

A second problem for Peking was that opposing "revisionism" was of somewhat limited interest to the members of the united front who were outside its Communist "core." To some of the "progressives," such as the national liberation movements, it appeared counterproductive, a theme on which Moscow played in its later calls for "united action" by Communists in Vietnam.[73] To the "national bourgeois" and other "middle forces," it was even less likely to appeal as a basis for unity than opposition to "U.S. imperialism." It was this last factor which was most responsible for prompting the first significant "adaptation" of the united front doctrine.

Until 1963, Peking had attempted to base its foreign policy on a united front conception which allocated the leading role to Third World armed struggle and secondary positions to radical Third World leaders, with any other forces involved in "contradictions" with the U.S. envisaged as having supporting roles. This image had the chief advantage of being easy to reconcile with the dual purposes required of an ideologically "correct" united front policy. It had the difficulties of being unlikely to win support from the more conservatively minded Third World leaders (particularly since they were liable to take exception to their "transitional" status) and of being unable to cope with the new Soviet problem. The majority of Chinese references to the international united front continued to employ this image until the start of the Cultural Revolution, but from 1963 they were joined by a second line of argument. In February 1963 Liu Ning-yi, in a speech at the AAPSO Conference at Moshi, declared,

> All countries, whether big or small, are equal and independent. The problems of the world must be solved jointly by all countries of the world. . . . The attempt to decide major problems of the world and to manipulate the destiny of mankind *by one or two countries* runs counter to the trend of our times and is against the interests of the people. . . . The countries of Asia and Africa as well as all peoples are *firmly opposed to the big powers bullying and oppressing and giving orders to the smaller countries* [emphasis added]. [74]

73. For Peking's reaction to the "united action" proposal, see *Letter of Reply Dated March 22, 1966 of the Central Committee of the Communist Party of China to the Central Committee of the Communist Party of the Soviet Union* (Peking, 1966).

74. *Peking Review*, 6 February 1963.

There are several points of interest in this statement. First, it suggests as a possible "principal enemy" of an united front not "U.S. imperialism" as such but a hierarchical international order dominated by a great power hegemony. Second, it implies both a different basis for unity—opposition to hegemony—and a new emphasis on the role of nation states, rather than revolutionary movements in an international united front. Third, although Liu specified only Afro-Asian countries, the phrase "smaller countries" can have a far wider application. Fourth, as the reference to "one or two" great powers clearly implies, this is an attempt to find a united front formulation which includes the Soviet Union as a target. Fifth, although the conception of an international united front in terms of small state antagonism to great power hegemony could be explained as an example of "making use of contradictions," it is nonetheless an "adaptation" of the united front doctrine in two ways. First, it has the effect of giving the revolutionary objective of a united front dual policy a less prominent place in the united front's order of priorities. Second, it suggests China's "socialization" within the international system in the sense that it reflects a concern with the traditional problems of the sovereign state and, more significantly, a tendency to look for their solution in the established patterns of operation of the state system.

It should again be emphasised that, until 1969 when a line similar to Liu Ning-yi's was revived, this new formulation remained very much secondary to that which saw "U.S. imperialism" as the "principal enemy" and the national liberation movement as the key component of the united front and allocated a place to revisionism mainly because of its "collaboration" with U.S. imperialism. It is possible that these two lines reflected a basic disagreement among Chinese leaders over foreign policy issues, with, to use a somewhat hackneyed but in this case appropriate terminology, the latter position representing a "radical," fundamentalist position and the former a "moderate," adaptive one. As will be seen, these appeared to be the lines drawn in Peking's foreign policy debate after 1969. For the moment, I shall return to Liu's line as it developed after February 1963 until its temporary demise during the Cultural Revolution.

In July 1963, an article by "Shih Ch'un"—a pseudonym also used by the author of an important "moderate" series of articles on China's foreign policy in 1972[75]—reintroduced the concept of the "intermediate zone" that had not been much employed since Lu Ting-yi's 1947 article. He wrote that

75. "Shih Chun," *On Studying World History* (Peking, 1973).

the U.S. was attempting to control the intermediate zone, "a zone that also includes the United States' allies."[76] This was amended in January 1964—in another "adaptation" of the united front doctrine—by a *People's Daily* editorial which announced the existence of two intermediate zones. The first consisted of "the independent countries and those striving for independence in Asia, Africa, and Latin America," while the second, essentially Western Europe, contained countries with a "dual character" since their ruling classes were simultaneously "exploiters and oppressors" and striving "to free themselves from U.S. control."[77] Western European developments had been receiving continuous attention from the Chinese press throughout 1963 with, unlike the Soviet position, a note of guarded approval for efforts towards Western European unity appearing in many comments.[78] The immediate context of the intermediate zones thesis was the recognition of the PRC by France on 27 January, a few days after the editorial was written.

It appears that the advocates of the new line had at least the partial support of Mao Tse-tung. On 12 January 1964, in a statement supporting the "Panamanian people," he made the following call for an international united front:

> *The people* of the countries in the socialist camp should unite, the people of the countries in Asia, Africa, and Latin America should unite, the people of all the continents should unite, all peace-loving countries should unite, and all countries *subjected to U.S. aggression, control, intervention, or bullying* should unite, and so form the broadest united front to oppose the U.S. imperialist policies of aggression and war and to defend world peace [emphasis added].[79]

Two points may be briefly noted about this statement. First, it called for unity only among "the people" of the socialist camp. Second, the phrase "U.S. aggression, control, intervention, or bullying" indicates an attempt to establish a broader basis for the united front. The anti-Soviet implication of

76. "Shih Chun," "Kennedy's 'Peace Strategy' Conspiracy Exposed," *Shih Chieh Chih Shih*, 10 July 1963.

77. *Peking Review*, 24 January 1964.

78. For example, in March 1963 *Red Flag* argued that the EEC should not be seen as a coalition of monopoly capital but as a coalition of governments and that it was directed primarily against the U.S.A. rather than the socialist countries (*Red Flag*, 16 March 1963).

79. *Peking Review*, 17 January 1964.

the new united front formulation was even more strongly suggested when Mao was quoted as saying to a French delegation, "If the Americans quit Formosa, there is no reason why they should not be our friends."[80] That this was probably an accurate report of what Mao said and that it was genuinely intended to signal Peking's readiness to negotiate with the U.S. may be inferred from a *People's Daily* editorial of 1 July 1964. This, after criticising U.S. policy, claimed, "However, China at all times exercised the greatest forbearance and restraint in the interest of relaxation of tension between the two countries."[81] It added that China had "again and again" proposed that the two governments reach an agreement, based on the five principles of peaceful coexistence, on a U.S. "guarantee to withdraw its armed forces from Taiwan." No demands were made for U.S. recognition of the PRC or the immediate American withdrawal from Asia. The U.S. was only required to guarantee the eventual removal of its forces.[82]

Most of these subtleties in China's line disappeared after the Tonkin Gulf incident in August 1964. However, the new themes which had emerged during 1963–1964—the notion of a "second intermediate zone," the depiction of the target of the international united front as great power "control, interference, aggression, or bullying" rather than "imperialism," the emphasis on Western Europe, and the readiness to have dealings with Washington—were all to reappear after the Cultural Revolution, which suggests that this event merely interrupted an existing trend, rather than produced an entirely new foreign policy orientation.

THE CULTURAL REVOLUTION
AND THE UNITED FRONT OF REVOLUTIONARIES

China's foreign policy setbacks during 1965 in Africa and Indonesia meant the collapse of Peking's united front strategy in the Third World. This was clearly recognised by Peking when, in October, it decided not to call for a Second Afro-Asian Conference, which Peking had apparently anticipated would be the high point and culmination of at least this phase in its strategy. By August 1966 the sinocentrism and xenophobia of the Cultural Revolu-

80. *New York Times*, 21 February 1964.

81. *Peking Review*, 3 July 1964.

82. See also my article "Peking's Foreign Policy: Perceptions and Change," *Current Scene*, June 1973, pp. 1–2.

tion were beginning to take over, with the tolerance that had been a hallmark of earlier approaches to forming a united front notably absent from such statements as the following: "It has become a law in international class struggles that one who is pro-U.S. inevitably opposes China and one who opposes China is bound to go over completely to U.S. imperialism."[83]

The effect of the Cultural Revolution on China's international united front policies is best illustrated by a formulation used by Mao in 1967: "Let the Parties and people of China and Albania unite, let the Marxist-Leninists of all countries unite, let the revolutionary people of the whole world unite and overthrow imperialism, revisionism, and the reactionaries of every country."[84] In this Mao abandoned not only the new line of 1963–1964 but the earlier formulation of 1960–1963, and indeed any reference to a united front which included "nations" or even nonrevolutionary "people."

It would be wrong to pay too much attention to China's foreign policy during the Cultural Revolution period, if indeed China can be said to have had a foreign policy then, since despite its liberal distribution of abusive messages to various governments, Peking in some respects simply lost significant contact with the outside world. Foreign visitors were limited to an assortment of "Marxist-Leninist revolutionaries" and a few government figures from Africa and Pakistan. Diplomats were withdrawn from most of their postings, and Foreign Ministry officials—on the occasions when they had control of their own department—were obliged to spend much of their time defending themselves and their minister from charges of "capitulationism" and so forth.[85]

Nonetheless, the Cultural Revolution is not without significance for this study. Absurd as much of Peking's international posturing was in this period, it represented an extreme form of the "struggle" aspect of united fronts. The united front doctrine combines a set of tactics for "uniting the many" with a strategy for the gradual revolutionising of a united front by means of "struggle" both against its "principal enemy" and intramurally. As Chou En-lai had demonstrated at Bandung, it was possible, by accepting the lowest common denominator of an Afro-Asian identity to obtain at least the preconditions for "uniting the many." One subsequent problem came

83. *People's Daily*, 7 August 1966.
84. *Peking Review*, 8 December 1967.
85. See M. Gurtov, "The Foreign Ministry and Foreign Affairs during the Cultural Revolution," *China Quarterly*, October–December 1969, for a detailed account of these factors.

with attempts to find a more relevant and substantial basis for unity than Chou's winning ways. It might have been valid to generalise about the KMT in terms of its left, centre, and right components and to believe that by winning over one part it might be possible to transform the whole. The Afro-Asian world, its supposed "national bourgeois" character notwithstanding did not have such a corporate identity and its problems were not reducible to a few simple formulae, such as "anti-imperialism." Another kind of difficulty—and one fraught with disaster—revolved around the concept of intramural "struggle" and the difficulties of applying it in the international arena where, unlike the position of the KMT in China, governments were completely sovereign in their own territory and, if they chose, could even refuse to acknowledge China's existence. Such consequences were not inevitable if "struggle" was given a subtle definition, and one more suited to international relations—such as gentle persuasion by example, "material benefits," and advice—but if it took the form which it did in 1967 severe damage to China's overseas influence was unavoidable.

"FRIENDS ALL OVER THE WORLD," 1968–1975

Towards the end of 1968 a number of subtle changes and additions began to appear in Chinese statements on international relations. "People's wars" were still given pride of place as the vanguard of struggle against the U.S. However, "U.S. imperialism" itself was now talked about increasingly as a spent force, already in its "death throes," rather than as something which would, at some future date, meet its inevitable doom.[86] The success of the Communist side in Vietnam and the growth of two types of "contradictions" were seen as largely responsible for this state of affairs. The first contradiction involved internal conflicts in American society. The Black Power movement, on which subject Mao himself had issued a special statement in April 1968,[87] and the anti-Vietnam War movement were thought to be of particular importance in this respect.[88] The second type of

86. See, for example, "Presidential Elections Farce Exposes U.S. Imperialism's Predicament at Home and Abroad," *Peking Review*, 20 September 1968.

87. *Peking Review*, 19 April 1968.

88. See, for example, "Revolutionary Mass Movement Surges Forward in West Europe and North America," *Peking Review*, 27 December 1968.

contradiction existed within the "imperialist camp." To some extent this was a revival of the "two intermediate zones" thesis of 1964, although it was not stated in these terms until August 1971. In 1968, Chinese statements had pointed to the financial crisis in the Western world, disputes in NATO, and French opposition to the U.S. as evidence of the developing contradictions between the U.S. and its allies.[89]

The Soviet invasion of Czechoslovakia in August and the enunciation of the Brezhnev doctrine of "limited sovereignty" for countries in the socialist camp produced several small but significant amendments in Peking's line on a number of issues. The U.S.S.R. was given the new designation of "social imperialist," which meant that it had taken a qualitative step away from revisionism to imperialism and now ranked with the U.S. as a leading oppressor state.[90] The term "social imperialism" was, of course, intended as a "reconciling" image, one which made it easier to give an ideological explanation of the necessity for opposing Moscow at least as much as Washington.

It was from about this time that Chinese comments began to refer to a "new stage" in Soviet-U.S. relations, and since this was one of the key factors behind China's foreign policy moves in 1971–1972, it deserves close scrutiny. An important CCP meeting held shortly after the invasion of Czechoslovakia spelt out the problems that most concerned Chou En-lai:

> While both colluding and struggling with each other, the U.S. imperialists and the Soviet revisionists are trying in vain to redivide the world. In their war of aggression against Vietnam, the U.S. imperialists enjoy the tacit consent and support of the Soviet revisionists, while in turn the Soviet revisionist renegade clique enjoys the tacit consent and support of the U.S. imperialists in openly dispatching troops to occupy Czechoslovakia.[91]

Several points in this statement are worthy of note. It refers, for example, to "struggle" as well as "collusion" between the U.S. and the U.S.S.R.

89. See "Financial Crisis in the West Testifies to Further Decay of Imperialism," *Peking Review*, 29 March 1968, and "Badly Split Imperialist Bloc Nears Its End," *Peking Review*, 12 April 1968.

90. "Diabolical Social-Imperialist Face of the Soviet Revisionist Renegade Clique," *Peking Review*, 25 October 1968.

91. "Communiqué of the Enlarged Twelfth Plenary Session of the Eighth Central Committee of the Communist Party of China, 31 October 1968," *Peking Review*, 1 November 1968.

Previously all the emphasis had been on the collaboration between these two, and the recognition that they might also have conflicts of interest implied that relations between them might be exploited by third parties. The statement may be seen as an attempt to define the emerging system of relations between the superpowers as it was seen from Peking. The reference to their "redividing the world," for example, could be translated into more conventional terminology as "détente."

The same 1968 meeting also produced a slightly altered united front formulation. It still gave "the peoples" the only role in opposing Moscow and Washington, but made U.S.-Soviet "domination" the principal target and gave the defeat of this precedence over winning "victory" and "liberation": "All peoples oppressed by U.S. imperialism, Soviet revisionism, and their lackeys should form a broad united front to smash the plots hatched by U.S. imperialism and Soviet revisionism in their vain attempt to dominate the world, so as to win victory and liberation more quickly."[92]

The 1969 New Year's Day joint editorial of China's three main propaganda organs managed for the first time since 1966 to give "nations" a role in the united front: "The struggle for liberation by the oppressed people and oppressed nations all over the world is advancing from strength to strength with great vigour."[93] However, the possible existence of high-level disagreement along radical/moderate lines over foreign policy matters was indicated by the appearance in the same issue of *Peking Review* of an article on "people's war." As well as continuing to give its principal emphasis to the role of "armed struggle," this talked only of U.S.-Soviet "collusion," with no mention of "contention," and advanced a united front formulation which excluded "nations" from any role: "All *peoples* oppressed by U.S. imperialism, revisionism, and their lackeys will further unite, form a broad united front, and *launch a violent sustained attack* on their common enemy" [Emphasis added].[94]

None of the formulations used to date had employed the phrase "broadest" or "broadest possible" united front to signal China's readiness to enter a new "unity" stage. This, however, came with Lin Piao's report to the Ninth National Congress in April 1969. Lin's report described the U.S. as "going downhill" and "less and less effective" with its "paper tiger" character "long since. . . laid bare," but the Soviet Union, while also seen as

92. Ibid.
93. *Peking Review*, 3 January 1969.
94. Ibid.

a "paper tiger," was not said to have already "laid bare" its true ineffectuality. In a significant section of his report, Lin declared that there were now four main contradictions in the world:

> The contradiction between the oppressed nations on the one hand and imperialism and social-imperialism on the other; the contradiction between the proletariat and the bourgeoisie in the capitalist and revisionist countries; the contradiction between imperialist and social-imperialist countries and among the imperialist countries; and the contradiction between socialist countries on the one hand and imperialism and social-imperialism on the other.[95]

The Soviet Union was now included for the first time and its "contention" with the U.S. was elevated to the status of "contradiction." Apart from the traditional Marxist contradiction between the proletariat and the bourgeoisie, the stress was entirely on contradictions among "countries." The same emphasis appeared in Lin's new united front formulation: "All countries and people subjected to aggression, control, intervention, or bullying by U.S. imperialism and Soviet revisionism unite and form the broadest possible united front and overthrow our common enemies."[96] With the addition of "Soviet revisionism" and the use of "broadest possible united front" instead of just "broadest," these words were identical to those employed by Mao in his call for a united front in 1964. Finally, Lin asserted China's desire for peaceful coexistence with countries having different social systems—again betokening a return to the "moderate" position of 1963–1964. It should be noted that Lin was advocating what amounted to a "moderate" line on foreign affairs on this occasion. Whether this represented his true views or whether, as Chinese sources have since hinted, he was compelled to abide by policies with which he personally disagreed must remain a matter for speculation.

The similarities to the "moderate" line of 1963–1964 were most sharply brought out in a Ministry of Foreign Affairs statement issued on 26 November 1968, which proposed a resumption of the Sino-U.S. ambassadorial talks. This used almost exactly the same words as the July 1964 *People's Daily* editorial cited earlier in this chapter:

> Over the past thirteen years, the Chinese government has consistently adhered to the following principles in the Sino-U.S. ambassadorial talks.

95. *Peking Review*, 28 April 1969.
96. Ibid.

First, the U.S. government undertakes to immediately withdraw all its armed forces from China's territory, Taiwan Province and the Taiwan Straits area, and to dismantle all its military installations in Taiwan Province; second, the U.S. government agrees that China and the U.S. conclude an agreement on the five principles of peaceful coexistence.[97]

This statement was clearly aimed at the incoming President Nixon, who had been declaring for some time his intention of ending the Vietnam War. From the start of Nixon's presidency, Peking paid close attention to his major foreign policy speeches and overseas visits. These were usually derided as "counterrevolutionary dual tactics," but equal emphasis was given to the fact that Nixon and his advisers recognised the need for changes. This was the dominant theme of articles on the subject of Nixon's inaugural address, which was described as a "confession by the imperialists that they are beset with difficulties both at home and abroad and are in an impasse."[98] The same theme was echoed in a discussion of an article by Henry Kissinger:

Nixon's high-ranking braintruster and senior foreign policy adviser Henry Kissinger had to confess . . . that U.S. imperialism's counter-revolutionary "global strategy" to dominate the world has met with disastrous failure. He lamented, "The United States is no longer in a position to operate programs globally," and "The U.S. can no longer impose its preferred solution."[99]

However, there seems to have been genuine concern on the part of some as to whether the U.S. could be trusted to adhere to the course which Nixon seemed to have set and complete opposition from others to any suggestion of having dealings with Washington. Both points of view appeared throughout 1969. One recurrent theme, for example, focussed on the possibility of the United States sponsoring a Japanese military build-up to prepare Japan to take over America's role in Asia. The American use of Japan as a military base was described as "an important source of tension" in Asia,[100] while Nixon's reference to an Asian "collective security system" in his 1969 Guam statement was seen as an "attempt to organise a new anti-China, anti-popular military alliance in the guise of regional

97. *Peking Review*, 29 November 1968.
98. *Peking Review*, 31 January 1969.
99. "Crisis-Ridden U.S. Imperialism Will Not Last Long," *Peking Review*, 14 February 1969.
100. "Most Servile Flunkey," *Peking Review*, 28 February 1969.

economic cooperation and with Japan as its mainstay."[101] Peking was particularly alarmed by the joint communiqué issued at the end of Premier Sato's visit to the U.S. in November 1969, which referred to Taiwan as "a vital factor in the security of Japan."[102] Other articles, however, stressed the increased attention being paid by the Soviet Union to Japan and argued that Moscow, in pursuit of its alleged policy of erecting a "sea cordon" around China, was itself "stepping up collaboration" with Japan.[103] In particular, Brezhnev's call for an "Asian collective security system" was greeted with outrage.[104]

Those who had been arguing in favour of an improvement of relations with the U.S. on the grounds of its decline and the emergence of the Soviet Union as the greater danger found their position strengthened after the Sino-Soviet incidents that began in March 1969. However, even open fighting did not convince some that the U.S. had lost its place as "principal enemy" of the "world's people." In one batch of articles, the U.S.S.R. was merely given the designation "Accomplice Number One" of the U.S.,[105] whereas in another, in contrast, it was referred to as a "common enemy" and listed in front of "U.S. imperialism."[106] One article, written by Chairman Hill of the Australian Communist party (Marxist-Leninist)—a man normally well attuned to the prevailing wind from Peking—and reprinted in *Peking Review,* described the U.S. as the collaborator of the U.S.S.R. rather than the normal reversal of this relationship.[107] One notable difference in formulations came in the National Day speeches of October 1969, when Chou En-lai mentioned, but Lin Piao did not, the five principles of peaceful coexistence, now apparently the codewords for China's readiness to negotiate with the U.S.[108]

101. "Asian People Strongly Rebuff Nixon," *Peking Review*, 15 August 1969.

102. See G. Clark, "Sino-Japanese Relations—An Analysis," *Australian Outlook*, April 1971.

103. "Stepped Up Collaboration With Japanese Reactionaries," *Peking Review*, 13 June 1969.

104. "System of Collective Security in Asia—Soviet Revisionism's Tattered Flag for Anti-China Military Alliance," *Peking Review*, 4 July 1969.

105. For example, "Soviet Revisionism Is U.S. Imperialism's No. 1 Accomplice," *Peking Review*, 21 March 1969.

106. For example, "Soviet Revisionism Heavily Besieged by Soviet and World Revolutionary People," *Peking Review*, 13 June 1969.

107. *Peking Review*, 1 August 1969.

108. *Peking Review*, 3 October 1969.

Two events shifted the balance back in favour of the "radicals": the Sino-Soviet boundary negotiations in October 1969, and the American invasion of Cambodia and resumption of the bombing of North Vietnam in 1970. Statements about the U.S. after this latter event tended to include the phrase "U.S. imperialism is not reconciled to its defeat,"[109] implying that the earlier impression of Nixon as one who was so "reconciled" might have been premature. One statement even came close to admitting Chinese disappointment that Nixon had not lived up to his earlier promise:

> After Nixon took office, faced as he was in an unprecedented predicament of crises besetting him both at home and abroad, the bankrupt anti-China policy has become even more discredited. It was for this reason that he made a posture as if he wanted to improve relations with China. But facts in the past year and more have shown clearly that this is nothing but a trick to deceive public opinion and to cover up his criminal, evil intention of stepping up the anti-China activities.[110]

The article stated that what was especially significant was Washington's attempt to use Japan to prevent China from "liberating" Taiwan and generally to form the "shock force" of its "anti-China activities." It may also be observed that in *Peking Review* during 1970 there were over a hundred full articles attacking the U.S., compared with less than twenty directed against the Soviet Union—fewer than the number directed against Japan.

Evidence of a high-level dispute over China's foreign policy continued to appear in 1970. The 1 January joint editorial for that year reiterated China's readiness to develop diplomatic relations with *all* countries on the basis of the five principles.[111] However, a series of articles in honour of Lenin's centenary in April advanced an opposing view. One made no reference at all to the five principles,[112] while another claimed that the "broadest united front" was being formed with "the people of the world" (with no mention of "countries") on the basis of "proletarian international-ism" rather than the five principles.[113] In June, the chief of staff of the

109. For example, *Peking Review*, 13 June 1970.

110. "U.S. Imperialism Must Get Out of Taiwan," *Peking Review*, 3 July 1970.

111. *Peking Review*, 2 January 1970.

112. *Leninism or Social-Imperialism*, Peking, 1970.

113. "People throughout China Commemorate Birth Centenary of the Great Lenin," *Peking Review*, 30 April 1970.

PLA, Huang Yung-sheng, who fell with Lin Piao in 1971, declared "relaxation of Sino-U.S. relations is, of course, out of the question."[114]

The most interesting contribution was Mao's statement of 20 May on the Indochina situation. This ostensibly was an attack on the U.S. and a statement of support for the "revolutionary armed struggles of the peoples of Southeast Asian countries." However, Mao reiterated the line that the U.S. was "in the throes of its deathbed struggle" and emphasized the role of "nations" in defeating aggression. The passage in the statement that was most frequently repeated afterwards argued, "The danger of a new world war still exists, and the people of all countries must get prepared. But revolution is the main trend."[115]

This could be taken to have the following meaning: Fears of a war between China and the U.S., which some may have suggested as a result of the expansion of the war in Indochina, were unjustified because the U.S. remained pinned down by the worldwide phenomenon of revolution—the main trend. Thus the thesis that in effect it was already defeated remained substantially correct. That at least one of the factions in Peking was concerned about this implication in Mao's statement became clear on the anniversary of Mao's statement, in 1971, when a joint editorial directly and almost contemptuously contradicted Mao's view:

> The dangers of a new world war still exist. We must maintain high vigilance and be prepared at all times. *It is dangerous if we see only the raging revolutionary flames, but not the enemy who is sharpening his sword*, and think that in view of the excellent situation we can lay our heads on our pillows and just drop off to sleep [emphasis added].[116]

"The enemy who is sharpening his sword" could in theory have been the Soviet Union, but there are many clues in the article which suggest that this was not its intended meaning. First, the Soviet Union was not mentioned by name, being referred to only once as "the other superpower" and once as "social imperialism." Second, the article spelt out in some detail its case against détente with the U.S.:

114. *Peking Review*, 3 July 1970.
115. "People of the World Unite and Defeat the U.S. Aggressors and All Their Running Dogs," *Peking Review*, 23 May 1971.
116. "A Programme for Anti-Imperialist Struggle," *Peking Review*, 23 May 1971.

... the aggressive nature of imperialism will not change. U.S. imperialism will never be reconciled to its defeat. It has not for a moment relaxed its arms expansion and war preparations, nor has it relinquished its aggressive ambitions in the least. To save itself from doom, U.S. imperialism will inevitably counterattack, make desperate struggles, and *even embark on a hazardous adventure* [emphasis added].[117]

Third, it employed a united front formulation which managed to name the U.S. no less than six times:

The international united front against U.S. imperialism is an important magic weapon for the world people to defeat U.S. imperialism and all its running dogs. In order to completely defeat U.S. imperialism, the common enemy of the world people, we should further expand and strengthen the international united front against U.S. imperialism, unite to the greatest extent with all forces that can be united with, mobilise to the fullest all the positive factors favourable to the struggle against U.S. imperialism, and isolate and strike at the chief enemy to the utmost, so as to push to a new high the struggle of the world people against U.S. imperialism and all its running dogs.[118]

The Second Plenary Session of the CCP's Ninth Central Committee, held at Lushan between 23 August and 6 Sepember 1970 seems to have shifted the balance back in favour of the "moderates."[119] The foreign policy section of the subsequent communiqué declared that Mao's 20 May statement was "a great programme" and repeated the crucial passage about revolution being the "main trend."[120] It also reiterated China's desire for peaceful coexistence on the basis of the five principles.

During the last six months of 1970 a number of elaborations were made, principally by Chou En-lai, to China's foreign policy line. The overall effect of these was decisively to shift the emphasis away from the pursuit of world revolution and towards more orthodox *ends* and a reliance on conventional diplomatic *means*. The elaborations were the use of the word "superpowers" to refer to the U.S. and the Soviet Union,[121] "hegemony"

117. Ibid.
118. Ibid.
119. See Mao's comments on the meeting published in *Issues and Studies* September 1972, pp. 18–24.
120. "Communiqué of the Second Plenary Session of the Ninth Central Committee of the Communist Party of China," *Peking Review*, 11 September 1970.
121. Chou first used this expression in an interview with French newspaper correspondents, *Peking Review*, 31 July 1970.

and "power politics" to describe the undesirable features of the super-powers, and "medium and small states" to denote one of the main forces seen to be antagonistic to "superpower hegemony."[122] These changes amounted unmistakably to a major "adaptation" of Peking's interna-tional united front line. "Imperialism," "oppressed nations" (and the ideological distinction among states according to their level of economic development), and the clearly dualistic nature of united front policies gave way to a simple, non-Marxian distinction between the superpowers and the rest. The former were to be opposed, not because they were "oppressors," "imperialists," or "revisionists," but essentially because they were powerful and the task of opposing them was not to fall to the "revolutionary peoples" but to the governments of any states which might have an interest in so doing. It is worth noting that Lin Piao's chief public involvement in foreign affairs in late 1970–early 1971 was to dispatch a series of messages to libera-tion movements and Communist governments. In one message, to Vo Nguyen Giap, Lin repeated the phrase, the U.S. "may even embark on a reckless adventure" that had appeared in the article cited earlier, which was interpreted as an attack on moves towards détente with the U.S.[123] No use of the new terminology was made in any of these messages. It may be noted that Lin was later charged with opposing "Chairman Mao's revolutionary diplomatic line," as the new approach came to be called.[124] By the begin-ning of 1971, the notion of a united front of medium and small states op-posed to "superpower hegemony" had been declared "an irresistible trend of history,"[125] thus "reconciling" the actual course of China's foreign policy with the ideological requirement that policy be based upon the dialectical unfolding of history.

The "radicals" were still able, in July 1971, to advance a united front formulation which gave primary emphasis to opposition to the U.S. and "imperialism," but significantly even this formulation could not avoid reference to the new "antihegemony" line: "The task of the Chinese Com-

122. First references in "Speech by Premier Chou En-lai," *Peking Review,* 13 November 1970.

123. *Peking Review,* 25 December 1970.

124. China's embassy in Algeria stated in 1972 that Lin had been "opposed to the revolutionary line of Mao Tse-tung and to the revolutionary foreign policy worked out by him, especially after the Ninth Party Congress" (*Canberra Times,* 29 July 1972). See also Chang Wen-chin's remarks on Lin in the Appendix.

125. "Advance Victoriously along Chairman Mao's Revolutionary Line," *Peking Review,* 1 January 1971.

munist Party is . . . to exert our greatest efforts to struggle together with the people of all countries to defeat the U.S. aggressors and all their running dogs, oppose the politics of hegemony pushed by the two superpowers, and oppose the imperialist policies of aggression and war."[126] Henry Kissinger's visit to Peking symbolised the victory of the new line. It also necessitated a full and public explanation of it.

The most obvious Chinese motivation in seeking détente with the U.S.A. was that this might provide some extra leverage in dealing with the threat from the Soviet Union. One Chinese article hinted in a somewhat oblique fashion that the United States had been incorporated into an international united front in accordance with the united front principle of isolating the "principal enemy":

> Applying the revolutionary dialectics of "one divides into two" in mak-
> ing a scientific distinction between the enemy camps, Chairman Mao
> most clearly distinguished between the primary enemy and the secondary
> enemy and between the temporary allies and the *indirect allies*. By mak-
> ing this concrete and meticulous distinction he isolated the primary
> enemy of the Chinese people at that time, namely, Japanese imperialism
> *which was committing aggression against China* [emphasis added].[127]

Privately, China's dealings with Nixon were also explained in terms of a "dual policy" aimed at revolutionizing the American people, with Nixon prophetically labelled a "transitional personage."[128] Publicly, the current international situation was said to be marked by its great complexity and by the phenomenon of "global upheaval"—a phrase intended to incorporate a broader range of circumstances than the word "revolution." In this situa-tion "the enemy" was employing "counterrevolutionary dual tactics" which had to be opposed by "revolutionary dual tactics." The long-term prospects for revolution remained good so long as "the people" were firm in their principles, but they had to "master the art of waging struggle in a flex-ible way."[129] As one article put it, "The people invariably want revolution, and the revolution is bound to win. But the road of revolution is tortuous,

126. "Commemorate the 50th Anniversary of the Communist Party of China," *Peking Review*, 2 July 1971.

127. "A Powerful Weapon to Unite the People and Defeat the Enemy—A Study On Policy," *Red Flag*, 2 August 1971.

128. *Issues and Studies*, April 1972.

129. "A Powerful Weapon," *Red Flag*, 2 August 1971.

progressing in the course of struggle which is full of twists and turns."[130]

This was tantamount to arguing that any "twist and turn" taken by Chinese policy was still a contribution to world revolution, and indeed one article stated just that: "Since the Chinese revolution is part of the world revolution, all the revolutionary tasks we undertake are closely linked to the revolutionary struggles of the world's people."[131]

It is possible that some in Peking may have genuinely seen China's détente with the U.S.A. as a united front dual policy in a more complex seting than had existed hitherto. However, the very fact that there was opposition in Peking to the new line suggests that the use of united front formulations to explain it reflected a need to "reconcile" policy with doctrine, rather than a mere shift in tactics, with the overall united front strategy remaining intact. Indeed, as has been noted, the united front doctrine had to be considerably "adapted" to fit the new circumstances—the only time any significant adaptation had been made since the introduction of the two "intermediate zones" thesis in 1964.

It is necessary at this point to consider in more detail the two lines on united fronts that emerged during 1969–1970. The new line, which was clearly associated with Chou En-lai, defined "superpower hegemony" as the target of the international united front, stressed the role of "medium and small nations" in combatting the superpowers, and urged a détente with the U.S. The author of an important series of articles in 1972, purportedly on the subject of understanding world history, implied that a détente was necessary in order to promote "contention" rather than "collusion" between the superpowers, that "contention" would work against their hegemonial designs, and that this in turn would assist the world revolutionary cause:

Looking back on the history of the imperialist countries contending for world domination and suffering continuous defeats and of U.S. imperialism and tsarist Russian imperialism is of great help in observing today's contention for world hegemony by the two superpowers and some other international problems. The nature of imperialism determines that while frequently colluding, the imperialist countries have no way of

130. Shih Chun [pseud.], "Again on Studying World History," *Peking Review*, 16 June 1972.

131. Shih Chun [pseud.], "Why It Is Necessary to Study World History," *Peking Review*, 26 May 1972.

reconciling their conflicts in contending for world hegemony. *Their col-lusion means greater suppression of the peoples, whereas their bitter rivalry provides favourable conditions for the victory of the revolu-tionary people* [emphasis added].[132]

As the preceding statement implies, opposition to "hegemony" was now to precede and prepare the ground for revolution, with the latter becoming a more distant objective. Another article by the same author, "Shih Ch'un," made this point even more strongly by stressing the role of Western Euro-pean countries in opposing "hegemony":

> In order to win victory for the national liberation movements, it is not only necessary for the Asian, African, and Latin American peoples to help and support each other, but it is also possible *and even compulsory* for them to unite with the antihegemony struggle of the Second Intermediate Zone and to unite with all the forces that can be united to form the broadest possible united front [emphasis added]. [133]

It seems clear that it was the diminished importance of the revolutionary objective of united fronts in these new formulations which was responsible for their being opposed by a group in Peking (which may have included Lin Piao, although there is no definite evidence of this). The opponents of the new line stressed the role of "peoples" rather than "nations" in the united front, defined as its target "U.S. imperialism," with the Soviet Union re-taining a secondary position because of its "collaboration" with the U.S., emphasised armed struggle, and rejected the policy of détente with the U.S.

Of the two positions, the latter is closer to the united front model than the former. Indeed it represented little more than a leftist (because it did not call for the "broadest possible" united front) version of the line of 1960–1963, which was the closest that Peking came to a comprehensive ap-plication of united front principles to international relations. Chou's line, as has already been argued, constituted a considerable "adaptation" of the original united front doctrine. Chou retained the basic conception of an international united front but altered its focal point, constitution, and *modus operandi*.

Chou's "adaptation" of the united front doctrine did not simply signify a change of tactics to take account of the Soviet threat, although this was

132. Shih Chun [pseud.], "Again on Studying," *Peking Review*, 16 June 1972.

133. Shih Chun [pseud.], "On Studying Some History of the National Liberation Movement," *Peking Review*, 10 November 1972.

undoubtedly a major factor. Chou's line also reflected an appreciation of changing international realities and in particular an awareness of the inadequacy of some traditional Maoist formulations for describing a complex world situation in which "hegemony" rather than classical "imperialism" was the prime danger and the often nonviolent "struggles" of smaller countries an important force resisting hegemony. Mao himself recognised this, and in one of his much-quoted statements of the early 1970s, "countries want independence, nations want liberation, and the people want revolution," he advanced an intricate set of world political processes in which "struggles" for independence against hegemony and liberation from imperialism complemented and aided the more traditional revolutionary struggle for socialism. Despite its greater complexity the world situation was still viewed as essentially a revolutionary one, in the sense that it was thought to be undergoing a fundamental transformation. However, this was a considerable departure from the earlier belief in the inevitability of Chinese-style revolutions in the Third World, and its significance will be assessed shortly.

One further amendment to Peking's line on the international united front needs to be noted. The 1972 New Year's Day joint editorial, after noting the opposition of "medium and small countries" to the "hegemony and power politics of the two superpowers," observed that "countries of the Third World are increasingly playing a positive role in international affairs."[134] By October this formulation had changed to "The Third World is playing an increasingly important role in international affairs."[135]

In 1973 China clearly identified itself as a Third World country, and Mao produced a quotation to reflect what was now China's major foreign policy emphasis: "We all belong to the Third World, we are developing countries."[136] By 1975, Chinese statements had gone so far as to declare that "the Third World countries have become the main force in the revolutionary struggle against the two hegemonic powers,"[137] and even that the Third World was "the motive force of revolution, propelling history forward."[138]

134. "Unite to Win Still Greater Victories," *Peking Review*, 7 January 1972.
135. "Strive for New Victories," *Peking Review*, 6 October 1972.
136. "Hegemony Cannot Decide the Destiny of World History," *Peking Review*, 30 November 1973.
137. "New Year's Message," *Peking Review*, 3 January 1975.
138. "Rise of Third World and Decline of Hegemonism," *Peking Review*, 10 January 1975.

In 1974, in one of the most important Chinese speeches on international affairs of recent years, Teng Hsiao-p'ing provided a comprehensive statement of Peking's perception of the unfolding world political situation and the role of Third World countries. Speaking on the theme that "profound changes have taken place in the international situation," he observed the following: "In this situation of 'great disorder under heaven,' all the political forces in the world have undergone drastic division and realignment through prolonged trials of strength and struggle."[139]

Specifically, the socialist camp was "no longer in existence" following the perfidy of the Soviet Union, and the "Western imperialist bloc" was also disintegrating. This had given rise to a situation in which there were now three worlds "that are both interconnected and in contradiction to one another." The First World contained the two superpowers, the Third World was the developing countries, and the Second World comprised the developed states sandwiched in between these two, who retained the dual character they had been given in their previous incarnation as the Second Intermediate zone. Since the Third World countries had the "strongest desire to oppose oppression and seek liberation and development," they were a "revolutionary motive force propelling the wheel of history and are the main force combatting colonialism, imperialism, and particularly the superpowers." Teng made it clear that the "revolution" to be brought about by the Third World lay in the area of international economic relations. He argued that, just as the Third World countries had won political independence through struggle, so they would be able "to bring about through sustained struggle a thorough change in the international economic relations which are based on inequality, control, and exploitation." For this purpose they needed to establish a closely knit united front on questions relating to the international distribution of wealth and resolve differences among themselves by consultation.

The reasons for China's stress on the Third World—also reflected in Chinese policies at the U.N. and other international organisations—are not hard to find. First, the Third World's elevation from having a "positive role" to being the "motive force of history" occurred at a time when the oil-producing states and other primary producers were successfully uniting in price-raising cartels, so in this sense Peking was merely following events.

139. "Teng Hsiao-p'ing's Speech at the Special Session of the General Assembly," *Peking Review*, 12 April 1974.

Second, China had faced, and in some cases overcome, many of the economic problems that were being encountered by Third World countries. Since development aid from the U.S. and the U.S.S.R. had not been notably successful in reducing the gap between rich and poor countries, China was well placed to offer itself as a "true friend" of the Third World, as opposed to "false friends" who were interested only in exploiting it. Third, in Peking's perception, parts of the Third World were prime targets of Soviet expansion and, as many Chinese statements made clear, Peking was mainly interested in the possible anti-Soviet implications of, for example, attempts by African and other countries to have the Indian Ocean declared a zone of peace.[140]

Apart from these considerations, there may have been some uneasiness about the ideological correctness of lumping together capitalist and "oppressed" nations under the same heading of "medium and small countries." Teng's new united front formulation was, ideologically, far more satisfactory. It rested securely on those foundations thought to be essential to any united front operation: a sophisticated analysis of contradictions, clear distinctions among the component parts of the united front, a principal enemy and a leading force in contention with it, a protracted struggle and a long-term conception of how the struggle was to develop and what were to be its outcomes. Perhaps of even greater importance, it provided practical and specific guidance for the day-to-day process of foreign policy decision making, and guidance which covered a wider range of potential foreign policy issues that had been the case of any previous international united front policy. Chinese decision-makers were to stress the need for unity in intra-Third World conflicts, to support Third World calls for greater economic justice, and to encourage Second World conflicts with the First World and also Second World efforts to reach amicable agreement with the Third World. It may be noted, however, that Teng's formulation emphasised unity within the united front and carefully refrained from suggesting the need for intramural struggle, except against "diehard" Second World countries. Hence, it did not amount to a drastic departure from Chou En-lai's earlier "adaptation" of the united front but represented rather a further elaboration of Chou's line, with the same objective of taking account of new

140. For example, "Soviet Social-Imperialism in 1974: More Exposure of Its True Colours," *Peking Review*, 31 January 1975.

international realities but with more attention paid to the need for policy formulations to be derived from eternal doctrinal truths.

It should be emphasised that Peking's discovery of the Third World did not simply denote a return to its early 1960s policy, when "national bourgeois" governments of Afro-Asian countries were accorded a significant role in China's international united front conception. One of the more startling changes in Peking's attitude to the world in the 1970s was the attention paid by the Chinese press not simply to the antihegemonic activities of Third World countries but to their internal and social development.[141] Hitherto Peking had consistently denied any possibility of significant internal progress in non-Communist countries and had specifically attacked the Soviet notion that such countries might make a "peaceful transition" to socialism. For this reason, Peking had carefully refrained from praising the domestic policies even of states with which it had close relations. Although China's new posture of encouragement for economic progress was not supported by any new theoretical generalisations, it did imply an acceptance of the possibility for "peaceful transition" in certain circumstances. This was not simply a policy of expediency to meet the new situation, because it had been foreshadowed in China's relations with Tanzania as early as 1967 (as is argued in Chapter 7). Once again, the shift in China's policy suggested a broader and more sophisticated conception of the range of situations which might be subsumed under the term *revolution*.

CONCLUSION

The alliance model presents China's foreign policy as primarily conditioned by two factors: a search for security and China's geopolitical location in the international system. This implies that, faced with a particular situation or problem, the "push" of security and the "pull" of the international system would tend to impel China towards a predictable course of action. In one sense, China's international behaviour has been predictable: a posture of total enmity towards the U.S. was softened when the U.S. became less of a threat and the Soviet Union emerged as the greater danger. However, even at this elementary level, there are difficulties which

141. For example, "Development of National Industries in Africa," *Peking Review*, 9 May 1975.

cannot be fully accounted for without an understanding of the effect of ideology on the preconceptions and predispositions of the Chinese leadership. The possibility that Peking might have overreacted for ideological reasons to a perceived threat from the U.S. in 1949 has already been mentioned. The Sino-Soviet conflict could be interpreted as essentially involving a struggle for leadership within the Communist movement combined with a more conventional border dispute—two factors which may be understood in terms of the alliance model. Yet, even this is not so straightforward. It could, for example, be questioned whether the conflict would have erupted at the time or developed in the way that it did had not both states derived their legitimacy and even their *raison d'être* from the doctrines of Marx and Lenin.

Of more significance for this study is the question of whether the manner of China's response to threats may be understood without reference to ideology, and specifically the united front doctrine. To put this point another way, it may be asked whether a non-Maoist Chinese state would have found the same answers to the same problems. As has been argued, China's foreign policy has at times—especially from 1960 onwards—seemed to have been strongly influenced by a belief on the part of some Chinese leaders that they could perceive the *long-term* direction of events. It may now be conventional wisdom that the United States was "certain" to lose in Vietnam, but it was not at a time when Peking attempted to base its foreign policy upon a long-term conception of an international united front whose core was to consist of national liberation movements—indeed, U.S. involvement in Vietnam had hardly begun. Hence, although China's policy in the 1960–1965 period, when the united front doctrine appeared most influential, may in part have been aimed at improving China's security (a "predictable" policy goal in terms of the alliance model), the *means* that were chosen to this end are not comprehensible from the perspective of the alliance model.

They are, however, comprehensible if three assumptions are made:

1. That revolution as well as security was a fundamental goal of the Chinese leadership.

2. That the Chinese leadership operated from a unique set of basic beliefs about the world, as outlined in Propositions One to Six of the united front model.

3. That the united front doctrine was thought by Peking to provide a useful operational code by which the general principles of the Maoist world

view could be translated into a specific strategy for China's international relations.

The main reason for the "adaptation" in 1968–1970 of the international version of the united front doctrine was its inadequacy as an operational code. The most obvious reason for this—China's perceived threat from the Soviet Union—has been fully discussed. There were also defects inherent in the doctrine itself, such as the points raised by L. P. Van Slyke mentioned earlier: the difficulty of applying "unity and struggle" internationally and the absence of a global "common programme" which Peking could use as the foundation stone of an international united front. Most fundamentally, the international arena was considerably more complex than revolutionary China had been.

It was argued in the Introduction that "if ideological tenets did not appear adequately to account for some event or to describe some situation, the ideologue could either *adapt* his doctrines to make them fit reality more closely or he could attempt to *reconcile* an apparent contradiction by depicting reality in such a way that it did fit the doctrine." "Reality," of course, can never be wholly explained by any doctrine, so to that extent "reconciliation" would be a consistent feature of any Chinese attempts to apply doctrine to international relations. However, in at least the 1960–1963 period, there are no signs that Peking was not confident in its view that revolutionary China did provide a model for understanding world politics which was valid in all important respects. When the Sino-Soviet rift had to be openly acknowledged in 1963, the response of at least some in Peking was to seek to adapt the united front doctrine in ways that would make it more appropriate to the new situation. This attempt at adaptation was short-lived because of the American escalation of the war in Vietnam and possibly because it was opposed by what, for convenience, I have termed a "radical" faction in Peking. It seemed for a time during the Cultural Revolution that Peking was going to react to foreign policy setbacks in the 1965–1967 period by an extreme form of "reconciliation." As China became more and more isolated in the world, so it was more and more insistently stated that the world revolution was developing apace, that China had "friends all over the world," and that Chairman Mao was universally loved. However, with the end of the Cultural Revolution, Chou En-lai and others, apparently in the face of considerable opposition, resumed and considerably developed the "minority" policy line of 1963–1964.

The major cause of Chou En-lai's adaptation of the united front doctrine was, as has been suggested, the Sino-Soviet conflict. To that extent, the security and geopolitical factors stressed in the alliance model were of great importance, and it would even be possible to represent the adaptation as simply involving a switch from the perspective of one model to that of another. However, at least two other significant factors were also involved in the adaptation. First, Peking had demonstrably achieved few benefits for China from its 1960–1965 foreign policy, partly because support for the revolutionary struggles of "peoples" did not win U.N. votes or influence from the *governments* with which China, as a state in a world of states, had to deal. Second, the Chinese revolution did not provide the all-embracing model of the world that it had been thought to in 1960. The Chinese conception of world politics had envisaged a process in which an interventionist "U.S. imperialism" would be gradually weakened by a series of costly involvements in "people's wars." As it came more and more to reveal its "ugly expansionist features," an increasing number of countries, especially in the Afro-Asian world, would oppose it. This would tend to push them away from a strict posture of nonalignment, and since imperialism was "inevitably" aggressive, some would find themselves the objects of U.S. intervention, which would create more opportunities for "people's wars" in which Marxist-Leninist groups would come to the fore. All over the world, including in the U.S.A. itself, the "people" would meanwhile be involved in a process of "consciousness raising" which would in the long run lead to further Marxist-Leninist victories. The total scenerio could be seen as an international united front, with armed liberation struggles at its core. Since the Chinese Communists had the best understanding of what was, after all, to be a repetition on the global scale of the Chinese revolution, their role would be to guide the united front in the correct direction.

It must first be acknowledged that the Maoist vision of world politics was not wholly unrealistic. Indeed Peking's predictions about future global developments were as accurate as any others and better than most. However, they had a failing that was also to be found in many Western analyses of Afro-Asian countries. The impression was frequently given in Chinese articles and statements that the Third World—and especially its African segment—existed solely for the purpose of proving Maoist theories correct. Although lip service was paid to the necessity for each revolution to follow its own course, the Chinese did not—unlike the Russians with their conception of "national democracy"—make any real concession to the possibility that a Third World country might be following an acceptable revolutionary path unless it mirrored the Chinese revolution in certain vital aspects: armed opposition to an imperialist power, "correct" leadership, and the use of rural base areas.[142] Underlying Chinese pronouncements on world affairs in the early 1960s was always the clear implication that Peking considered the vast majority of governments with which it had dealings to be merely "transitional." To many Third World leaders, particularly in Africa, this was an attitude quite as insulting as any Western condescension, as Chou En-lai discovered to his cost when he praised Africa's "ripeness for revolution" during his 1964 tour of Africa.

Hence, Chou's adaptation of the international version of the united front doctrine and Teng Hsiao-p'ing's later elaborations should not be seen simply as reactions to a new threat but as attempts to find a new formulation to guide China's international relations that would both enhance China's own status and come to terms with the complexity of the world in the 1970s. The principal facets of the new line, it will be remembered, were its definition of "the enemy" as "superpower hegemony," its emphasis of the role of "countries" rather than "peoples" and, perhaps most important of all, its stress on political, diplomatic, and economic "struggles." Implicitly, China was now to have the thoroughly respectable and virtuous role of supporting and hopefully leading the medium and small against superpower "bullying" and economic injustice and thereby gain prestige and influence. Taken together, these changes represent an *evolution* of the Chinese world view from a narrowly based set of concepts which looked *inwards* to the Chinese Communist experience for their inspiration to a broader and more sophisticated set which looked outwards to the world as it was. The evolution was in this sense Darwinian: It was prompted by the need to change in order, if not to survive, at least to cope more effectively with the environment in which China was obliged to function—the nation-state system.

In this sense, too, the evolution may be seen as part of the socialization of China into the international system. The objective of the new united front—resisting hegemony—and the mainly nonviolent means that it was to employ both indicate a shift towards a conventional approach to China's international relations. This is not to say that Peking has ceased to have

142. See Chou En-lai's speech to the Algerian FLN, *Peking Review*, 3 January 1964.

a revolutionary outlook on the world. Peking's view is that political and economic conflicts between the superpowers and the rest are "contradictions" which will therefore be agencies of revolutionary change. However, insofar as the new line implies an acknowledgement by Peking of the need to adopt—even for ultimate revolutionary purposes—the conventional practices and norms of the international system, it also implies an acceptance of the need to conform to the rules of the game of international society. In short, by deciding to pursue national and revolutionary goals from within a framework determined externally by the nature of the international system rather than internally by China's revolutionary experience, Peking has to that extent accepted Peking's membership in something which in Marxist terms simply does not exist: a social system of states with its own rules, norms, and acceptable patterns of behaviour.

CHAPTER FOUR

China and Indonesia, 1961-1965: The Failure of a Dual Policy

The remaining chapters are devoted to a detailed consideration of China's relations with four specific countries: Indonesia, Pakistan, Cambodia, and Tanzania. In each case a basic question is asked: Was the relationship predominantly an alliance or a united front, in the sense in which these two terms are defined in Chapter 2.

The countries to be examined were chosen primarily for three reasons. First, these four states had established closer relations with China than any other non-Communist states. Second, all four relationships developed mainly during the period 1960–1965, which was the period when the united front doctrine exercised its greatest influence over China's foreign policy. Third, all four countries are, in Chinese Communist parlance, governed by "national bourgeois" regimes and hence could be expected to be prime targets for specific united front policies.

The three Asian states are also important because they are the only non-Communist countries to have received from China any kind of commitment to their defence—the minimum necessary condition for a relationship to be considered an alliance, as defined in Chapter 2. Tanzania did not receive such a commitment but is included because of the special place given to revolutionary prospects in Africa by Chinese statements during the early 1960s.

The same basic format is followed in each chapter. First, a brief historical outline of the main developments in the relationship is given, focussing, in the case of the three Asian countries, on the circumstances which led to the Chinese commitment of support. Next, a general assessment of Chinese motivations is made, forming the basis for the final section of each chapter, which considers the relationship from the perspective of the alliance and united front models.

In the case of Indonesia, the chief purpose of the historical outline is to trace the developments which took Sino-Indonesian relations from their considerably strained state in 1960 to the position in January 1965 when China was the only major country giving full support to all of President Sukarno's foreign policy escapades. The outline will concentrate mainly on Chinese motives. This will inevitably necessitate some oversimplification of an exceedingly complex series of events which involved, on the Indonesian side, many different actors. However, this book is about China's foreign policy, not Indonesia's, and there already exist many analyses of internal Indonesian politics during this period. Most of the discussions of Sino-Indonesian relations to date tend to emphasise the internal Indonesian factors that brought Sukarno into a quasi-alliance with China, so that several puzzling aspects of China's diplomacy and objectives have been barely touched upon.

THE FORMATION OF AN INFORMAL ALLIANCE, 1961–1965

China's diplomatic activity in the Third World in the 1953–1956 period revolved around certain immediate and basic objectives: obtaining recognition, isolating Taiwan, securing admission to the United Nations, opening trade relations and, in short, breaking out of the political and economic isolation which Washington had attempted to impose upon it. Indonesia was one of several Asian states upon whom Peking's diplomatic offensive concentrated in this period. By 1957 China had achieved some success in these endeavours and began to direct its efforts towards those states with strained relations with the United States. Once again Indonesia fitted its requirements in several ways, especially in 1958 when the CIA was allegedly involved in several separatist revolts which broke out in Indonesia during that year. China was reported to have offered "volunteers" to assist Indonesia in quelling these revolts, but (even if this report is accurate) it is unlikely that the Chinese offer amounted to anything more than a gesture.[1]

1. D. Mozingo, *Sino-Indonesian Relations: An Overview, 1955–1965* (Rand Memorandum 4641–PR), p. 18.

The essential fragility of the relationship up to this point was demonstrated during 1959–1960, when the two states collided over the issue
of Indonesia's Overseas Chinese population. This had been a potential
source of tension for some time and erupted into an open quarrel in 1959,
following Indonesian moves to reduce the economic power of Indonesia's
Chinese population.[2] Peking claimed the right to "protect the rights and
interests of the Overseas Chinese" and accused Indonesia of persecuting
them.[3] Jakarta, on the other hand, protested an alleged "anti-Indonesia
campaign" being conducted by Peking Radio and also the involvement of
two Chinese consuls in inciting the Overseas Chinese to disrupt the
Indonesian economy.[4] The dispute continued to sour relations between the
two countries throughout 1960.

Some observers have seen the informal alliance of 1965 as the culmination of ten years of patient diplomacy on the part of China.[5] The interpretation offered here is somewhat different. I will argue that until late in
1964 the relationship between the two sides was marked by a high degree of
caution on both sides and that China's willingness to enter into potentially
far-reaching commitments with Indonesia at the end of 1964 constituted a
dramatic departure from the previous course of China's policy towards
Indonesia that has not been adequately explained.

Sino-Indonesian relations were certainly warmer in 1961 than they had
been during the previous year, but there is no evidence to suggest that
either side was interested in developing a closer *entente*. For Indonesia,
China was at this stage merely one of several states whose support was being
sought for the West Irian campaign against the Dutch, and whose attitude
towards the West Irian question was far less crucial than that of the Soviet
Union, which financed the campaign, or the United States, which was in a
position to influence the Dutch. Similarly Peking, while anxious to end its
quarrel with this major Third World state at a time when the Sino-Indian
dispute was growing more acrimonious, did not appear to regard either
Indonesia or West Irian as areas of vital concern. Some of Sukarno's

2. For the background to this question, see D. Mozingo, "The Sino-Indonesian
Dual Nationality Treaty," *Asian Survey*, December 1961, and the same author's
"New Developments in China's Relations with Indonesia," *Current Scene*, 5
February 1962.

3. *People's Daily*, 12 December 1959.

4. *Times of India*, 23 May 1960.

5. Mozingo, *Sino-Indonesian Relations*, p. 18.

policies, in particular his call in March 1961 for a second Afro-Asian conference, did coincide with Chinese interests, but Sukarno was not yet acting in collaboration with the Chinese on this issue.

In March 1961 China's foreign minister, Ch'en Yi, went to Jakarta for a visit that was designed mainly to symbolise the end of the quarrel between the two states. In his first statement in Jakarta Ch'en Yi hinted that Indonesia should not allow its obsession with West Irian to prevent it from supporting liberation struggles elsewhere in the world that were clearly thought by China to have a more far-reaching significance: "We not only have our own tasks—China and Indonesia both have territories, Taiwan and West Irian respectively, not yet liberated—we also have greater tasks: the national liberation movement waged by our brothers in Asian, African, and Latin American countries need our help."[6]

Ch'en secured a friendship treaty at the end of his visit, but if he had been looking for verbal support of China's line on the struggle between the national liberation movement and "U.S. imperialism" he must have been disappointed. The joint communiqué issued after his talks with Indonesian leaders stated that both countries supported "each other's anti-imperialist stand," but qualified this statement by linking it specifically to the Taiwan and West Irian issues. Indonesia gave its backing, as before, to China's claim for admission into the United Nations, and the communiqué vaguely denounced "foreign interference" in Laos and the Congo, but did not mention Algeria, which was also on the Chinese list of important liberation struggles at this time. However, the two sides were able to agree on the one issue in which both had a special interest: the convening of a second Afro-Asian conference.

The Chinese press after the visit asserted that it heralded a "new stage" in Sino-Indonesian relations,[7] but this was a standard formula and signified very little. One Chinese newspaper sounded a more realistic note when it suggested that no "insurmountable" differences existed.[8] A North Vietnamese newspaper thought that the Sino-Indonesian treaty added up to "another defeat of U.S. imperialism in its attempts to isolate China,"[9] which was in a limited sense true, but was also about the sum of advantage that did accrue to China. In any case the Americans could not have been too

6. New China News Agency (NCNA), 29 March 1961.
7. *People's Daily*, 4 April 1961.
8. *Kuang-ming Jih-pao*, 4 April 1961.
9. *Nhan Dan*, 4 April 1961.

alarmed by the visit. Foreign Minister Subandrio had earlier in 1961 expressed his belief to American Ambassador Howard P. Jones that China was the only real threat that Indonesia faced—a remark that he repeated on several subsequent occasions.[10]

Ch'en Yi's visit was followed up in June by a two-day stopover in Peking by Sukarno at the end of an extensive world tour. It is interesting to note in passing that China was not on Sukarno's original itinerary, being added only as an afterthought towards the end of Sukarno's tour, and that while the Chinese press gave extensive coverage to the tour it made no mention of Sukarno's visit to Washington. Liu Shao-ch'i, in his speech of welcome at Peking airport, praised Sukarno's foreign policy but did not mention the domestic aspects of his leadership.[11] A speech by P'eng Chen listed numerous world issues thought by China to be important and on which it was obviously hoped that Sukarno would take a stand.[12] However, in the joint communiqué issued at the end of the visit, while West Irian was referred to, being linked as usual with Taiwan, the only other international issue specifically mentioned was Laos, where the two states expressed their opposition to "foreign interference *in whatever form or manifestation*" [emphasis added].[13] This formulation may have been inserted by Sukarno against Chinese opposition, since it was similar to the compromise wording that had been arrived at after a long debate at the Bandung Conference, whose final declaration opposed imperialism "in all its manifestations."[14] This had been intended by the pro-Western delegates at Bandung to imply condemnation of imperialism by the Communist as well as the Western powers. Sukarno had used a similar wording in previous declarations in an attempt to demonstrate his even-handedness.[15]

Peking's own view of the importance of its association with Indonesia in 1961 may be inferred from the relatively weak and unenthusiastic epithets used by the Chinese leadership and press in their references to the relationship and also from their treatment of the West Irian question. Both

10. H. P. Jones, *Indonesia: The Possible Dream* (Hoover Institute Publications, 1971), p. 192.

11. NCNA, 13 June 1961.

12. These included Laos, Algeria, the Congo, the Cameroons, Kenya, Zanzibar, Angola, and Cuba (NCNA, 14 June 1961).

13. Ibid.

14. G. H. Jansen, *Afro-Asia and Non-Alignment* (London, 1966), pp. 214–215.

15. Jones, *Indonesia*, p. 195.

Sukarno and PKI leader Aidit, who had arrived in Peking several days before him, had described China and Indonesia as "comrades in arms."[16] This expression did not find its way into Chinese statements until two years later, with far less positive terms such as "friendly cooperation" being employed instead. On the West Irian question, Peking's line throughout 1961 was that China "resolutely supported" Indonesia's claim, but the support given was only verbal. On one occasion the *People's Daily* asserted that the Chinese people were Indonesia's "most reliable friends" on the West Irian question, perhaps arguing indirectly that Indonesia's armourers in Moscow would be unreliable when the crunch came.[17] However, Jakarta in 1961 could see little reason why it should accept MIGs from Peking rather than Moscow—even if China had been in a position to offer them—and MIGs were what it needed, no matter how "resolute" China's words might sound.

Even China's verbal support for the West Irian compaign requires closer inspection. It might be expected that China would regard with some ambivalence an issue that was likely to strengthen both Soviet influence in Indonesia and the internal position of the Indonesian army vis-à-vis the PKI, and this does appear to have been the case. The issue was never singled out by the Chinese media for special attention as a major aspect of the global confrontation with imperialism, which Peking was now claiming to be the main "contradiction" in the world. Moreover, on the occasions when the Chinese press reported Indonesian statements on West Irian, it selected, in the great majority of cases, comments emanating from the PKI rather than the Indonesian government. The reason for this was that the PKI tended fictitiously to represent the U.S.A. as being closely associated with the Dutch, whereas the Indonesian government did not make this connection. This suggests that another, perhaps more important, reason for Peking's ambivalence over West Irian was that Indonesia's "struggle against imperialism" was not directed specifically against China's principal enemy. This of course did not prevent the Chinese propaganda organs from representing it as such or from discovering other, mostly trivial, examples of anti-Americanism on the part of the Indonesian government.[18] Indeed

16. Sukarno's statement in NCNA, 13 June 1961; Aidit's in NCNA, 19 June 1961.

17. NCNA, 4 April 1961.

18. For example, when Indonesia banned *Time* and *Life* magazines in May (NCNA, 5 May 1961).

the Chinese would presumably have backed up these assertions by arguing that *all* anti-imperialist struggles were directed against the United States in some fashion, but in practice some had to be selected as having special significance and West Irian was not among them.

By the end of 1961 the only facets of Sukarno's foreign policy that had been fully endorsed by Peking were his calls for a second Bandung Conference and the line he took on the question of peaceful coexistence at the September Belgrade Conference of nonaligned countries. Peking Radio broadcasts on the Belgrade Conference stressed Sukarno's "fundamental differences" with President Tito and Prime Minister Nehru, which was an exaggerated but not wholly untrue version of what had actually happened in Belgrade.[19] Even greater attention was paid to Sukarno's remarks on "peaceful coexistence," on which a *People's Daily* editorial had this to say:

> The important speech made at the conference by President Sukarno carried great weight among the public of all countries. He stressed that the source of international tension was "imperialism and colonialism and the forcible division of nations." He stated clearly, "History in the past and the realities of today prove that different social systems can coexist, but there can be no coexistence between independence and justice on the one side and imperialism-colonialism on the other."[20]

The editorial also reported Sukarno's assertion that the nonaligned conference "is not a rival to the Afro-Asian Conference but must be complementary to it." Both Sukarno's positions on peaceful coexistence and the sources of international tension were of course similar to the line China was taking in the ideological dispute with the Soviet Union but it is unlikely that Sukarno was influenced by this, given Indonesia's dependence on the U.S.S.R. at this time.

Throughout 1962 the Chinese press continued to give most coverage on the West Irian question to PKI reports that linked the U.S.A. with Dutch policy.[21] Some alarm was shown by both the PKI and China when Robert

19. The report of "fundamental differences" appears in NCNA, 15 September 1961. NCNA also mentioned an incident at the beginning of the conference when the Indonesian journalists present protested to Belgrade that they had been discriminated against in only being allowed three seats when India had six.

20. NCNA, 9 September 1961.

21. For example, in March it quoted a *Washington Post* editorial supporting Holland, and suggested that Dutch intransigence at this time had American backing (NCNA, 28 March 1962).

Kennedy visited Indonesia in February in an attempt to resolve the West Irian question. He was referred to by the Chinese media as a "ruthless fascist" and an "old hand" at anti-Communist persecution, with his work in connection with the prosecution of Owen Lattimore being advanced in support of these statements.[22] Although these remarks were not directed specifically against the Indonesian government, they are an indication of China's uneasiness about the extent of Indonesia's commitment to the "real" anti-imperialist struggle at this time. Peking had similar feelings about Indonesia's acceptance of an American mediator, Ellsworth Bunker, whose proposals were castigated as being no different from those of the intractable Dutch Foreign Minister Luns.[23] After the settlement of the West Irian question—which Peking hailed as a victory won by the Indonesian people's struggle, with no mention of Soviet aid—the Chinese press again tended to repeat the PKI line that the anti-imperialist struggle had to continue. Aidit's comment in August, "Around Indonesia are countries under the control of imperialism," was widely quoted in the Chinese press.[24]

Several other incidents during 1962 fed China's ambivalence towards Indonesia. Indonesian-Yugoslav relations had improved considerably during the year after some minor setbacks in 1961, with one highlight being the visit of Yugoslav Vice-President Kardelj in December. Peking did not comment directly on this, but NCNA, on the day of Kardelj's arrival, reprinted an editorial from the PKI newspaper *Harian Rakjat,* which accused Yugoslavia of supporting India in the Sino-Indian dispute.[25] An even more sensitive spot was touched when Taiwan was invited to attend the Asian games to be held at Jakarta in August 1962. After keeping silent for some months, during which time covert pressure may have been brought to bear on the Indonesian government, both the Chinese and PKI propaganda organs were brought into play in July. The Chinese media managed to combine a veiled threat of the possible damage to Sino-Indonesian relations that could be caused by this incident with a hint that it would generously heap the blame for it on Taiwan and the U.S.A. if Indonesia refused entry to the Taiwanese, as it eventually did: "Indonesia will certainly see through completely the political intrigue of U.S. imperialism to antagonise the Chinese

22. Peking Radio, 19 February 1962.
23. NCNA, 14 April 1962.
24. NCNA, 23 August 1962.
25. NCNA, 12 December 1962.

people and undermine the friendly relations between China and Indonesia."[26]

Several observers have seen Subandrio's visit to Peking in January 1963 as the real beginning of the Sino-Indonesian alliance. The most definite statement of this thesis appears in a recent study of the period by A. C. A. Dake, who had access to confidential documents as well as to interviews with the highest levels of the Indonesian leadership. Dake asserts, on the basis of an interview with Adam Malik in 1972, that in autumn 1962 Indonesia had applied to the Soviet Union for small arms which it wished to provide to guerrillas in North Borneo, the request apparently having been made "as a result of an informal consensus between Aidit and Subandrio with Sukarno in the background." However, "Moscow declined, not seeing sufficient reason for supporting Indonesia's undercover activities in the area," so Indonesia turned to China, the "result" being Subandrio's visit and a promise of arms and instructors in guerrilla warfare.[27]

There are a number of difficulties in the way of accepting this as a wholly convincing interpretation. The first must be the reliability of Malik's evidence in a matter which implicated Subandrio, who had been made a major scapegoat for the events of 1965. Second, China's attitude on the Malaysian question was still uncertain at the time of Subandrio's visit. Dake himself observes that Peking "was still trying to sort out its policy line before being more explicit in its commitments,"[28] and in the light of this and the doubts about Indonesia which I have argued were present in Peking throughout 1962, it is not immediately obvious why China should so readily agree to provide arms in January 1963. If there was such an agreement, it suggests an anti-Soviet move rather than support for Indonesia's anti-Malaysia policy, a point I will return to later. Third, there is some doubt as to whether Indonesia's plans for Malaysia in autumn 1962 had really advanced to the stage of contemplating large-scale subversion. A fourth problem with Dake's interpretation arises out of his assertion that Subandrio's visit to China was the "result" of the Soviet Union's refusal to supply arms in autumn 1962. Subandrio, in common with all of the delegates to the Colombo Conference except Ne Win of Burma, had visited both Peking and New Delhi in January in order to discuss conference deliberations on the Sino-

26. NCNA, 3 August 1962.

27. A. C. A. Dake, *In the Spirit of the Red Banteng* (The Hague, 1973), pp. 174–175.

28. Ibid., p. 174.

Indian conflict. This did not preclude the possibility of talking about other matters while he was there, but the suggestion that this was the main reason for the visit is unfounded. Finally, there is no evidence that China sent guerrilla warfare instructors to Indonesia before 1965, although there may have been some consignments of machine guns.

In any case, whether there was an agreement or not, it is an exaggeration to say that close cooperation followed as a result of it. What did happen in 1963 was that Indonesia received a higher priority in Peking and the two states collaborated on a limited range of issues, but without losing any of the ambivalence with which each regarded the other. This ambivalence was apparent from the beginning of the year, when Ch'en Yi, in his welcoming address for Subandrio at Peking airport, could find nothing more enthusiastic to say about relations between the two countries than that they were "satisfactory." Subandrio's reply, in which he spoke of "this period of development in which it is so easy to have conflicting interests among ourselves," similarly did not appear to herald a new era in Sino-Indonesian relations.[29] Ambivalence was also evident during Liu Shao-ch'i's visit to Jakarta in April, which was accompanied by widespread anti-Chinese rioting, causing Liu in his farewell address to express his regret about the "difficulties and obstacles" between the two countries. Ambiguity reached a peak in the middle of the year when Indonesia moved towards a peaceful settlement of the Malaysian question, supported the conception of a regional grouping to be known as Maphilindo, which had various anti-Chinese undertones,[31] and appeared to be drifting in the direction of a more pro-Western posture as evidenced by its granting of a twenty-year guarantee to British and American oil companies in Indonesia.[32] Perhaps the sharpest comment on China's commitment to Indonesia is provided by the fact that during 1963 China's trade with Malaysia increased by 400 percent—a statistic that did not go unremarked in Moscow.[33]

29. Both quotes from NCNA, 1 January 1963.
30. *Indonesian Herald*, 22 April 1963.
31. For a convincing argument that this was at least the Filipino view of Maphilindo, see R. Abell, "Philippines' Policy towards Regional Cooperation in South-East Asia, 1961–1969" (Australian National University Ph.D. thesis, 1972). For the similar opinion of Maphilindo held by the Kennedy administration, see R. Hilsman, *To Move a Nation* (New York, 1967), p. 406.
32. *New York Times*, 8 July 1963.
33. Dake, *Spirit of the Red Banteng*, pp. 276–277.

All this does not prove that the relations between the two states were antagonistic, but merely that they were not yet close. There was some genuine cooperation between the two where their interests coincided—notably at the Afro-Asian Solidarity Conference at Moshi, Tanganyika, in February 1963[34]—and the Chinese press was still able, by diligently searching, to find evidence that Indonesia's real "confrontation" was with the United States.[35] Liu Shao-ch'i was probably pleased with the contrast between the warm welcome he received in March and the cool and formal reception that had been accorded Marshal Malinovsky a few weeks earlier.[36] Perhaps it was this that prompted Liu finally to accept Sukarno's epithet of two years earlier and refer to the relationship as one between "comrades in arms."[37]

If, however, the Chinese statements made in 1963, about Sino-Indonesian relations having reached a "new stage," were more justified than those that had been made earlier, the relationship could not yet be termed an alliance. China did not appear to be willing to undertake any large commitments to the Indonesian government, and Sukarno still attached more importance to his relationship with Moscow. This became clear towards the end of the year when Adam Malik made an unannounced visit to Moscow in search of economic aid that was urgently needed after some PKI extremists together with Overseas Chinese oilworkers sabotaged the Shell Company's installations in Borneo. Malik was reported to have said privately that he intended to represent this to the Russians as part of a move towards revolution by a China-oriented PKI.[38]

The last four months of 1964 witnessed several crucial developments in Sino-Indonesian relations, but for at least the first six months of that year the circumspect attitude of the two states towards each other was still very much in evidence. The year began inauspiciously from China's viewpoint, with Sukarno declaring a cease-fire in Malaysia after discussions with Robert Kennedy. However, things soon improved when the cease-fire had virtually no effect, and the Americans began to back out of their economic aid commitments to Indonesia. Peking was pleased with these develop-

34. See *Far Eastern Economic Review*, 14 March 1963, for a report of this conference.

35. For example, Sukarno's annoyance about American criticism of his foreign policy was noted (NCNA, 26 May 1963).

36. *Bangkok Post*, 17 June 1963; see also *Djakarta Daily Mail*, 26 March 1963.

37. NCNA, 13 April 1963.

38. *Sunday Times*, 29 December 1963.

39. *The Nation*, 29 March 1964.

ments, since it had by this time overcome any initial doubts it might have had about confrontation in Malaysia. The conflict was now being declared an "integral part" of the struggle against imperialism, a description which Peking had not applied to the West Irian issue.[39] However, although many of Sukarno's actions could meet with the approval of Peking, they did not eliminate other sources of tension between the two states. This became apparent in April 1964 when the Indonesian government came under pressure from the PKI because it had not invited China to the preparatory meeting for the Second Afro-Asian Conference, which was to be held in Jakarta.[40] Only ten days before the meeting was due to begin in April, the Indonesian Foreign Ministry was still insisting that China would not be invited and, as had been the case in the Asian Games incident, it was not until the last minute that an invitation finally was issued.[41] It is possible that Indonesia had a secret arrangement with China to the effect that China's name would be kept off the list of delegates until very late, so as to ensure maximum attendance, but if this was the case it was strange that the PKI had not been informed. If Jakarta really did intend to exclude China and only backed down because of pressure from the PKI, then this suggests that Indonesia did not regard China as a partner in the Afro-Asian movement but as a rival—a possibility that would not be surprising.

A further incident in April that might have caused some tension was the nationalisation of the Peking-controlled Bank of China in Jakarta, although both sides played this down.[42] However, these minor irritations were not enough to prevent a steady growth in the intensity of the relationship between the two states during the first six months of 1964. In June the leader of a Chinese friendship delegation visiting Jakarta gave the first hint that China might support Indonesia in the event of a war. The actual expression he used—that China "would not remain silent" if Indonesia were attacked—was weak but it marked an advance from the "resolute support" which was all that had been offered since 1961.[43]

Sukarno did not appear very grateful for China's promise of support. In his 17 August speech in 1964, which heralded a more militant foreign policy line, he listed the states in Asia which were favourably regarded by Indonesia, including China, but went on to declare that nothing would pre-

40. *The Nation*, 4 April 1964.
41. *Straits Times*, 9 April 1964.
42. *New York Times*, 5 April 1964.
43. *Indonesian Herald*, 3 June 1964.

vent "Korea, Vietnam, Cambodia, and Indonesia from becoming friends and uniting."[44] The omission of China is all the more intriguing as, a few days before Sukarno's speech, PKI leader Aidit, who often anticipated what the president was going to say, had declared that Jakarta, Phnom Penh, Hanoi, Pyongyang, *and* Peking constituted the "defence axis of the new emerging forces."[45] However, it was in this speech that Sukarno for the first time directed his anti-imperialist remarks specifically at the U.S.A.—a development that did not go unnoticed in China.

Sukarno's conversion to anti-Americanism combined with an expansion of British forces in Malaysia to spark off some debate in Peking about the possibility of China's becoming more involved in Indonesia's defence. In September 1964 several statements appeared from different sources in Peking which all seemed to agree on the need for a more positive stand, but disagreed on the question of exactly *how* positive this was to be. The first shot was fired by a *People's Daily* editorial on 9 September, headed "Victory Belongs to the Indonesian People." The New China News Agency's English translation of this contained the following key passage: "Should U.S. imperialism dare launch aggression against Indonesia, the Chinese people will back Indonesia *with all their might*" [emphasis added].[46]

Some Western observers were alarmed by this, since it appeared to them to imply a similar sort of commitment to that which China had been recently declaring in the case of Vietnam. In fact, such fears were unfounded. Chinese statements on Vietnam, including one which had appeared in the same issue of the *People's Daily* as the editorial just mentioned, were far stronger in tone and degree of commitment than this statement on Indonesia.[47] There are several further points of interest in the statement. First, it referred only to support against the U.S.A., whereas the states that actually had military forces opposing Indonesia were Britain and Australia. Second, shortly after, when another translation of the editorial appeared in *Peking Review*, its wording was altered with the effect of weakening the original commitment. The phrase "all their might" vanished, and the statement now read as follows: "If the U.S. imperialists are rash

44. *Indonesian Herald*, 21 August 1964.
45. *Straits Times*, 10 August 1964.
46. NCNA, 9 September 1964.
47. The statement on Vietnam read, "The Chinese people will resolutely stand by the people of Vietnam and the other Indo-Chinese states and, together with them, fight to the end until the complete defeat of the U.S. aggressors" (*Peking Review*, 11 September 1964).

enough to unleash aggression against Indonesia, the Chinese people will do *all they can* to support the Indonesian people" [emphasis added].[48]

On 16 September China's Chief of Staff Lo Jui-ch'ing entered the fray. He assured visiting Indonesian Air Chief Marshal Suryadarma that "the Chinese people are always the most faithful and reliable friends of the Indonesian people in their struggle against U.S. imperialist policies of aggression and war" [emphasis added].[49] However, Lo felt certain that, if the imperialists did attack, the task of defeating them could safely be left to "the heroic Indonesian people who have a glorious tradition of fighting against imperialism" and did not suggest that China's faithfulness and reliability might be translated into concrete action. Suryadarma must have felt perplexed at a banquet in his honour a few days later when a Chinese air force general, Liu Ya-lau, appeared to commit China's armed forces to Indonesia's defence: "In the just struggle against the U.S. imperialist intervention and aggression and against 'Malaysia,' product of neocolonialism, the Chinese people *and the Chinese People's Liberation Army* will unswervingly stand on the side of their Indonesian comrades in arms" [emphasis added].[50]

Meanwhile in Indonesia Ti Tzu-tzai, an obscure Chinese functionary, who was perhaps out of touch with developments in Peking, had made the most positive statement of all at a meeting of the PKI-controlled Indonesian trades union congress (SOBSI): "If the *U.S. and British* imperialists dare to launch aggression against Indonesia, the Chinese people will *muster all their strength* to support the Indonesian people *until the imperialists are completely defeated*" [emphasis added].[51] On balance, however, those in Peking who were reluctant for China to become too heavily involved in Sukarno's adventures appear to have succeeded in restraining their more enthusiastic colleagues on this occasion. Further evidence for this conclusion is provided by the fact that NCNA in its report of a speech made by Aidit on 13 September cut out all his references to China's support for Indonesia in the event of a major conflict.[52] The Indonesians, too, still had some doubts about China. Subandrio, for example, in a radio interview in

48. Ibid.
49. NCNA, 16 September 1964.
50. NCNA, 2 October 1964.
51 NCNA, 25 September 1964.
52. S. W. Simon, *The Broken Triangle: Peking, Djakarta, and the PKI* (Baltimore, 1969), p. 240.

October, expressed some misgivings about China's recent explosion of a nuclear device.[53]

The sequence of events that did lead to a definite Chinese commitment—albeit a limited one—began in late September. During 1964 Indonesia's relations with the Soviet Union had been becoming increasingly strained for several reasons: Indonesia had been falling behind in its debt repayments to the Soviet Union; it had opposed the Soviet claim to be admitted to the proposed Second Afro-Asian Conference; and the Russians were equivocal in their support for confrontation in Malaysia. Mr. Mikoyan had been dispatched to Jakarta in June to put some hard facts before the Indonesians on these subjects, and there were various unconfirmed rumours that the two sides had reached a deal involving Russian missiles and stronger backing for confrontation in return for Indonesian support for Russian admission to the Afro-Asian conference.[54] In late September Sukarno himself had gone to Moscow, partly to keep an eye on General Nasution, who was negotiating another arms deal.[55] While there he had a bitter quarrel with Mr. Khrushchev[56] but appeared to agree to advance a Soviet line on the questions of peaceful coexistence, disarmament, and the test ban treaty at the forthcoming Cairo conference of nonaligned nations.[57] However, at the conference he forgot his promise and in his main speech came closer to the Chinese position on all these points.[58] Shortly after the conference Khrushchev "resigned" on the same day as China exploded a nuclear device, and a new element of uncertainty entered into Moscow's policy towards Indonesia. Meanwhile, in Sukarno's absence some of the rivals of the PKI, headed by the anti-Chinese, national Communist Murba party, had initiated a tactical manoeuvre designed to reduce the influence of the PKI.[59]

It was against this background that Sukarno, who had begun another world tour after leaving Cairo, was suddenly invited to visit China before returning home. There is little publicly available information about what he

53. *Straits Times*, 22 October 1964.
54. *Sunday Telegraph*, 5 July 1964.
55. Dake, *Spirit of the Red Banteng*, pp. 289–290.
56. U. Ra'anan, *The U.S.S.R. Arms the Third World* (Cambridge, Mass., 1969), p. 240.
57. Dake, *Spirit of the Red Banteng*, p. 290.
58. Ibid., pp. 291–292.
59. See ibid., pp. 300–306, for an account of the so-called "Body for the Promotion of Sukarnoism."

actually discussed with Chou En-lai at Shanghai, but it appears that this meeting did produce a genuine "new stage" in Sino-Indonesian relations. Sukarno received fulsome praise for the line he had taken at Cairo and a promise of economic and military assistance.[60] However, Chou apparently told Sukarno that he could not expect the same kind of help as he had been receiving from the Soviet Union—advanced planes and naval vessels—and suggested that Sukarno concentrate more on conducting a guerrilla campaign, for which venture China could provide substantial help. According to Dake it was at this point that Chou En-lai urged the formation of a "fifth force" or "people's militia"—a significant proposal whose implications will be discussed later.[61] Chou's authorship of the proposal was confirmed by Sukarno himself when, some months later, he discussed with army leaders the possibility of creating a "fifth force."[62]

The Sino-Indonesian relationship was further cemented when China's Foreign Minister Ch'en Yi and Chang Wen-chin, a departmental director of the Foreign Ministry, visited Jakarta in December. The joint communiqué issued at the end of this visit declared that all anti-imperialist struggles constituted "a single struggle" and that the two sides had discussed "ways of raising the level of the struggle."[63] It also stated that "various problems" relating to the Second Afro-Asian Conference, scheduled to begin in March at Algiers, were discussed. While Ch'en was in Indonesia, the *Indonesian Herald*, which usually reflected Foreign Ministry opinion, accused "a country geographically not belonging to the Afro-Asian world" of trying to drive a wedge between Africans and Asians.[64] This was a sign that Indonesia was now fully committed to supporting China's efforts to counter Soviet influence in the Afro-Asian world. A further pointer to this was the statement in the joint communiqué to the effect that both sides would abide by the decisions of the April preparatory meeting for the Afro-Asian conference. While not explicitly stated, this almost certainly referred to one decision alone—the exclusion of the Soviet Union.

The most important and prolonged meeting between Chinese and Indonesian leaders was held in January 1965 at Canton between Chou En-lai and Subandrio. This came after Sukarno withdrew Indonesia from the

60. NCNA, 4 November 1964.
61. Dake, *Spirit of the Red Banteng*, pp. 326–327.
62. *Bangkok Post*, 1 June 1965.
63. NCNA, 3 December 1964.
64. *Indonesian Herald*, 11 November 1964.

United Nations, a decision to which some believed Ch'en Yi had prompted him in November. This allegation is almost certainly unwarranted. Suban- drio gave the following version of the decision shortly after it was taken: "The question was not discussed with Peking in any way. It was Pres- ident Sukarno's decision alone. When I was at the U.N. in late De- cember, even I did not know it would be taken."[65] In fact Peking, in spite of its public support for Sukarno's move, might even have preferred Indonesia to remain in the United Nations, which at least provided the partnership with a forum that was denied to China.

There were various rumours circulating at the time of Subandrio's visit to Canton to the effect that Indonesia had already sealed a secret military pact with China which would range Chinese manpower behind a full-scale thrust into Malaysia. The most persistent of these had Subandrio informing a group of Indonesian diplomats about this "pact" at a secret meeting in New York in December 1964.[66] Subandrio was said to have placed this pact in the context of a grand strategic design

> . . . aimed at dividing the British from the Americans and eliminating all remaining "imperialist" bases in South East Asia. Subandrio not only spoke of the combined Chinese-Indonesian thrust against Malaysia but also envisaged the cooperation of the Vietcong in South Vietnam, pointing out that they already controlled most of the Mekong Delta and the peninsula to the south of it—which, he explained, would serve as a staging area for an attack against Malaysia across the Gulf of Siam.[67]

Parts of this scenario are nothing short of fantasy—especially the points about the Vietcong, who probably felt they had enough on their hands already—but whether the fantasy was in the mind of Subandrio or those who printed the rumour will be discussed shortly. However, the suggestion that there was a *formal* alliance would more appropriately be considered in this historical outline. The evidence for the existence of a formal military alliance is rather flimsy. When Subandrio left for China he let it be known that he was going to find out exactly what aid Indonesia could expect from China in the event of a war with Britain, but insisted that Indonesia would not form a military alliance because it did not want to jeopardise its nonaligned status.[68] On his return he told a press conference that he had

65. *Bangkok Post*, 23 January 1965.
66. *Japan Times*, 8 February 1965.
67. R. Shaplen, *Time Out of Hand* (London, 1969), p. 80.
68. *London Times*, 21 January 1965.

been offered assistance but that China and Indonesia had not signed a pact.[69] Although one cannot know for certain, it is likely that this is nothing short of the truth. Even the reason given by Subandrio for not signing a treaty is plausible, since it would serve the interests of both Peking and Jakarta if Indonesia were able to continue to participate in the non-aligned forums. Indonesian students who raided the offices of the Indonesian Foreign Ministry in 1966 claimed to have appropriated a document establishing a secret alliance between Indonesia and China, but this was later found to be no such thing.[70]

However, the appellation "informal alliance" is justified. The Subandrio-Chou meeting produced the strongest official commitment yet by China to Indonesia's defence, a significant Chinese role in the planning of con-frontation and in the training of Indonesian troops, and a common front between the two countries over a wide range of issues. It should be noted, however, that even after January China's support of the Indonesian govern-ment was qualified in several ways. By the beginning of January the Chinese press had still not agreed on a common formula in their references to China's commitment to Indonesia. One typical article was able to go only so far as to declare that if the U.S. and Britain carried out "armed prov-ocations" against Indonesia they would meet with "resolute" opposition from "the peoples of other Asian countries and peace-loving countries and peoples throughout the world."[71] Chou En-lai finally ended the confusion by enunciating the line that was to be the standard formula until October 1965: "Should the British and U.S. imperialists dare to impose a war on the Indonesian people, the Chinese people will absolutely not sit idly by."[72]

Not only was this the first statement by a top Chinese official to back Indonesia against Britain as well as the U.S.A., but the phrase "impose a war" covered a much wider range of possibilities than "aggression," including a war that was actually initiated by Indonesia. However, the wording of China's commitment is vague—there are many stages between sitting by and going to war, and this might have been deliberate. An ad-ditional qualification may have been intended by the use of the term "British *and* U.S.," since a combined Anglo-American stand was less likely

69. *Straits Times*, 15 February 1962.

70. T. Vitachi, *The Fall of Sukarno* (London 1967), pp. 162–163.

71. "The Indonesian People Will Not Tolerate Insults," *Peking Review*, 8 January 1965.

72. *Peking Review*, 5 February 1965.

than one involving Britain alone. That Subandrio himself was aware of these qualifications is apparent from his own statement acknowledging China's promise of aid, in which he merely associated China's support with that of other "progressive peoples": "Progressive peoples, *particularly the Chinese people,* will certainly defend Indonesia if it is subjected to aggression" [emphasis added].[73]

Nonetheless Chou had given Indonesia a far more positive pledge of support than any previous statements had done. I have attempted to show in the analysis up to this point that the informal alliance of 1965 should not be seen, as most observers have seen it, simply as the culmination of a gradual process during which the two states came together over the previous ten or even the previous three years, but as involving a rather sudden shift in China's position. The problem that now remains is why China thought it necessary to alter its policy.

THE QUESTION OF CHINESE MOTIVATION

The "common ideology" thesis

Several analysts of Sino-Indonesian relations have stressed the importance of what they believe to be the similarity between the world views of the Chinese Communists and Sukarno. J. M. Van der Kroef, for example, sees the two states as sharing a "revolutionary nationalist élan."[74] A similar point is made by S. W. Simon, who refers to the "susceptibility" of the Chinese and Indonesian elites to an informal alliance arrangement and sees the downfall of that alliance as the consequence of the coming to power in Indonesia of another elite with different values.[75]

There is some superficial resemblance between Sukarnoist and Maoist ideologies. Sukarno saw Indonesian society as a continuing revolution with worldwide implications. Like Mao he believed that revolution brought to the fore mental and spiritual as well as physical qualities in man.[76] Both stressed the need for unity among all potentially revolutionary forces,

73. *Manchester Guardian,* 26 January 1965.
74. J. M. Van der Kroef, "Sino-Indonesian Partnership," *Orbis,* summer 1964.
75. Simon, *Broken Triangle,* p. 20.
76. J. R. Angell, "The New Emerging Forces in Indonesian Foreign Policy" (Australian National University Ph.D. thesis, February 1970), pp. 55–58.
77. J. S. Mintz, *Mohammed, Marx and Marhaen* (London 1965), p. 185. See also Feith and Castles, *Indonesian Political Thinking, 1945–1965* (Ithaca, N.Y., 1970), pp. 37–38.

domestically as well as internationally.[77] Sukarno had called for an international united front against imperialism as early as 1933.[78] Both Mao and Sukarno de-emphasised the special role of the industrial working class in favour of a broader conception of "the people," symbolised in Sukarno's case by the semimythical Indonesian peasant Marhaen, the embodiment of the virtues of the common man. Both had a "dialectical" view of international relations, which they saw as a constant struggle between declining and rising forces, labelled, in Sukarno's case, the "old established forces" and the "new emerging forces."

However, it should not take much familiarity with the history of the relations among different European socialist movements to find cause to doubt the assertion that an apparent similarity of ideologies might predispose two elites to form an alliance. Even if, in this case, one accepts the depiction of both ideologies as "revolutionary nationalist," it is difficult to see how two nationalisms both out to change the world could be anything but exclusive and indeed opposed. China, as the preceding analysis has shown, was very circumspect in its approach to Indonesia throughout the period considered here. Ideology, far from facilitating a close relationship, was one of the barriers to it. To an orthodox Communist, Sukarno's opinions about the universe could be regarded only as the "false ideology" of bourgeois nationalism. It is significant that until 1965 the Chinese media paid little attention to Sukarno's "revolutionary" domestic policies, and relied on the PKI for analyses of the internal Indonesian situation. Even after January 1965 reference was only very occasionally made to Sukarno's domestic achievements, and when the two sides issued joint statements the generalisations in them about the "world situation" did not embody a synthesis between the Chinese and Indonesian world views but the juxtaposition of two distinct formulations carefully interwoven so as to present a façade of unanimity.[79]

The "grand strategy" thesis

A version of the "grand strategy" argument already cited envisaged a simultaneous thrust by Indonesia, China, and the Vietcong against Western positions in Southeast Asia combining conventional and guerrilla tactics. It is not wholly clear whether China's role in this operation was to have been one of support or participation. There were, however, reports that China

78. Angell, "New Emerging Forces," p. 180.

79. For example, the Subandrio-Chou En-lai joint statement consistently has Sukarno's new and old forces dichotomy side by side with a more orthodox Chinese presentation of the conflict between imperialism and revolution.

and Indonesia had reached an agreement to divide Southeast Asia into separate spheres of influence following the success of this venture.[80]

A less dramatic grand strategy thesis is outlined by D. Mozingo:

> For a decade Communist China has sought to bring about Indonesia's alignment with a Peking-led Asian "anti-imperialist coalition" designed to remove the influence of the Western powers and ultimately to clear the way for the establishment of a China-centred political order in the Far East. This grand design began to unfold in 1954 and was predicated on a Chinese estimate that the aims of Asian nationalism would result in a long period of conflict with the interests of the Western powers.[81]

The key phrases in Mozingo's analysis are "ultimately" and "long period of conflict," which suggest a Chinese aim of gradually whittling away at Western influence rather than a concentrated effort at a certain point in time. It should be noted that both grand strategy theses postulate the central concern of China's foreign policy to have been its enmity with the United States, although Mozingo, by using the phrase "Western powers" is able to include the Soviet Union at a later stage in his analysis.

It is difficult to take the first version of the grand strategy seriously. Apart from the obvious question of why the great assault did not materialise, there are several reasons to doubt that the Chinese or Indonesians ever envisaged a major conflict in North Borneo, as opposed to a gradual process of attrition. From the perspective of the Indonesian army an invasion of North Borneo was a daunting prospect. Even in the periods when North Borneo was not drenched by monsoons—which lasted longer than usual in 1965—it offered considerable difficulties to an army contemplating an invasion by land against well-trained and armed troops. There is a natural mountain barrier between much of Malaysian and Indonesian Borneo, except for one region, then the British first administrative division around the town of Kuching, which was where the Indonesians concentrated their soldiers. However, there were no all-weather roads between Kuching and the border and only two passes through which an invasion could be mounted, both of which were heavily defended by the British.[82] A sea-borne invasion was a hypothetical possibility since the Indonesian navy was, on paper, very well equipped but in practice it lacked

---

80. *Sunday Times* (London), 4 July 1965.
81. Mozingo, *Sino-Indonesian Relations*, p. 12.
82. *London Times*, 7 November 1964.

the necessary skills to make full use of its hardware. A naval invasion became even less likely after March 1965, when Britain heavily reinforced its own fleet in the area. Finally, the internal Indonesian political context should not be ignored. The army was presumably well aware that the closer a major war appeared to be, the more strongly would the PKI press its case for a "people's militia," which, if permitted, could decisively swing the Indonesian balance of power in favour of the Communists.

It is worth remembering that Sukarno, in his confrontation with the Dutch over West Irian, had not counted on Indonesia's ability to gain victory in battle, but on the prevailing anti-imperialist international climate, on the Dutch unwillingness to spend a fortune defending West Irian, and on America's influence over its NATO ally. It is probable that he believed the same factors to be operating in his favour in the Malaysian confrontation since, until 1965, he followed a similar strategy. As has been seen, it was in part due to the urging of Chou En-lai that he switched from a West Irian strategy, which might have had some chance of success, to a protracted war strategy. If, therefore, China allied itself with Indonesia in the hope of assisting Indonesia to gain control of North Borneo, it seems strange that Peking prompted the Indonesians to move away from a strategy that had already proved successful in another context.

This does not negate the argument that China's enmity with the U.S. was a factor in its relations with Indonesia. Chapter 3 discussed how China's general line on international united fronts moved after 1956 in a more vehemently anti-American direction, with Peking tending to concentrate its efforts on those Afro-Asian states which adopted an "anti-imperialist" foreign policy line. It is clear that this provides at least part of the explanation for China's Indonesian policy. Peking's doubts about Jakarta's relatively good relations with the Kennedy administration, the constant search of the Chinese press for trivial pieces of information purporting to prove the existence of bitter American-Indonesian disputes, and its unconcealed delight at the anti-American turn in Indonesia's foreign policy in 1964 all demonstrate the extent to which China's attitude towards Indonesia hinged upon Indonesia's relations with the United States.

However, the American factor does not provide a sufficient explanation of why China became so heavily committed to Indonesia towards the end of 1964. While Peking constantly looked for and encouraged anti-American policies on the part of other states, it was normally satisfied with the adoption of a militant verbal posture and often with less than this. Moreover, it

was generally wary about any form of collaboration with non-Communist
states that went much beyond declarations of unity in the common cause.
As has been seen, its notion of an international united front often entailed
little more than the assertion of an "objective" unity between different
"struggles" in the sense that they all helped to overstretch the forces of
imperialism. In the case of Indonesia, this was all that was claimed during
the West Irian campaign, as well as in the first two years of the Malaysian
confrontation. While in January 1965 Peking was ostensibly responding to
a request for more support for Indonesia in the face of a military build-up
by Britain, this does not account for its equivocation in September 1964,
shortly after the build-up had begun. Moreover the Malaysian confrontation, like the West Irian campaign, was directed against what, for the
Chinese, was a secondary imperialist power, and the well-known Anglo-
American differences over the issue suggested that the U.S. would not
automatically become involved even if major hostilities did break out.[83] In
addition, China already had a growing commitment to what for Peking was
a more important conflict in Vietnam that *was* directed against the U.S.A.
Finally, it is difficult to believe that China would have entirely welcomed the
prospect of an enlarged Indonesia, with potential irredenta stretching to
Singapore and beyond.

The Sino-Soviet dispute
as a factor in Sino-Indonesian relations

The Sino-Soviet dispute had a fivefold significance in the formation of
China's policies towards Indonesia. First, Indonesia had become increasingly reliant on Soviet aid, and it would have been a considerable coup for
China if it could assist in driving a wedge between the two countries. Sec-
ond, Sukarno inclined towards the view that the Soviet Union should not
be admitted to the Second Afro-Asian Conference, an issue on which Pe-
king had expended a considerable diplomatic effort since 1962. Third, the
PKI was the largest and one of the most prestigious of the nongoverning
Communist parties in the world, and its support was eagerly sought by both
China and the Soviet Union in the ongoing debate in the international
Communist movement. Fourth, Peking believed that Soviet policies in Indo-
nesia adversely affected the position of the Indonesian Communists in the

83. For an account of these differences, see M. Leifer, "Anglo-American
Differences over Malaysia," *World Today*, April 1964.

internal balance of power in Indonesia. Indeed at one point in the Sino-Soviet polemics the CCP accused the CPSU of "ganging up with the Indonesian reactionaries in order to injure the CP of Indonesia which upholds Marxism-Leninism."[84] This statement is interesting, since it contains one of the few public references by Peking to "reactionaries" in a country with which it enjoyed close relations. In this case it may have been intended to refer to the Indonesian army, the main opponents of the PKI and the recipients of considerable quantities of military aid from Moscow. Finally, Indonesia was one of two Asian countries, the other being India, on whom the Soviet Union had concentrated a great deal of attention since 1960 with what may have appeared to the Chinese the aim of building them up as counterweights to China.

An intriguingly large number of Chinese initiatives towards Indonesia were made shortly after a similar Soviet move or one made by Indonesia which had implications for the Sino-Soviet dispute. Chen Yi visited Jakarta after an important mission by General Nasution to Moscow in 1961,[85] Liu Shao-ch'i's visit followed one by Malinovsky, and President Sukarno was unexpectedly invited to Peking after Sukarno had clearly gone against Soviet wishes at the 1964 Cairo Conference. The transcript of the January 1965 talks between Chou En-lai and Subandrio which came into the hands of A. C. A. Dake shows clearly the extent to which Peking had one eye on the likely effects on Moscow of China's alliance with Indonesia. As Dake puts it, "All through the conversations, Chou was trying to egg Subandrio on in respect to Moscow, suggesting at one point to 'have our joint declaration ready exactly in time so that we can give it to the Soviet Union. Then we can fully discuss it when Kosygin comes to Peking.' " The transcript also reports Chou as saying, "Don't pay your debt to the Soviet Union, they do not help Indonesia. Do not only not repay your debt of one billion dollars, but even ask for more, 90 percent for arms."[86]

A united front interpretation

So far I have considered China's alliance with Indonesia as a function of China's relations with other states. A third factor that has to this point been

84. "CCP Central Committee's Reply to CPSU's Letter of 15 June 1964," *Peking Review*, 31 July 1964.
85. For details, see G. J. Pauker, "General Nasution's Visit to Moscow," *Asian Survey*, March 1961.
86. Dake, *Spirit of the Red Banteng*, pp. 330–331, 338.

only touched upon is China's relations with the PKI and the extent to which China was motivated by considerations relating to the internal situation in Indonesia, in particular by the desire to assist the PKI.

The PKI was important to China for three reasons. First, its support was coveted by both sides in the Sino-Soviet dispute. Second, it had real influence on the making of Indonesian foreign policy and on Sukarno, especially after leading PKI member Njoto was given an important cabinet position in 1964. Third, it appeared to have a good chance of winning power in Indonesia. It is with the third of these factors that this section is concerned. It considers the question of how far China's policies towards Indonesia are explicable in terms of its support for the PKI in the Indonesian power struggle. It should, however, be noted that although these three factors may be separated analytically, it is unlikely that Peking drew such clear distinctions among them. If, for example, China could have assisted in bringing about a PKI victory in Indonesia, this might have greatly increased its prestige vis-à-vis the Soviet Union in the international Communist movement.

Hard evidence of what went on in the many meetings between PKI and CCP leaders is impossible to come by, so what follows will necessarily involve a high degree of speculation. Four hypotheses about China's policy towards Indonesia will be advanced:

1. That Peking, throughout the 1961–1965 period, attached at least as much importance to its relations with the PKI as it did to those with the Indonesian government.

2. That in 1963, and partly as a result of Chinese persuasion, the PKI decided to switch away from its constitutional strategy for winning power and towards a more Chinese-style strategy.

3. That Peking used the opportunity presented by Sukarno's rift with both Washington and Moscow to adopt the role of Indonesia's major international ally for the purpose of urging upon Sukarno a confrontation strategy that was aimed at establishing in Indonesia the conditions for a Chinese-style revolution.

4. That China's informal alliance with the Indonesian government therefore fully deserves the title "united front" to the extent that it incorporated an alliance "from below" with the PKI to overthrow that government.

After Aidit won control of the PKI in 1951, following the party's decimation in the Madiun rebellion of 1948, he laid down a new set of doctrines establishing the party's post-Madiun strategy. The key facet of these was an emphasis on "peaceful transition" to socialism.[87] As Aidit expressed the new doctrine in 1957, "If it depends on the Communists, the best way, the ideal way, for transition to the system of people's democratic power . . . is the way of peace, the parliamentary way."[88] The main thrust of Aidit's doctrine thus anticipated the changes in the Soviet line on the Third World after the death of Stalin. Indeed, Indonesia was one of the models for the later Soviet concept of "national democracy," which was intended to refer to Afro-Asian countries which were anti-imperialist and which allocated the local Communists a role in domestic policy making.[89] This was, in theory at least, to be a feature of Sukarno's 1957 conception of "Guided Democracy," which Sukarno announced on his return from a visit to the Soviet Union and which was immediately endorsed by Moscow.[90]

It is plain that a major factor behind the evolution of the new Soviet position on Afro-Asian countries was Moscow's increasing reluctance to endanger its relations with the governments of such states for the sake of local Communists. In 1959, Chinese analysts were writing in the Soviet journal *International Affairs* that, while cooperation between Communists and governing national parties was permissible if the nationalists' foreign policy was "positive,"[91] this did not negate the necessity for armed struggle in order to achieve "complete independence," that is, Communist governments.[92] In contrast, Soviet contributors to this journal insisted that, while "a common stance on fundamental questions of foreign policy" was the only bond between local Communists and governing nationalists,[93] nationalist "progressiveness" in foreign policy matters could be translated

87. For discussion of the PKI's post-Madiun strategy, see D. Hindley, *The Communist Party of Indonesia, 1951–1963* (Berkeley, 1964), and R. T. McVey, *The Rise of Indonesian Communism* (Ithaca, N.Y., 1965), especially pp. 616–617.

88. Cited in R. T. McVey, "PKI Fortunes at Low Tide," *Problems of Communism*, January–April 1971, p. 28.

89. G. F. Hudson, R. Lowenthal, and R. MacFarquer, *The Sino-Soviet Dispute* (London 1961), p. 194.

90. See "President Sukarno's Plan," *New Times*, 28 February 1957, and "The New Indonesian Cabinet," *International Affairs* (Moscow), no. 3, 1957.

91. For example, Yi Li-yu, "People's China Relations with Asian and African Countries," *International Affairs*, no. 3, 1959, pp. 77–78.

92. For example, Hsin Tu, "The National Liberation Movement and the Defence of Peace," *International Affairs*, no. 3, 1959, pp. 83–84.

93. V. P. Nikhamin, "Some Features of the Foreign Policy of the Eastern Non-Socialist Countries," *International Affairs*, no. 3, 1959, pp. 85–86.

into "progressive" domestic policies,[94] thus facilitating a "peaceful transition" to socialism. Similarly, E. M. Zhukov contended that the "national bourgeoisie" would not capitulate to imperialist pressure and pointedly declared that the "real friends" of Afro-Asian countries should support their efforts to industrialise and implement land reform, whereas Wang Chia-hsiang, in a later Chinese publication, argued that the "national bourgeoisie" *would* capitulate under imperialist pressure.[95] In effect, Moscow was implying that Afro-Asian Communists should refrain from the use of violence against their governments where those governments were pursuing "positive" foreign policies, whereas Peking's position was that violence was inevitable since "complete independence" in the Third World and genuinely "progressive" domestic policies were possible only through a "people's democratic revolution" led by the Communist parties and following a Chinese strategy.

The specific ramifications of the Soviet line on Indonesia were apparent as early as the mid-1950s. In 1956, for example, Moscow not only praised Sukarno's anti-imperialist outlook but also the Indonesian government's domestic economic policies, including its "progressive" labour legislation.[96] Aidit, in contrast, though he still adhered to his "parliamentary road" to power, expressed a somewhat more pessimistic view of Indonesia's internal economic prospects.[97] Moreover, although Aidit, like Moscow, supported the inauguration of Guided Democracy and the government's suppression of a rebellion in Sumatra in 1958, he was aware that both events had tended to enhance the internal position of the PKI's main opponent, the Indonesian army. However, throughout his major ideological work, *Indonesian Society and the Indonesian Revolution*, Aidit failed to acknowledge the extent of PKI dependence on nationalist forbearance and continued to insist that the nationalists could be enticed leftward if they were not frightened into an anti-Communist position by a premature act of violence.[98]

94. V. Avarin, "Economic and Political Progress in the Underdeveloped Countries," *International Affairs*, no. 3, 1959, pp. 80–82.

95. E. M. Zhukov, "The Bankruptcy of the Imperialist Colonial System," *International Affairs*, no. 3, 1959, pp. 64–68; Wang Chia-hsiang, "The International Significance of the Chinese Revolution," *Ten Glorious Years* (Peking, 1960), p. 272.

96. A. Baturin, "New Economic Trends in Indonesia," *New Times*, 6 September 1956.

97. D. N. Aidit, "Unite to Achieve Demands of the August 1945 Revolution," *Supplement to Review of Indonesia*, September 1956, pp. 4–5.

98. Harris, "Communist Strategy toward the National Bourgeoisie in Asia and

As the Sino-Soviet dispute became increasingly acrimonious during 1960–1961, the PKI at first sought to take a neutral position between the two sides.[99] However, even this was sufficient for it to earn the gratitude of Peking, which had few allies of any significance in the dispute. Moreover, in March 1962 PKI members joined the Indonesian cabinet for the first time and so were in a position to assist in building up relations between China and Indonesia. Both points were acknowledged in a CCP cable to the Seventh Congress of the PKI in March 1962, which thanked the PKI for its "important contributions to the defence of Marxism-Leninism, the upholding of the Moscow Declaration and Statement, and the strengthening of international Communist unity" as well as for its efforts in "promoting friendly cooperation between the two countries."[100] During these two years the number of visits to China by PKI members greatly outnumbered all other Indonesian visits.

By 1963, the PKI had shifted closer to a pro-Chinese stance, as evidenced by Aidit's report of 10 February 1963 entitled "Courage, More Courage," in which he declared that revisionism was the "main danger" in the Communist movement.[101] The PKI openly criticised the CPSU on only a few isolated occasions. However, on several important issues, such as the 1963 test ban treaty and the Soviet call for a world meeting of Communist parties, the PKI's position was essentially the same as that of the CCP.[102] At the end of 1963, Aidit's report "Ignite the Banteng Spirit" refuted "the idea that the struggle for national independence will not succeed without the help of the socialist countries," which, as Chinese commentary on the report pointed out was an idea being "deliberately disseminated in order that the Communists struggling for national independence would not dare to express opinions different from those of a certain socialist country, because that would lead to the denial of assistance to their own country."[103]

the Middle East 1945–1961," Columbia University Ph.D. thesis, 1966, pp. 260–261, 258.

99. See D. Hindley, "The Indonesian Communist Party and the Conflict in the International Communist Movement," *China Quarterly*, no. 19 (July/September 1964).

100. NCNA, 25 April 1962.

101. NCNA, 14 February 1963.

102. On the test ban treaty, see Hindley, "Indonesian Communist Party," p. 112; on the meeting of Communist parties, see *Indonesian Herald*, 16 December 1964.

103. NCNA, 31 December 1963.

104. *Melbourne Age*, 3 July 1964.

In 1964 the PKI was reported to have snubbed Soviet Deputy Premier Mikoyan during his visit to Indonesia,[104] and at the beginning of 1965 Aidit openly challenged Moscow to prove that its opposition to "imperialism" was genuine.[105]

It seems probable that a major factor in the PKI's switch in line was its growing conviction in 1962–1963 that a peaceful strategy for attaining power would earn it no more dividends than it had already and that Moscow's overriding emphasis on Sukarno's foreign policy was at the expense of the PKI's internal ambitions. I will show that, in spite of the improvement in its relations with Jakarta, Peking consistently stressed the inevitability of a split between the Indonesian "national bourgeoisie" and the Communists, as well as the necessity for armed struggle. That it did this by calling attention to the PKI's own references to the need for "struggle" within its united front with the nationalists and ignoring the PKI's much stronger (at least until 1963) advocacy of the "peaceful road" suggests that it was implicitly pointing out to the PKI the dangers of pursuing a "revisionist" course domestically while opposing "revisionism" internationally. Moreover, the decisive switch in PKI strategy came during a lengthy visit by Aidit to China, which indicates a direct Chinese involvement in the PKI's change in line.

During 1962 the PKI began to express publicly its doubts about its present strategy and to indicate that more "struggle" was required within its united front with the Indonesian nationalists. Although it continued to emphasise the "peaceful road," Chinese reports of PKI activities drew attention only to the former aspect. The tone was set in the CCP's cable to the PKI's Seventh Congress, cited earlier, which praised the PKI's struggle for Indonesia's "full independence," its "persistent and tireless efforts to consolidate and enlarge the national united front," and to "defend the people's democratic rights."[106] A lengthy NCNA report of Aidit's speech to the congress focussed on Aidit's criticism of "revisionism" but also quoted remarks of his which suggested that the PKI viewed its internal strategy in Chinese "unity and struggle" terms: "The progressive forces have developed further. . . . The unity between the progressive forces and the middle-of-the-road forces, and especially with its left wing, has become stronger. The role of the left wing in the middle-of-the-road forces and their courage in opposing the diehards have grown."[107]

105. *Straits Times*, 1 February 1965.
106. NCNA, 25 April 1962.
107. NCNA, 11 May 1962.

Later in the year, Peking Radio reported Aidit as having criticised the "narrow nationalism" of the Indian working class during the Sino-Indian conflict, and as having drawn the following lesson from this experience: "We are all the more convinced that dialectics should be applied to the national front which we are establishing together with the bourgeoisie; that is, it is necessary to implement the policy of both uniting with the bourgeoisie and struggling against it."[108]

Early in 1963, *Red Flag* published a lengthy analysis of Indonesian Communist strategy. This was primarily devoted to pointing to those elements in PKI strategy which most resembled the Maoist conception of revolution, and particularly Mao's injunctions concerning "unity and struggle" and armed struggle. For example, a long extract from Aidit's book *The Founding and Growth of the Indonesian Communist Party,* which included no reference at all to the "peaceful road," dealt largely with the party's inadequate grasp of united front tactics in the 1940s:

> The August Revolution (1945–1948) failed because the Indonesian Communist Party was unable to evaluate its experience in the united front work before the revolution began; nor was it experienced in armed struggle and party construction. . . . One valuable experience it gained from the revolution is that it has learned to understand the inherent wavering attitude of the national capitalist class. . . . In the course of cooperating with the national capitalist class, the party must never lose its independence, nor can it overlook its most dependable and numerically strong ally—the peasantry. . . . Another lesson it learned is that armed struggles are the most important form of struggle in the course of the revolution.[109]

In a later section, the article stressed the qualifications which the PKI had laid down regarding its participation in "parliamentary struggles" and added, "The Indonesian Communist Party does not take the work in parliament as the most important work, nor does it regard parliamentary work as the only form of struggle."[110]

The importance which the PKI was coming to have in Peking's perspective was clearly demonstrated by the compliments lavished on the PKI during 1963–1965. Aidit was said to have "Indonesianized Marxism-Leninism"[111] and to have contributed to the enrichment of "the world's

108. Peking Radio, 15 November 1962.

109. "The Revolutionary Struggle of the Indonesian People and the Indonesian Communist Party," *Red Flag,* 20 May 1963, p. 108.

110. Ibid., p. 123.

111. Peng Chen's speech on the forty-fifth anniversary of the PKI, *Peking Review,* 4 June 1965.

theoretical treasury of the fight for socialism and national democratic revolution."[112] He also received the honour of having his *Selected Works* published in China.[113]

One of the purposes of the singling out by Peking of what it regarded as the "correct" aspects of PKI strategy and its ignoring the "incorrect" aspects was, it has been suggested, to draw the attention of the PKI to the dangers of internal revisionism. Later in 1963 Aidit went to China on a visit that was to last for several weeks and indicated, in a remarkable series of "reports," his acceptance of China's implicit criticism of the PKI. He declared that Indonesia was still a "semifeudal society pending its full independence" and went on to state that the "character of the Indonesian revolution was a bourgeois democratic revolution" which was a prelude for a "socialist revolution." He added that to strive for the leading role in the revolution was the "historical task of the proletariat" and that after studying Mao Tse-tung's ideas on the conditions for "striving for the leading role in the revolution leading to the revolution" he was now in a position to say that "recently the working class and the Communist Party of Indonesia have achieved these conditions."[114] He also had much to say on the subject of the PKI's united front strategy:

> The August Revolution taught the Communists of Indonesia the nature of the revolution in Indonesia; what the classes are that support it and the classes that oppose; the reason the National United Front is indispensable for the victory of the revolution; who the reliable allies of the proletariat are, and those allies that waver and, under certain circumstances, would betray the revolution . . . [and] that armed struggle is the most important form of struggle in making revolution.[115]

Aidit's last week in China was spent in Canton, with Chou En-lai and Lo Jui-ch'ing accompanying him on his journey south—a considerable honour. While there he declared bluntly that "the national bourgeoisie is vacillating by nature," and added that the peasants were the Communists' "most reliable ally and the main revolutionary force."[116]

112. NCNA, 23 May 1963.

113. NCNA, 20 March 1963.

114. D. N. Aidit, "The Revolution of Indonesia and the Urgent Tasks of the Indonesian Communist Party," NCNA, 2 September 1963.

115. D. N. Aidit, "A Number of Questions in the Indonesian Revolution and the Communist Party of Indonesia," NCNA, 4 September 1963.

116. D. N. Aidit, "The Revolution of Indonesia Is an Inseparable Part of the World Socialist Revolution," NCNA, 25 September 1963.

It is unlikely that the PKI had any clear notion of how it was going to translate its change in line into specific policies for attaining power, particularly since any precipitate action would be certain to provoke the Indonesian army into retaliating in force. The major problem for the PKI was that, though its influence extended into all areas of Indonesian society, it had no military strength. However, the PKI apparently saw Indonesia's confrontation with Malaysia as providing favourable conditions for a gradual improvement in the Communist position, much as the CCP had been able to build up its strength during the anti-Japanese war. This was why, despite the PKI's dependence on Sukarno for protection from the army, it openly criticised his participation in the Bangkok talks with the Malaysian leaders over a possible end to confrontation.[117] Moreover, in accordance with its new emphasis on the countryside, the PKI blamed the government for the near famine conditions in several rural areas and called for the admission of more Communists into Sukarno's "NASAKOM" cabinet as essential to the solution of this problem.[118] Later in the year, Aidit ordered the campaign against the "farmers' enemies" to be stepped up.[119]

During Sukarno's visit to China in 1964 some of the political parties most hostile to the PKI had commenced an anti-PKI campaign, but on Sukarno's return to Indonesia he took decisive action against the non-Communist parties, leaving the PKI at the beginning of 1965 as the only organised political force in Indonesia—except of course for the army.[120] This prompted a major stepping up of the PKI's propaganda and agitation. In January 1965 Aidit challenged Britain to invade Indonesia, adding that if this happened a series of revolutions would follow.[121] In May he issued a report to a PKI plenum entitled "Step Up the Revolutionary Offensive in All Fields."[122] In the same month the party's journal, *Harian Rakjat*, asserted that the PKI nationalist united front was "the most effective weapon for eliminating imperialism and feudalism and for completing the national revolution—it paves the way for Indonesia to advance towards socialism."[123] In July, Foreign Minister Subandrio issued the so-called

117. Jakarta Home Service, 24 January 1964.

118. *The Nation*, 20 February 1964.

119. *Indonesian Herald*, 30 May 1964.

120. For a detailed account of these developments, see Dake, *Spirit of the Red Banteng*.

121. *Straits Times*, 1 February 1965.

122. *Indonesian Herald*, 14 May 1964.

123. NCNA, 24 May 1965.

"Gilchrist letter," which allegedly proved the existence of an Anglo-American "plot" to attack Indonesia. This was immediately seized upon by the PKI as a pretext for urging closer "unity between the people and the armed forces" and the establishment of a commissar system in the army, which would, of course, have given the PKI effective control of the army's lower echelons.[124] In the same month, PKI leader Lukman called on the peasants to free themselves from "feudal exploitation so as to carry out the national and democratic revolution through to the end."[125]

It is impossible to say exactly what role Peking played at each stage of these developments. Aidit retained a relatively independent (though somewhat inclined to the Chinese side) position in the Sino-Soviet dispute from 1963–1965,[126] and it is probable that his decision to change PKI strategy in 1963 was influenced only marginally by Chinese pressure, although the changes must have been discussed with the Chinese leaders during Aidit's long visit to China in the same year. What is clear is that when Sukarno came into conflict with both Moscow and Washington in 1964, Peking used this opportunity both to increase China's involvement in and influence over Indonesia and to urge Sukarno to concentrate more on the guerrilla war side of "confrontation." Peking's most significant initiative was the suggestion that Indonesia form a "people's militia" or "fifth force," and the implications of this proposal provide the strongest support for the contention that China's policy towards Indonesia was significantly influenced by its desire to help the PKI.

That the proposal was so strongly resisted by the army, and even initially by Sukarno himself,[127] offers the clearest indication that the establishment of a well-armed "people's militia" had implications far beyond the usefulness of such a force for confrontation. Indeed the utility of a "fifth force" for defensive purposes against an external enemy was slight. Significantly, when Sukarno, in July 1965, instructed that the Indonesian "volunteers'" movement (which the PKI began to emphasise when it seemed that the "fifth force" would not materialize) be developed and consolidated,

124. NCNA, 9 July 1965.

125. NCNA, 14 July 1965.

126. See Dake, *Spirit of the Red Banteng*, pp. 204–219, and R. Mortimer, *Indonesian Communism under Sukarno* (London 1974), pp. 329–363.

127. *Djakarta Daily Mail*, 1 January 1965.

he stated that this was to be done primarily for internal reasons, "in order to preserve the compactness of NASAKOM at home" and only secondarily to "deal with the U.S.-British invasion plot."[128]

Peking believed that certain components of the situation in Indonesia bore resemblance to those which had brought the CCP itself to power: an external threat and a large mass-based Communist party able to turn the threat to advantage in its struggle for power. P'eng Chen used this analogy in a speech he made during his visit to Indonesia in June 1965. He also linked the development of the internal revolutionary situation in Indonesia with the struggle against the external enemy: "The political consciousness, fighting capacity, and discipline of the broad masses of the Indonesian peasants have grown rapidly with this struggle."[129]

The chief component missing from the Maoist equation for winning power was Communist military power, hence the "fifth force" proposal. There can be little doubt that the proposal was made for this internally directed reason rather than from a genuine conviction that a "fifth force" was necessary for confrontation. It is unlikely that whereas Sukarno, the PKI, and the army all viewed the "fifth force" suggestion in the light of its effect on the internal balance of power in Indonesia, Chou En-lai alone was unaware of this implication when he put the proposal before Sukarno. In two lengthy articles which appeared in *Peking Review* in August 1964 and February 1965 Liu Yun-cheng reiterated Mao's doctrines on the role of the people's militia in the Chinese revolution and made it clear that the purpose of the people's militia in China had been precisely that of building up revolutionary base areas, raising the political consciousness of the peasantry, and in short preparing the ground for a Communist victory.[130] That at least the second of these articles may have been partly written with Indonesia in mind is indicated by a quotation from Lenin which Liu had managed to unearth: "It would be a deceitful and lying evasion to say that it is superfluous to arm the proletariat when there is a revolutionary

128. Jakarta Home Service, 10 July 1965.
129. *Peking Review*, 4 June 1965.
130. Liu Yun-cheng, "The Militia in the Chinese People's Revolutionary Wars," *Peking Review*, 21 August 1964, and "The Role of the People's Militia," *Peking Review*, 5 February 1965.
131. Liu, "Role of the People's Militia."

army, or that there are 'not enough arms.' "[131] Both of the objections listed
by Lenin had also been advanced by the Indonesian army.[132]

The fact that China attempted to influence the strategy of confrontation
in ways that would assist the PKI does not necessarily mean that Peking
supported or helped plan the attempted coup of 30 September 1965. It
rather suggests the opposite. Peking appeared to have in mind the development of a revolutionary situation in Indonesia over a long period of time
during which the PKI would prepare itself for an eventual armed struggle
with the army, and the army itself would be infiltrated to a sufficient extent
by PKI supporters to make it likely that the PKI would find considerable
support from within the army. A putsch of the Gestapu type had no part in
such a strategy, and especially not one which took place before the PKI was
in a position to defend itself. Although there are still some mysterious
aspects to the Gestapu affair, as yet only circumstantial evidence has been
advanced to prove China's complicity in it.[133] Indeed, even the exact nature
of the PKI's involvement is still a source of controversy.

Nonetheless China's alliance with Indonesia was in fact a dual alliance
with both government and PKI, and as such it derived its ideological
inspiration from Mao's united front doctrines. Not only was the relationship conceived of in united front terms, it offers one of the clearest examples of an attempt to translate into concrete and specific terms the broad
generalisations of the united front theories. Often when Peking talked
about its relations with non-Communist countries in united front terms,
this signified little more than that the governments of such countries were
regarded as not wholly reliable and that at some distant date in the future
they would be overthrown. In the Indonesian case a Communist victory
seemed somewhat closer than this, which made it necessary to work out exactly how the specific case of the Indonesian revolution related to the
general theories—how ideology and practice were to be combined. The
result was an attempted "reconciliation" of theory and practice in which
two stages are apparent. In the first stage, which reached its culmination
with Aidit's visit to China in 1963, the "practice" of the Indonesian revolution was simply written and spoken about as if, in fact, the PKI were following an essentially "Chinese" road to power: the facts were distorted

132. *Indonesian Herald*, 20 May 1965.
133. See R. P. L. Howie, "China and the *Gestapu* Affair in Indonesia: Accomplice or Scapegoat" (unpublished paper, Australian Political Studies
Association Conference, Canberra, 1970).

somewhat in order to fit the ideology. In the second stage, beginning in late 1964, an attempt was made to change the facts in a more fundamental sense. Peking attempted to influence the strategy of confrontation in ways that would make the situation in Indonesia resemble more closely that which had obtained in China in the 1930s and 1940s.

CONCLUSION

I have subtitled this chapter "The Failure of a Dual Policy." It would perhaps be more accurate to say that China had several dual policies towards Indonesia. It believed that its interests in opposing the Soviet Union and possibly the United States were served by its alliance with Indonesia at the same time as the revolutionary aims of the PKI were being advanced. Indeed it even had a "dual policy" towards the PKI: its support was needed against the CPSU and because of its influence with Sukarno.

Hence, when the Sino-Indonesian relationship is considered from the perspective of the united front model, the complexity of a situation which involved several interacting and interdependent motivations should not be ignored. The model does offer a comprehensive interpretation which fits China's policy towards Indonesia in several important respects. At the most general level, China's perception of the internal political situation in Indonesia reflected a tendency to equate Indonesia with revolutionary China. Essentially this meant that Peking was influenced by an assumption that the Indonesian situation was unfolding in a predictable direction with the main participants—"diehard," "middle," and "progressive" forces—playing their expected parts ("acting according to type" in the terms of the united front model).

The propositions of the united front model outlined under the heading "specific united fronts" are also applicable to China's policy towards Indonesia. One of China's objectives in establishing a closer relationship with Indonesia towards the end of 1964 was to encourage revolutionary tendencies within Indonesia "at the same time as and partly by means of an alignment with it against an external enemy" (Proposition 12, united front model). Proposition 13, that Peking took account of the revolutionary possibilities in Indonesia, is essentially a subclause of Proposition 12, and is valid to the same extent. Proposition 14, that Peking established a "united front from below" with the PKI is more difficult. In one sense it is applicable, since Peking and the PKI had a very close relationship which included consultations over Indonesia's revolutionary strategy. However, despite many rumours in 1965 that Peking was secretly supplying the PKI with small arms (which never materialised during the post-Gestapu purge), there is little evidence that Peking was extensively engaged in activities that would give the term "united front from below" a more concrete meaning.

"Confrontation" could not really be termed a vital part of China's "broad united front" strategy except in the sense that it might encourage emulation in other situations where the U.S. might become involved. Hence, Peking's opposition to moves by Indonesia to end the Malaysian confrontation in 1964 needs some explanation other than such marginal advantage to the United States as might flow from an end to confrontation. Proposition 15 of the united front model suggests that Peking would encourage its united front partners to adopt radical postures on international issues partly as a means of aiding local "progressive" forces. The proposition is based on the Maoist assumption that conflict with an external enemy provides beneficial "consciousness-raising" side effects as well as tactical opportunities for the progressive forces. Both factors appear to have been present in Chinese thinking during 1964–1965, as evidenced in particular by P'eng Chen's speeches.

It cannot be said that a wide range of united front *tactics* were employed by China in its relationship with Indonesia (Proposition 16). This perhaps illustrates the difficulties of translating the details as opposed to the broad outlines of a united front strategy to the international arena. However, Peking's most significant initiative, the "fifth force" proposal, was clearly aimed at altering the balance of forces inside Indonesia. It may thus be seen as a tactic with the classic united front motives of "isolating the diehards" (Indonesia's army) and "developing the progressive forces."

As the united front models fits, to a certain extent, China's policy towards Indonesia, so the alliance model is basically inapplicable. Indonesia's "imperialist" enemy was not threatening China, and China gained no additional military or diplomatic advantages (rather the opposite) from its commitment to Indonesia (Propositions 6 and 7, alliance model). China *did* interfere, albeit in a subtle way, in Indonesia's internal affairs despite the generally acceptable international stance of its ally (Proposition 8). A strong, stable, and anti-American Indonesia might have balanced, to a limited extent, American power in Asia (Proposition 9) but, given the actual condition of Indonesia at the beginning of 1965, it would be difficult to maintain that this entered into Chinese calculations.

However, as suggested earlier, the united front model does not tell the whole story of China's objectives in its relations with Indonesia. Peking *was* interested in the revolutionary prospects in Indonesia, but always with one eye on the effect that a victory by Communists who adopted a Maoist strategy and subsequently established a close relationship with China would have on the Sino-Soviet conflict. Hence, an external enemy factor was present in China's policy towards Indonesia but the means chosen by Peking to counter Moscow were, to say the least, unconventional and strongly influenced by the united front doctrine.

CHAPTER FIVE

China's Alliance with Pakistan

The Sino-Pakistani relationship is perhaps the most significant and interesting of the four case studies. This is so for four reasons:

1. The northwestern area of the Indian subcontinent is of great strategic importance to both China and the Soviet Union. Thus, their vital interests are involved there in a way that they are not in, for example, Indonesia.

2. The Sino-Pakistani relationship is the only one of the four to have been confronted with the essential test of any alliance: war. Moreover, the fact that Pakistan fought two wars during the period under consideration makes it possible to compare China's reactions to each crisis.

3. Unlike both the Indonesian and Cambodian cases the relationship did not end abruptly as a result of internal political change, but endured throughout a period that witnessed dramatic upheavals in both China and Pakistan.

4. The subcontinent is one of the few areas of the world in which all three major powers have been closely involved in rivalry with one another and in which China has competed on a relatively equal footing with the two superpowers.

1954–1962

The most striking feature of the Sino-Pakistani relationship is that it has enjoyed greater continuity and stability than any other relationship between China and a non-Communist Asian state. Since 1954 Pakistan has been singled out for public criticism by Chinese propaganda organs only in a few isolated instances, all of them before 1960. This is all the more strange since, by the criteria that Peking has employed in respect to other states, Pakistan is the very epitome of a "reactionary" Third World state. It committed the most serious offence in the Chinese book by entering into an alliance with the United States and permitting an American base to be established in the strategically important area of Peshawar; its *raison d'être* was a fiercely anti-Communist religion; from 1958 it was governed by an increasingly oppressive military dictatorship. Peking's attitude towards Pakistan may be contrasted to that of Moscow, which, on various occasions, criticised Pakistan's alliance with the U.S.A., described Pakistan as an artificial state, deplored the repressive policies of the Pakistani government, and for most of the period after 1955 supported India's position on the Kashmir issue, as well as taking Afghanistan's side in its dispute with Pakistan.[1]

Pakistan recognized the People's Republic of China within a few months of its establishment, but this did not immediately cause the CCP to move from the rigid line which depicted all of the newly independent countries as "imperialist lackeys." When China did begin to shift its position on the former colonies in 1951, it turned to India rather than Pakistan. However, Pakistan's voting behaviour at the United Nations may have suggested to Peking that Pakistan was not prepared to toe an American line on all questions and that it was especially reluctant to offend China if this could possibly be avoided.[2] On Pakistan's side, China's image improved when, following a drastic slide in Indo-Pakistani trade, China greatly increased its imports from Pakistan during 1952.[3] According to Chou En-lai, speaking in 1963, an unspecified "preliminary understanding" was reached between China and Pakistan through the efforts of General Raza, Pakistan's first ambassador to China, who took up his post in 1951.[4] It was probably as a

1. For Soviet foreign policy in the Indian subcontinent, see I. Clark, "Soviet Policy towards India and Pakistan, 1965–1971" (Australian National University Ph.D. thesis, 1974). See also V. S. Budhraj, "Moscow and the Birth of Bangladesh," *Asian Survey*, May 1973; R. H. Donaldson, "India: The Soviet Stake in Stability," *Asian Survey*, June 1972; S. P. Seth, "Russia's Role in Indo-Pak Politics," *Asian Survey*, August 1969.

2. Pakistan supported the resolutions denouncing Korea, but abstained on the resolutions calling China an aggressor in Korea and placing an embargo on trade with China. S. M. Burke, *Pakistan's Foreign Policy* (London, 1973), p. 102.

3. Ibid.

4. Interview with the Pakistan press, *Dawn*, 11 April 1963.

result of this that China's first public comments on the Kashmir issue were strictly neutral, taking the line that tension between India and Pakistan was caused by "U.S. imperialism" and applauding the 1953 talks between the two sides.[5]

It was clearly this "understanding" which caused China to take such a tolerant view of Pakistan's membership in SEATO. During the Bandung Conference of 1955, Chou En-lai revealed that he had had a conversation with Pakistan's premier, Bogra, who had reassured him about Pakistan's membership in SEATO.[6] However, Peking's lenient attitude on this issue dates back much earlier than the Bandung Conference. Even before the Baguio meeting which established SEATO, Chinese newspaper articles discussing the meeting failed to make any critical references to Pakistan's participation. A *Kuang Ming Jih-bao* editorial, for example, stated, "Five out of the eight countries planning to participate in the Baguio Conference are not Asian states, while the ruling clique of Thailand and the Philippines can hardly be regarded as representing their peoples."[7] Other Chinese articles in August 1954 stressed the fact that Pakistan had avoided making any prior commitment to join SEATO.[8]

Even after Pakistan joined SEATO, the Chinese press tended to refrain from direct attacks on the Pakistani government, emphasising instead the domestic opposition in Pakistan to SEATO and the occasions when Pakistan took an independent line within SEATO itself.[9] A British writer on Pakistan claims that he was assured "on unimpeachable authority" that Peking sent a private message to the Pakistan government shortly after the Bandung Conference which assured Pakistan that "there was no conceivable clash of interests between the two countries which could imperil their friendly relations; but that this position did not apply to Indo-Chinese relations, in which a definite conflict of interests could be expected in the near future."[10]

5. NCNA, 28 August 1953.

6. G. McT. Kahin, *The Asian-African Conference* (Ithaca, N.Y., 1956), p. 51.

7. NCNA, 17 August 1954.

8. For example, NCNA, 25 August 1954.

9. For example, Pakistan was praised in 1956 for "having wisely held itself aloof" from SEATO manoeuvres in February (*People's China*, 16 March 1956). Later in the year *People's Daily* attributed the political upheaval in Pakistan and the fall from favour of the Muslim League to the unpopularity of Pakistan's membership of SEATO (NCNA, 4 June 1956).

10. L. F. Rushbrook Williams, *The State of Pakistan* (London, 1962), p. 120. It is worth noting that Krishna Menon was later to express his disbelief in the ex-

The implication of this interpretation is that China was seeking friendly relations with Pakistan from an early stage because Pakistan was the most obvious ally for China in an expected confrontation with India.

The assertion that Peking was aware of the possibility of future conflicts of interest with India in the mid-1950s is probably correct,[11] and this may well have entered into Peking's calculations at this time. However, the point should not be exaggerated. First, China's policy towards Pakistan during the Bandung period should be seen in the context of its general Asian policy at this time. While Pakistan fared better in the Chinese press than the other two Asian members of SEATO, China's attitude towards both Thailand and to a lesser extent the Philippines was far more restrained in 1954–1956 than it was later to become. In addition, unlike Thailand and the Philippines, Pakistan had recognised China and supported the admission of China to the United Nations. Moreover, because of its less than single-minded devotion to America's anti-Communist crusade it was likely to be a source of weakness within the two alliances of which it was a member. Fourth, the relations between the two states were correct and formal rather than close, and there is no evidence that China attempted in the 1950s to take them beyond this. As will be seen, the impetus for a closer association came from Pakistan in 1959 and 1960, with Peking at first responding somewhat cautiously. Fifth, the claim in the alleged "private letter" that there was "no conceivable clash of interests" between the two countries is not justified logically or historically. The two countries did have a disputed border, and some minor incidents had taken place on this from as early as 1953.[12]

Moreover, despite Peking's restraint on the subject, the pro-Western orientation of Pakistan's foreign policy remained a potential source of tension between the two countries. In 1957 Pakistani Prime Minister Suhrawardy was criticised by the Chinese press for "hostile remarks" that he was supposed to have made on the subject of China during a visit to the U.S.A.[13] A series of more serious incidents in 1959 caused relations between the two countries to reach their lowest point. Ayub Khan's military

---

istence of such a letter. See M. Brecher, *India and World Politics* (London, 1968), pp. 58–59.

11. Chou En-lai was reported to have said that there had been a "dark side" to Sino-Indian relations from the first. See *The Sino-Indian Boundary Question* (Peking, 1962), p. 12.

12. F. Watson, *The Frontiers of China* (London, 1966), p. 140.

13. NCNA, 24 July 1957.

coup was believed in China to presage a more pro-Western turn in Pakistan's foreign policy, and several events early in 1959 were seen as confirming this view.[14] Most alarming from China's perspective were Ayub's call for India and Pakistan to combine for the collective defence of the subcontinent and his conclusion of a bilateral defence pact with the U.S.A. under which the Americans were to set up a base at Peshawar. Peking contrived several pretexts during the year to demonstrate its displeasure with the Pakistan government. For example, in February the Chinese Committee for Afro-Asian Solidarity sent a belligerent cable to Ayub protesting the arrest of two Pakistani leftists and "resolutely demanding" their release.[15]

Matters came to a head in July when Peking issued a sweeping condemnation of Ayub Khan's policies in the course of a series of protests against Pakistan's granting permission to a Muslim group from Taiwan to tour the country. A *People's Daily* "Observer" article asserted that ever since 1951 Pakistan had "adopted an unfriendly attitude towards China on many issues" and that since Ayub's coup Pakistan's "hostile attitude" had become even worse.[16] The specific issues singled out for criticism included Pakistan's shift in the U.N. debates on the China question towards support of American resolutions calling for the matter to be postponed, and Pakistan's 1959 pact with the U.S.A.[17] However, the strongest remarks were directed against Pakistan's comments on the Tibetan revolt and its joint defence offer to India: "In April and May the Pakistan Foreign Ministry made repeated statements at home and abroad slandering the Chinese people, interfering in China's internal affairs, sowing discord in the relations between China and India, and agitating for the Cold War."[18]

It is worth noting that Peking made it clear in these protests that it regarded the preservation of good relations between China and Pakistan as important to China and that it had resorted to public denunciations only after what it believed to have been a deliberate and sustained "anti-China campaign" on the part of Pakistan. The *People's Daily* revealed that, "To avoid open criticism and charges, the Chinese government has on several occasions through diplomatic channels made friendly representations and

14. *Peking Review*, 28 July 1959.
15. NCNA, 27 February 1959. A more temperately worded cable was sent by the All China Journalists Association shortly afterwards (NCNA, 9 March 1959).
16. *Peking Review*, 28 July 1959.
17. Ibid. See also NCNA, 23 July 1959.
18. Ibid.

lodged protests with the Pakistan government." It gave the reason for this restraint: "The Chinese people have always attached a great importance to Sino-Pakistani friendship and waited patiently to see a change of stand by the Pakistani government."[19]

The conclusions reached to this point about China's policy towards Pakistan may be summarised as follows: Pakistan was seen as belonging to a different category from Thailand and the Philippines, and China was willing up to a point to turn a blind eye to certain unwelcome aspects of Pakistan's foreign policy; however, an explanation of this based solely or even principally on Peking's belief in the inevitability of a future Sino-Indian rift is inadequate. In Leninist terms, Pakistan was a "weak link" in the imperialist chain and a potential source of "contradictions within the imperialist camp." It was also a Muslim state, and for both domestic political reasons and because the Muslim countries had produced some of the most radical Third World leaders, Peking was anxious to avoid policies that could be interpreted as anti-Islamic.[20] However, it is probable that China's Pakistan policy was based mainly on much less complex calculations than these. The area of Kashmir controlled by Pakistan bordered a region of China both politically unstable and of considerable strategic importance. It is not unthinkable that the policy which appeared to make most sense to China in the mid-1950s was that of seeking friendly relations with *both* India and Pakistan rather than playing one off against the other. The same policy was to be attempted by both the Soviet Union and the U.S.A. at different times in the 1960s—and with the same lack of success.

Pakistan's foreign policy revolved around one central concern: its fear of India. It was this that had caused it to enter SEATO rather than any apprehensions about China—as Peking itself clearly understood. Pakistan's apparent shift in 1959 towards closer links with the U.S.A. and its proposal for a joint defence system with India should also be interpreted as opportunistic moves in the context of India-Pakistan relations rather than as caused by newly aroused fears of China. The joint defence offer was made conditional on the Kashmir question being resolved by a plebiscite, which Pakistan believed would go in its favour. Nehru rejected the offer on the grounds that Pakistan's real objective was not to restrain China but to secure Kashmir.[21]

19. Ibid.
20. China's delegation to the Bandung Conference had included a Muslim.
21. M. Ayoob, "India as a Factor in Sino-Pakistan Relations," *International Studies*, January 1968.

Pakistan, which could ill-afford to have two hostile neighbours, was quick to try to restore the damage that had been done to Sino-Pakistani relations in the early part of 1959. A further motive was its growing awareness that China would be Pakistan's natural ally against India if Sino-Indian relations continued to worsen. An additional impetus to this was given when the Kennedy administration began in 1960 to improve its relations with India.

Ayub Khan states in his memoirs that informal approaches were made to China over the possibility of the two states negotiating a boundary agreement towards the end of 1959,[22] while the first diplomatic note on this subject was sent by Pakistan on 28 March 1961.[23] China did not reply to this note until eleven months later, on 27 February 1962, and it did not respond at all to the earlier approaches. Negotiations finally began during December 1962, shortly after the Sino-Indian conflict had ended. Although the actual demarcation took some years to complete, an agreement in principle was reached by March 1963. The Indians claimed that by this agreement Pakistan had given away thousands of square miles of Kashmiri (and therefore Indian-claimed) territory, but in fact the agreement appears to have been favourable to Pakistan, since it gained 750 square miles of economically valuable territory which had been controlled by China.[24]

The reason for China's initial reluctance to enter into negotiations over the border was probably its desire to avoid further alienation of India by appearing to give some legitimacy to Pakistan's control of part of Kashmir. The same conciliatory posture was apparent even after the 1962 Sino-Indian war. For example, the text of the 1963 border agreement emphasised that the agreement was provisional and would be renegotiated with "the sovereign authority concerned" if India and Pakistan resolved their Kashmir dispute.[25] The Chinese Foreign Ministry emphasised after the agreement had been reached that China's position on the Kashmir dispute remained one of noninvolvement and impartiality.[26]

It should thus not be automatically assumed that the *sole* reason China eventually responded to Pakistan's request for negotiations was the deterioration in Sino-Indian relations, although this was obviously of great

22. M. Ayub Khan, *Friends not Masters* (London, 1967), p. 162.

23. *Dawn*, 3 March 1963.

24. The area gained by Pakistan contained a salt range and grazing ground (*Dawn*, 7 March 1963).

25. *Peking Review*, 15 March 1963.

26. NCNA, 2 March 1963.

importance. The agreement was only one of several reached by China in the early 1960s, and although one motivating factor may have been the desire to demonstrate the contrast between China's reasonableness and India's obstinacy,[27] China seems to have been genuinely concerned to prevent any further conflicts with its neighbours over disputed boundaries. Another factor in the Sino-Pakistani case might have been that Pakistan offered to support the annual United Nations resolution proposing that China's entry into the U.N. be decided on the basis of a simple rather than a two-thirds majority in return for China's agreement to demarcate the boundary. This is hinted at by Ayub Khan in his memoirs, where he relates a meeting he had with the Chinese ambassador to Pakistan in December 1961:

> I asked him about our suggestion of demarcating the undefined border between China and Pakistan. He said that that was a very complicated matter. I told him that if border demarcation was a complicated matter, China's admission to the United Nations was even more complicated. . . . I think the Chinese ambassador was very impressed by what I told him.[28]

1963–1965

Ayub claims that the sole purpose of the border agreement was to "eliminate a possible cause of conflict in the future."[29] However, it can be argued that Pakistan saw the agreement as having implications that went far beyond this, and indeed regarded it as the first stage in the formation of an informal alliance between China and Pakistan against India. Despite the disclaimers in the text of the agreement, it undeniably brought China closer to a legal recognition of Pakistan's de facto control of part of Kashmir, and Pakistan may have calculated that it was only a step beyond this for China to become committed to the status quo in Kashmir (if not indeed to Pakistan's claim on the whole of Kashmir) and thereby to the defence of Pakistan itself. Chou En-lai in an interview with a Pakistani journalist did not confine himself to the pragmatic justification for the agreement—that it

27. This was a point made in Chou En-lai's communications with Afro-Asian leaders on the subject of the Sino-Indian dispute. See "Premier Chou En-lai's Letter to the Leaders of Asian and African Countries on the Sino-Indian Boundary Question," *Sino-Indian Boundary Question*, pp. 6–10.

28. Khan, *Friends not Masters*, p. 162.

29. Ibid., p. 164.

was a means of preventing future conflict—but argued that the actual demarcation that had been arrived at was legally defensible because it followed the boundaries shown on British maps in the nineteenth century.[30] This suggests that Peking would be unwilling to make any further territorial concessions should the boundary have to be renegotiated with India. Since India was almost certain to demand such concessions, Pakistan's calculation that China could probably be drawn into a commitment to the status quo on the subcontinent appears to have been soundly based.

Of course it would be too much to expect to find a public statement by Pakistan's Foreign Ministry of this scenario. However, the strongest evidence for its existence is the fact that soon after the border agreement was signed several Pakistani leaders began to talk as if China had become involved in the defence of Pakistan. The most famous of these statements was contained in a speech by Foreign Minister Bhutto to Pakistan's National Assembly on 17 July 1963: "An attack on Pakistan's territorial integrity also involved the territorial integrity and security of the largest state in Asia."[31] This statement was particularly significant because of the general context of Bhutto's speech, in which he talked of the need for a reappraisal of Pakistan's foreign relations and alliance policy in the wake of increased Western arms deliveries to India following the Sino-Indian war. It is also deliberately vague. It did not suggest that there was a defence pact between the two countries but merely that China's "territorial integrity" would be involved if India attacked Pakistan—which, it was suggested earlier, was the effect Pakistan believed the border agreement would have.

Similarly, in a press conference in the United States during which he was asked if Pakistan had entered into an alliance with China, Bhutto denied the existence of either a formal or informal alliance but pointed out that "in case of conflict the area's geopolitics might come into play, and it was not possible to predict exactly how the situation would develop."[32] On another occasion Bhutto gave the lie to Pakistani protestations that Pakistan's friendship with China had no military connotations by asserting that what had brought the two countries into a closer relationship were "the impelling considerations of national security."[33]

It is clear that Bhutto thought that an actual *treaty* of alliance between

30. *Dawn*, 11 April 1963.
31. *Asian Almanac*, 17–20 July 1963, p. 36.
32. *Dawn*, 9 October 1963.
33. *Dawn*, 13 September 1963.

China and Pakistan was unnecessary. On one occasion, when asked if Pakistan was China's ally, he replied evasively, "Ally is a technical word," while on another occasion he said that Pakistan did not need to enter into military collaboration with China to obtain Peking's support on the Kashmir issue.[34] The Pakistanis clearly believed not only that they could count on China's support without having to sign an alliance treaty but that this informal arrangement served their interest best for three reasons. First, it created uncertainty in the minds of India's leaders as to the extent to which China would go in aiding Pakistan. Second, it enabled Pakistan to avoid the embarrassing position of being a party to two pacts, one against, the other with China. Third, it allowed Pakistan to keep its options open in terms of winning support from the two superpowers, since Pakistan could hold out the threat of a closer involvement with China in order to bring pressure to bear on the United States and the Soviet Union. Ayub Khan did precisely that when, in an interview, he denied that Pakistan and China had concluded a secret military pact but said on being asked about the possibility of such a pact being signed in the future,

> *The answer to that lies with the U.S. authorities.* If India grows menacingly strong, we shall be in a great predicament and shall have to look around for someone to help us. If we are attacked by India, then that means India is on the move and wants to expand. We assume that other Asian powers, especially China, would take notice of that [emphasis added].[35]

It is significant in this context that, although the Soviet Union began to improve its relations with Pakistan in 1961, it was not until 1963–1964 that it shifted towards a policy of neutrality on the Kashmir question.[36]

The publicly stated Pakistani view in 1963 was, then, that China's own security requirements would inevitably involve China on Pakistan's side should Pakistan's security be seriously threatened. For the relationship between the two countries to deserve the title "informal alliance" it would be necessary for China to have the same understanding of the situation as Pakistan and for there to be some evidence that the two countries had reached a private agreement that could be interpreted as establishing an informal alliance.

34. *New York Times*, 27 February 1964, and *Guardian*, 20 February 1964.
35. *Dawn*, 13 September 1963.
36. Clark, "Soviet Policy," p. 94.

During 1963 there were no Chinese statements of support for Pakistan which implied the same degree of commitment as Pakistani speeches were suggesting. However, a commitment of sorts was given by China's trade minister at the end of the year when he said that China would support Pakistan in the event of "fresh aggression" by India.[37] It should also be noted that Peking on no occasion refuted the claims that were being made in Pakistan concerning China's support, which suggests at least a degree of tacit acceptance by China of the role in which Rawalpindi had cast it.

It was suggested earlier that Pakistan's leaders had calculated that China could be drawn into a commitment to the defence of Pakistani-controlled Kashmir, if not of other parts of Pakistan, as a logical consequence of the Sino-Pakistan border demarcation. Events do appear to have developed in this way during 1963–1964. In March 1963, Ch'en Yi had declared with reference to the Kashmir issue, "The Chinese government has all along maintained a position of not getting involved in this matter and hoped that it would be settled peacefully. . . . This attitude of ours is open and above board and consistent."[38] However, throughout 1963 and the first part of 1964, Rawalpindi sought to demonstrate its usefulness to China in a number of ways, with what may be assumed was the objective of causing China to shift from its neutrality on the Kashmir question. In the April 1963 meeting of the SEATO Ministerial Council, the Pakistani delegation clashed with the Anglo-American delegation over, among other matters, SEATO's attitude towards China.[39] Ayub Khan also offered his good offices to China and the U.S. to assist in bridging the gulf between them.[40] During the 1964 Laos crisis Ayub was used as an intermediary for the exchange of messages between the two sides.[41]

Pakistan received its reward for these endeavours on China's behalf in February 1964, when Chou En-lai visited Pakistan. The joint communiqué issued after this visit stated, "The two sides expressed the hope that the Kashmir dispute would be resolved in accordance with the wishes of the people of Kashmir, as pledged to them by India and Pakistan."[42] This

37. *Times* (London), 2 December 1963.
38. NCNA, 2 March 1963.
39. *Dawn*, 13 April 1963.
40. This was stated by Ayub Khan during his visit to London in 1964 (*Dawn*, 14 July 1964).
41. *Far Eastern Economic Review*, 23 July 1964.
42. NCNA, 24 February 1964.

formula was to be repeated in all subsequent Sino-Pakistani joint communiqués. Although its wording was relatively innocuous, it did represent a considerable change of line by China, since the references to "the wishes of the people" was meant to imply that the question should be decided by a plebiscite among the mostly Muslim Kashmiri people.

It is notable that during the discussions between Chou and the Pakistani leaders, the Pakistan side stressed that Pakistani control of the whole of Kashmir would mean that India would have no land route to Ladakh—one of the key areas of contention in the Sino-Indian boundary dispute.[43] It is also interesting that the joint communiqué did not say that the Kashmir question should be settled peacefully, even though just before the passage on Kashmir cited here, the communiqué stated that "the Prime Minister and the President agreed that the border dispute between India and China should and can be resolved *peacefully* through negotiations."[44] Finally, Chinese public statements on Pakistan after this meeting generally contained an (albeit vague) verbal commitment to Pakistan's "national independence and state sovereignty" as well as an expression to the effect that the two countries shared a "common cause of opposing foreign aggression and intervention."[45]

Taken together these points raise the question of whether the Sino-Pakistani alliance could be considered an *offensive* alliance, that is, one which involved minimally some Chinese connivance at a Pakistani policy aimed at securing Kashmir by military means.

To judge whether a particular treaty constituted an offensive alliance often involves also a judgement about who was the aggressor in any subsequent conflict. This in the case of Indo-Pakistan relations has not proved a fruitful exercise, and indeed the Indo-Pakistan wars demonstrate the ambiguities and complexities that are inseparable from questions of this kind. However, without denying that for some years India had been consolidating its hold on Kashmir in a manner that would have appeared provocative in Pakistan, it is clear that the crucial move which stepped up the tension in Kashmir in August 1965 was made by Pakistan.[46] Moreover,

43. *Sunday Telegraph*, 23 February 1964.
44. NCNA, 24 February 1964.
45. For example, NCNA, 12 October 1964.
46. See W. J. Barnds, *India, Pakistan, and the Great Powers* (New York, 1972), pp. 197–203; also R. Brines, *The Indo-Pakistani Conflict* (London, 1968), pp. 287–293.

Pakistan appeared to act with a confidence in 1965 that had been lacking earlier and that some believed stemmed from the assurances it received from China. Three other points might be made in support of the argument that China and Pakistan had in effect formed an offensive alliance: that the Rann of Kutch incident in April 1965 closely followed visits to China by Ayub Khan and to Pakistan by Chou En-lai and Ch'en Yi and that Ch'en Yi visited Pakistan unexpectedly in the first days of the Kashmir conflict in September 1965; that Pakistan chose to assert its position in Indian-controlled Kashmir by infiltrating guerrillas in a vain attempt to stir up an internal war; and of course that China made its strongest intervention ever on the side of a non-Communist state in the course of the war.

The problem with the argument that China connived at a Pakistani forward policy is that it cannot be proved without access to secret Pakistani and Chinese documents detailing what actually went on in the various high-level discussions in 1965. Without this, the most that can be said on the basis of the available information is that, while Pakistan may have received encouragement from the very *fact* of its friendship with China, there is no evidence to suggest that China had any great influence on Pakistan's policy in 1965.

Taking the first point, Ayub's increased confidence—overconfidence, as it turned out—which led him to a policy of "leaning on India" in 1964–1965, there is no evidence to show that China contributed to this other than indirectly. The Sino-Indian war revealed some of the deficiences of the Indian army, and Ayub could have assumed that Pakistan's friendship with China raised apprehensions in India. However, many other circumstances contributed to the creation of a war atmosphere in Pakistan. The riots in Kashmir during 1963 had encouraged the Pakistanis to believe that a determined move by Pakistan would meet with considerable local support.[47] Nehru's death in May 1964 left India with a prime minister in Shastri who was regarded by many as much weaker than his predecessor. Moreover, the international climate was more favourable to Pakistan than it had been for some time, with the Soviet Union working towards an improvement of its relations with Pakistan and the United States beginning to have doubts about its post-1962 arms aid to India.[48] Finally, Pakistan's success during the Rann of Kutch incident, the growing internal pressure in Pakistan for something to be done about Kashmir, and Ayub's self-con-

47. Ibid.
48. Seth, "Russia's Role."

fidence because of his "record of almost unbroken successes since 1951"[49] all contributed to Pakistan's decision to send guerrillas into Kashmir in August 1965.

Any connection between the high-level Sino-Pakistan talks in March 1965 and Pakistan's forward policy is of course impossible to prove or disprove. The sole passage relating to Kashmir in the joint communiqué issued after Ayub's visit in March 1965 is open to differing interpretations: "The two parties noted with concern that the Kashmir dispute remains unresolved, and considered its continued existence a threat to peace and security in the region. They reaffirmed that this dispute should be resolved in accordance with the wishes of the people of Kashmir as pledged to them by India and Pakistan."[50]

The reference to the "threat" from the continued existence of the Kashmir dispute combined with the absence of the word "peaceful" in the call for the dispute to be resolved can be read as either ominous or innocuous, and only knowledge of the details of the Sino-Pakistani talks would make it possible to say which it was. In the absence of this, there are a few pointers which seem to suggest that if Ayub revealed to his Chinese hosts any plans that he might have had regarding Kashmir the Chinese side may have tried to restrain rather than encourage him. A *People's Daily* editorial described the talks as "frank," which was the usual code word for indicating disagreement.[51] As will be discussed later, the disagreement appears to have centred on the attitudes of the two countries to various international issues, but it may also have referred to their discussions on the Kashmir question.

More significant is that both the official communiqué and the speeches made by China's leaders during the visit lacked the customary reference to China's support for Pakistan's "sovereignty and independence." This phrase had been used by China to indicate its commitment to Pakistan's survival and to imply that China could be considered as Pakistan's ally if that survival were threatened. Its omission was of great significance, especially if Peking had been informed that Pakistan intended to force the Kashmir issue, and may have been seen in Peking as a way of warning Pakistan and reassuring India of the limits of China's commitment to Pakistan. This point is reinforced by an examination of the speeches made by both sides

49. Barnds, *India, Pakistan*, p. 201.
50. *Peking Review*, 12 March 1965.
51. NCNA, 9 March 1965.

during Ayub's visit. On one occasion Liu Shao-ch'i used a weaker phrase than the customary one to assert China's support for Pakistan: "[The Chinese people] firmly support Pakistan in her just struggle to uphold national dignity and oppose foreign pressure." Ayub in his reply to Liu ignored the discrepancy between Liu's speech and earlier Chines estatements of support and blandly reminded China of its earlier line: "The Chinese people staunchly support Pakistan's just struggle to oppose foreign intervention and threats and to safeguard independence and sovereignty."[52]

Ayub also made an unusual reference to the need for Asian unity against "imperialism," which might either have been intended as a polite bow to China's ideological preoccupations or as a specific plea for Sino-Pakistani unity against India: "The present situation in Asia is excellent. But imperialism is still making trouble. The Asian countries have to strengthen their unity and cooperation and make joint efforts to oppose imperialist aggression and intervention and safeguard peace in Asia."[53] No such statement had been made by Ayub during Chou En-lai's visit to Pakistan in 1964. It should further be noted that when the Rann of Kutch incident broke out in April the Chinese government statement on it, while expressing support for Pakistan, drew attention to Pakistan's public posture of desiring a peaceful solution to her border dispute with India: "The Chinese government and people fully sympathize with and support the solemn and just stand of the Pakistan government in opposing the Indian policy of military expansion and *advocating settlement of the border dispute through peaceful negotiations*" [emphasis added]. Peking also remarked that if India widened the conflict, it would "certainly come to no good end," which can hardly be seen as embodying a major commitment to aid Pakistan.[54]

The attempt by Pakistan to spark off a "people's war" in Kashmir in August was a strategy of which China might have approved, but there is no evidence to suggest that Peking had any direct influence on the decision. Indian reports that the guerrillas in Kashmir had been trained and armed by Peking were not independently confirmed, and it appears that Chinese instructors in guerrilla warfare did not arrive in Pakistan until 1966. However, Ch'en Yi's denial of the Indian accusations is interesting because

52. NCNA, 2 March 1965.
53. Ibid.
54. Quotes from NCNA, 4 May 1965.

he appeared to be saying that China would have played the role that India
had cast it in if it had had the capacity to do so:

> The Indian papers have even joined the Western press in linking any
> struggle for freedom and independence in the world with China and
> alleging that it is instigated by China, which supplies arms and trains its
> cadres. By so doing, they heap on China the honour of supporting all
> freedom, independence, and liberation struggles. But China has yet
> neither the ability nor the qualification to accept such honour.[55]

The essentially defensive and limited nature of the Sino-Pakistani
alliance became clear during the Indo-Pakistani war of 1965. The Chinese
press had ignored the earlier stages of the conflict in August partly because,
as was suggested here, it did not wholly approve of Pakistan's adventurism,
partly because the conflict was limited to skirmishes in Kashmir, and partly
because the Pakistanis appeared to be enjoying some success. The first
official statement on the conflict did not appear until 7 September, the day
after India had dramatically escalated the conflict by launching an offensive
into West Pakistan itself and ordering a general mobilisation. This, the
Chinese statement declared, "enlarged the local conflict between India and
Pakistan into a general conflict between the two countries." The statement
left no doubt about the seriousness with which China regarded India's
move. It declared that it was "a grave threat to peace in this part of Asia"
and went on, "The Chinese government sternly condemns India for its
criminal aggression, expresses firm support for Pakistan in its just struggle
against aggression, and solemnly warns the Indian government that it must
bear responsibility for all the consequences of its criminal and extended
aggression."[56]

The veiled threat in this passage was reiterated at the end of the
statement: "India's aggression against any one of its neighbours concerns
all its neighbours. Since the Indian government has taken the first step in
committing aggression against Pakistan, it cannot evade responsibility for
the chain of consequences arising therefrom." It was hinted that the "chain
of consequences" might include increased Chinese pressure on the Sino-Indian border: "The Chinese government has served repeated warnings
[about Indian border violations], and it is now closely following the

55. NCNA, 4 September 1965.
56. *Peking Review*, 10 September 1965.

development of India's acts of aggression and is strengthening its defences and heightening its alertness along its borders."[57]

This statement set the tone for China's subsequent moves and declarations on the war. On 10 September the PLA units in Tibet were ordered "to be highly vigilant against provocations on the part of the Indian reactionaries,"[58] and after a series of warnings China issued its dramatic ultimatum of 16 September demanding that India withdraw its alleged "military works for aggression on the Chinese side of the China-Sikkim boundary or on the boundary itself" within three days, or face the consequences.[59] Three days later, after what Peking chose to interpret as a "conspicuous change of tune" by the Indian government,[60] the ultimatum was extended to 22 September and later abandoned because, according to Peking, the intruding Indian soldiers had "all run away."[61]

Peking's behaviour during the crisis exposed China to a great deal of ridicule as well as charges of attempting to inflame the situation. Many Western observers believed that China's aims were to prolong the war and obtain the maximum gains for China at minimum risk.[62] If correct, this interpretation would support the contention that the Sino-Pakistani alliance was offensive rather than defensive. However, it is difficult to see how the course of action chosen by China really assisted her in these aims. China did not extend her territorial control beyond the post-1962 line during the conflict. Nor did China's ultimatum encourage Pakistan to continue fighting. It is also noteworthy that the first Chinese arms shipments to Pakistan did not take place until after the war had ended. Given that the Western powers had stopped sending arms to the subcontinent the moment the war broke out, this is hardly consistent with the charge that China wanted to prolong the conflict. Unless China was acting irrationally, some other explanation is needed.

China's aims appear to have been threefold: to warn India that, while it would not support Pakistan's adventurism, it could not countenance a major shift in India's favour in the subcontinental balance of power; to demonstrate China's credibility and usefulness as an alliance partner; and to

57. Ibid.
58. NCNA, 10 September 1965.
59. *Peking Review*, 24 September 1965.
60. Ibid.
61. NCNA, 23 September 1965.
62. Brines, *Indo-Pakistani Conflict*, p. 372.

serve notice that China's interests must be taken into account in any international settlement of the Kashmir question. As already noted, the Chinese media ignored the crisis until India enlarged it into a general war in which Pakistan's survival might have been at stake. Furthermore, Peking confined itself to vague and general warnings until the war appeared to be turning against Pakistan. Although China's ultimatum caused alarm throughout the world when it was delivered, its effect was precisely what Peking had probably foreseen it would be: to increase the international pressure on both India and Pakistan to agree to a ceasefire. The ultimatum was extended on the day the Security Council put ceasefire proposals before the two sides and forgotten about when the ceasefire was agreed to. I have already argued that Peking was well aware of and had probably opposed Pakistan's earlier provocations, which had led to the war. However, once Pakistan itself was endangered, China could no longer maintain a disapproving silence, since its own security interests were at stake. As it had by now come to define these interests in terms of its alliance with Pakistan, it needed to act in such a way as to demonstrate the credibility of its support for Pakistan. Once again China's calculated exercise in brinkmanship met this requirement.

China's third concern was that its general diplomatic isolation, and in particular its lack of a seat on the Security Council, might prevent it from having any influence on the negotiations which would follow the war. Indeed it is clear from Chinese propaganda during September that Peking believed—with some validity—that U.S. and Soviet diplomacy during the war had taken them a step further towards China's chief fear: a tacit U.S.-Soviet "joint hegemony." This, in the Chinese view, would not only take no account of China's interests but could turn into a specifically anti-China combination. A related fear was that the war might enable the Soviet Union to increase its influence with both India and Pakistan. Thus the Chinese line on the superpowers' role stressed three related arguments:

1. The superpowers were "colluding and conspiring" in the Security Council.

2. Despite their show of impartiality, they were in fact opposed to Pakistan and by supporting India against China had done much to strengthen India's "truculent and arrogant" attitude against Pakistan.

3. Both superpowers, but especially the Soviet Union, saw in the conflict a way of hitting at China by accusing her of inflaming the conflict.[63]

If Peking had hoped that its ultimatum would win it some influence on the postwar negotiations it was to be disappointed, since the Soviet Union's offer of good offices was accepted by both sides. However, it is possible that China's action had some immediate impact. Pakistan's Foreign Minister Bhutto even went so far as to claim after the war that China had played a decisive role in the U.N. handling of the conflict, and he called the 20 September resolution "China's resolution," as he believed it had shaken the U.N. into realising the need for a permanent settlement of the Kashmir question, but this may have exaggerated China's significance.[64]

1966–1971

Some observers believe that Sino-Pakistani relations began to deteriorate after the September war.[65] This is true only in the sense that Pakistan moved after 1965 to improve its relations with the two superpowers, with the inevitable effect of a relative decline in the significance of its relationship with China. However, no absolute decline occurred and indeed in 1966 Sino-Pakistani relations reached a peak, if measured by cultural, economic, and military exchanges. On Pakistan's National Day, 23 March 1966, Chinese tanks and aircraft were put on display for the first time, to the consternation of the U.S. and the Soviet Union, who were concerned that China's new arms aid might upset the military balance in the subcontinent.[66] Also in March, Liu Shao-ch'i visited Pakistan for the first time and reiterated China's pledge of support for Pakistan: "Pakistan can rest assured that when Pakistan resolutely fights against foreign aggression in defence of its national independence, sovereignty, and territorial integrity, 650 million Chinese people will stand unswervingly on their side and give them resolute support and assistance."[67]

The reference in the statement just quoted to Pakistan's "territorial integrity" was new and was probably intended to refer to Pakistani-controlled

63. For China's attitude towards the roles of the U.S.S.R. and U.S.A., see in particular Chou En-lai's speech of 9 September 1965, NCNA, 9 September 1965. See also "U.N.—Sanctuary for the Indian Aggressor," *Peking Review*, 17 September 1965, and "Who Backs the Indian Aggressors," *Peking Review*, 24 September 1965.

64. *London Times*, 6 October 1965.

65. For example, Budhraj, "Moscow and Bangladesh."

66. *Dawn*, 6 April 1966.

67. *London Times*, 28 March 1966.

Kashmir, on which issue China's stand had edged even further towards support of Pakistan.[68] This pledge was, however, to prove embarrassing to China when a different threat to Pakistan's "territorial integrity" emerged in 1971. At the time the Chinese may have believed that it was necessary for them to give Pakistan a particularly firm assurance in order to make up for their equivocation in the first half of 1965 and to counterbalance the Soviet Union's recent rapprochement with Pakistan during the Tashkent talks.[69] It is significant that Liu Shao-ch'i made no public reference to the Tashkent declaration, although Ayub had described it in his presence as "a framework and a procedure for settling outstanding disputes between India and Pakistan."[70] Ch'en Yi during a visit to Pakistan in 1966 was quite specific about Peking's apprehensions concerning the possible effect of improved Indo-Pakistani relations and the increased influence of the Soviet Union: "The United States and the Soviet Union are trying by every possible means to plot joint Indian-Pakistan opposition to China, and this is detrimental to China and harmful to Pakistan as well." He was assured by a Pakistani minister that Pakistan would not be lured away from its friendship with China.[71]

Further references to China's support for Pakistan's territorial integrity were made during 1966, with the last one being made by China's ambassador to Pakistan, Chang Wen-chin, in November.[72] After this, however, no such references were made until December 1971. Pakistan was the only one of China's non-Communist friends not to be publicly criticised during the Cultural Revolution, but the exchange of visits between the two countries did slacken off considerably. Hence, although China and Pakistan remained on good terms during this period, the Cultural Revolution must

68. The Sino-Pakistani joint communiqué following Liu Shao-ch'i's visit referred to China's support for the "righteous stand of the Pakistani government on this dispute" (NCNA, 31 March 1966).

69. There was even a report after Liu's visit that in response to complaints from East Pakistanis that Rawalpindi was concentrating on the Western segment of the country, Ayub Khan had claimed that he had ensured East Pakistan's safety by getting China to warn India that if there were any moves against East Pakistan, the Chinese would intervene (*London Times*, 17 May 1966).

70. NCNA, 26 March 1966.

71. Quotation and response from NCNA, 28 July 1966.

72. *Dawn*, 16 November 1966.

73. Donaldson, "India," p. 477.

inevitably have caused concern in Rawalpindi about China's usefulness as an ally. This was an important factor in prompting Pakistan to bring pressure on the Soviet Union to prove its neutrality by supplying arms to Pakistan as well as India, which the Soviet Union did for the first time in 1968.[73]

The period 1969–1971 was one of fluctuating alignments between the major powers and the subcontinent. In January 1969 Indira Gandhi made the first of several moves towards normalization of relations with China, and although there was no reply from Peking to the letter she sent with this aim, it appears that Peking began to consider the possibility of a rapprochement with India. One small move in this direction occurred when Mao Tse-tung exchanged affable remarks with India's chargé d'affaires in Peking during the May Day celebrations of 1970.[74] However, Peking was anxious to avoid giving the impression to Pakistan that any improvement of its relations with India would be at the expense of Pakistan. Pakistan had proved to be highly sensitive to marginal shifts of position by the major powers and usually had attempted to balance any such shift by one power by moving closer to another. In 1969 the Soviet Union had proposed the formation of an Asian collective security system and although Pakistan eventually rejected this, it did so only after appearing to give the proposal serious consideration.[75] In this way Pakistan implicitly indicated to Peking that a Chinese rapprochement with India could result in closer ties between Pakistan and the Soviet Union.[76] An additional factor inhibiting Peking from moving too quickly towards a détente with India was the fact that Pakistan had by this time become an important intermediary between China and the U.S.A. Early in 1970 a Pakistani minister, in a speech whose significance was not apparent at the time, hinted at this: "We have reason to believe that there is now in the U.S. a better understanding of our equation with China. There is even a realisation that Pakistan's friendship with China could be useful in building bridges between the East and the West."[77]

74. *Asian Recorder*, 10–16 December 1971.

75. Budhraj, "Moscow and Bangladesh," p. 483.

76. This is also suggested by the fact that during a visit to China in July 1969 by Air Marshall Nur Khan, Chou En-lai attacked the Soviet proposal but Nur Khan did not mention it (*Peking Review*, 18 July 1969).

77. *Dawn*, 31 January 1970. Pakistan was the staging post for Henry Kissinger's famous visit to China.

Throughout 1970 several Indian-inspired rumours appeared suggesting that Sino-Pakistani relations were deteriorating. There was some factual foundation to these reports, since certain high-level Pakistanis had begun to express their fears that Peking might be involved in fomenting unrest in East Pakistan. Indeed China had felt compelled to go to the lengths of issuing a statement denying such involvement.[78] However, the rumours were almost certainly an aspect of India's long-term campaign to create divisions between China and Pakistan, as was clearly understood by the Pakistani government, which engaged in several months of intensive diplomacy, climaxed by Yahya Khan's visit to China in November 1970, to strengthen Sino-Pakistani ties.[79] The visit was not wholly successful for Pakistan. A Pakistani spokesman said that the talks had resulted in a "*proximity* of views on *most* issues" [emphasis added].[80] In the heyday of the Sino-Pakistani relationship, talks had usually been followed by the claim that there had been an "*identity* of views." Nonetheless, China continued to assert its support for Pakistan's "sovereignty and independence"—but not territorial integrity—throughout 1970. Moreover China's ability to come to Pakistan's aid in Kashmir was enhanced by the opening of two roads linking the countries in August 1970 and January 1971.[81]

Peking's behaviour throughout the Bangladesh crisis of 1971 was far more restrained than it had been in September 1965. In the early stages of the crisis Yahya Khan sought a pledge of support from China against an Indian attack. This was given in the form of a letter from Chou En-lai, dated 12 April, which stated that, should India "dare to launch aggression against Pakistan, the Chinese government will, as always, firmly support the Pakistan government and people in their struggle to safeguard state sovereignty and national independence."[82] However, this letter contained no reference to China's support for Pakistan's territorial integrity—the issue at stake in the Bangladesh breakaway movement—and it did not receive wide coverage in the Chinese media after it was delivered.

On the day before this letter was sent, a *People's Daily* "Commentator"

78. New Delhi Radio, 28 October 1970.
79. *Far Eastern Economic Review*, 17 October 1970.
80. *Pakistan Times*, 12 November 1970.
81. The Sinkiang-Pakistan road passed through Pakistan's part of Kashmir, thus providing China with a further interest in preserving the status quo in Kashmir.
82. *Far Eastern Economic Review*, 7 August 1971.

article had spelt out the limits of China's commitment even more clearly. The article asked rhetorically, "As is known to all, if the independence, sovereignty, unification, and territorial integrity of a country are encroached upon, then what is left of the interests of the people?"[83] However, when it came to the usual declaration of China's support for Pakistan, the article again left out any reference to territorial integrity. Similarly in May, at a reception to mark the establishment of diplomatic relations between China and Pakistan, Pakistan's ambassador stated, "Today when our very existence as a nation has been threatened by hostile outside interference in our internal affairs, the People's Republic of China has come out with unflinching and forthright support to our *national solidarity, integrity,* and sovereignty" [emphasis added].[84] However, the speech from the Chinese side by Vice Foreign Minister Han Nien-lung simply reiterated China's early pledge of support for Pakistan's "just struggle to safeguard state sovereignty and national independence and oppose foreign aggression and interference," with again no mention of "integrity."[85]

A notable feature of China's policy until December 1971 was the conciliatory posture that Peking adopted towards India. Several signs of this appeared throughout the year. During a visit in June by Pakistani Air Marshal Abdul Rahmin Khan, the Chinese press deleted from their reports of his speeches all of his hostile references to India's internal policies.[86] Later in the year an Indian ping-pong team toured China, while in November Chou En-lai cabled Indira Gandhi thanking her for India's support for China's admission to the U.N. and expressing the hope that the friendship between India and China might "grow and develop daily."[87] India's representative to the United Nations, in a speech thanking Chou for this message, referred to the "historic ties" between the two countries.[88]

The event which did most to upset China's gradual progress towards normalization of its relations with India was Henry Kissinger's visit to Peking in July. Pakistan had played a considerable role in arranging this, and the announcement of the visit caused apprehension in India at the possibility that, in a future crisis between India and China or Pakistan, the U.S. would not, as in 1962, support India or, as in 1965, suspend its arms aid to Pakistan. It was in part for this reason that India signed its treaty with the Soviet Union on 9 August. Although not an alliance pact in form, the effect

83. *Peking Review*, 16 April 1971.
84. *Peking Review*, 18 May 1971.
85. Ibid.

of the treaty was to make clear the Soviet Union's interest in the security of India—in other words, it involved much the same kind of relationship as that between China and Pakistan. Peking did not launch a verbal offensive against the treaty immediately after it was signed, possibly because it still hoped for some improvement in Sino-Indian relations. However, the treaty undoubtedly constituted another element impelling China towards a more cautious attitude in 1971 than it had shown in 1965.

Even as late as November 1971, although Peking publicly criticised India's interference in the Bangladesh crisis, it also called on both countries to hold consultations with a view to reducing tension.[89] Later in the month Foreign Minister Bhutto went on an urgent trip to China, presumably in an attempt to persuade Peking to take a more positive stand with the aim of deterring an Indian attack on East Pakistan. His visit was fruitless, with the two sides not even able to reach agreement on a joint communiqué. There were even reports that Bhutto had been subjected to a "spontaneous" demonstration against Islamabad's policies in East Pakistan.[90]

There are four basic explanations of China's guarded attitude during 1971. First, as already noted, Peking was interested in the possibility of improving its relations with India.[91] Second, a crisis was developing in East Pakistan in which China did not have a direct interest. Third, Peking found it difficult to condone behaviour on the part of Pakistan which had been almost universally condemned by the rest of the world. Specifically, a group of scholars from the Australian National University which visited China in 1973 was assured by Assistant Foreign Minister (and former ambassador to Pakistan) Chang Wen-chin that China did not approve of Pakistan's behaviour.[92] Finally, the Indo-Soviet treaty increased the danger to China of becoming too heavily committed to the defence of what was, in any case, an untenable position by West Pakistan. This last point should not be

86. *Far Eastern Economic Review*, 31 July 1971.

87. *Asian Recorder*, 10–16 December 1971.

88. *Peking Review*, 3 December 1971.

89. *South China Morning Post*, 8 November 1971.

90. T. J. S. George, "Peking's Pre-War Message to Bhutto," *Far Eastern Economic Review*, 5 February 1972.

91. See also Chang Wen-chin's remarks, cited in Appendix, "[in 1971] the Indian government made some gestures to improve relations, and we gave these serious consideration and took some steps to respond—for example, we indicated our willingness to exchange ambassadors."

92. See Appendix.

overemphasised since China's policy lines had been laid down much earlier than August 1971, when the treaty was signed.

China was faced with a somewhat similar situation in December 1971 to that which had obtained in September 1965—a war initiated by India but largely provoked by Pakistani policies that had not been supported by Peking. There were, however, four major differences: China was now in the United Nations; Kashmir was not endangered; West Pakistan had little chance of winning; and China found itself on the same side as the U.S.A. In fact both China and the U.S.A. were impotent in the face of an Indian move which had the support of the overwhelming majority of the population of East Pakistan. In both cases their decision to come down on the side of Islamabad was determined largely by two factors: the fact that the only great power beneficiary of the war seemed likely to be the Soviet Union, and the commitments which both had undertaken to support Pakistan. To the delight of Moscow, they were faced with two unenviable choices: to leave an ally in the lurch or to support it in a war which it had no chance of winning and in which world opinion was somewhat in India's favour. They could not emerge creditably whatever choice they made, and in the event the lesser of the two evils seemed to be the course which at least did not make India's (and indirectly Moscow's) victory even easier.

As in September 1965, once the December 1971 war had commenced Peking discarded its earlier, cautious attitude and issued a strong statement of support for Pakistan which, for the first time since 1966, contained a reference to "territorial integrity": " . . . the Chinese people resolutely support the Pakistani government and people in their just struggle to defend state sovereignty and territorial integrity and to counter foreign aggression."[93] However, on this occasion China did not immediately begin to direct threatening remarks towards India but confined itself to arguing Pakistan's case at the United Nations. Here the dominant theme in all Chinese speeches was the hidden hand of the Soviet Union that was seen to be behind India's "aggression." Few arguments were adduced in support of Pakistan's earlier policies, other than the assertion that the Bangladesh issue was the internal affair of Pakistan.

The Chinese speeches in the United Nations concentrated on the possibly dire implications for world peace if India's aggression were to go unchallenged. The frequent analogy was drawn between Bangladesh and the

93. NCNA, 16 December 1971.

Japanese puppet state of Manchukuo, which had been established after the invasion of Manchuria in 1931. China pointed out that the Manchurian invasion had been the first move in the succession of events leading to the Second World War and reminded the United Nations of the League's failure to act early enough to prevent the world war. It gave as the reason for the League's failure its domination by "certain powers" who believed that their interests would best be served if Japan became embroiled in a war with the Soviet Union.[94] The implication here was obvious: The United States should not make the same mistake as Britain and France in the 1930s. Huang Hua in one speech pointedly informed the United States that it could not expect to gain from a Sino-Soviet conflict, observing that the Soviet aim was to "gain control over the subcontinent, encircle China, and strengthen its position in contending with the other superpowers for world hegemony."[95] On another occasion, after attacking India's pretext for going to war—the thousands of East Pakistani refugees in India—he referred to an exodus of refugees from China ten years earlier: "In 1962 the Soviet government engineered a counter-revolutionary rebellion in China's Sinkiang province, carrying out subversion and splittist activities against China."[96] This, he said, had resulted in tens of thousands of refugees—or as he put it, "Chinese civilians who were forcibly taken away by you under coercion"—ending up in the Soviet Union, and he asked Moscow if it intended to use this as a pretext for attacking China.

On 16 December, when Pakistan had all but lost the war, Peking suddenly stepped up its verbal offensive against India. In a slightly farcical repetition of its behaviour during the Kashmir crisis, Peking accused Indian troops of crossing China's border with Sikkim.[97] However, it did not issue an ultimatum as it had in 1965 but contented itself with making vaguely threatening remarks such as the following: "If a timely stop is not put to such aggression committed by the Indian government, Pakistan will not be the only country to fall victim; inevitably, other countries neighbouring on India will also be endangered." Peking also issued a somewhat empty-sounding warning, which was repeated on several occasions, that "henceforth there will be no tranquillity on the Indian subcontinent."[98]

94. *Peking Review*, 17 December 1971.
95. Ibid.
96. NCNA, 4 December 1971.
97. NCNA, 16 December 1971.
98. Quotations from ibid.

Most of these remarks simply reflected Peking's sense of frustration at its inability to influence events which appeared to it to be developing in a way that was beneficial to the Soviet Union. On this occasion there was some truth in a Soviet article which referred to China's "very noisy" but "politically absurd" position.[99] It should be added, however, that Peking was well aware of the "absurdity" of its position, as evidenced by its very clear disdain for Pakistan's actions in Bangladesh during 1971.

THE INSIGNIFICANCE OF IDEOLOGY

For China's relations with Pakistan to fit a united front perspective, two criteria would have to be fulfilled. China and Pakistan would need to have been aligned on a broad range of issues and clear evidence of Peking's interest in revolutionary possibilities in Pakistan would have to be available.

On the first point, there were very few international issues on which China and Pakistan were able to present a common stance, mainly because Pakistan's alliance with the United States continued to be of great importance to it throughout the period considered here. Pakistan supported China's call for nuclear disarmament in 1963 and also gave some backing to China's campaign to keep the Soviet Union out of the proposed Second Afro-Asian Conference.[100] As had been seen, Pakistan also represented China's case at various international forums, such as SEATO or Commonwealth meetings. On other questions, however, there was a clear divergence of views between China and Pakistan. This was notably so in the case of Pakistan's attitude towards America's policy in Vietnam, as demonstrated during Ayub Khan's visit to China in 1965. In one speech he said, "We believe that the conflict in Vietnam should not be allowed to escalate into another world war. It can be settled peacefully through negotiations. . . . The U.S. and China, which are great pacific powers, must arrive at an understanding on the basis of equality and mutual recognition of their legitimate interests."[101] There were several things wrong with this from China's perspective. In the first place, since Mao's 1957 "East Wind" speech it had been almost a matter of sacred doctrine that the Vietnam conflict or any other "national liberation war" could not possible "escalate

99. Cited in Clark, "Soviet Policy," p. 243.
100. *Dawn*, 13 April 1963, and NCNA, 7 March 1965.
101. *Dawn*, 6 March 1965.

into another world war." Second, the proposal that it be settled peacefully would not have met with China's approval at this time.[102] Third, the suggestion that the U.S. had any "legitimate interests" in Vietnam must have been greeted with horror. In the event, in a most unusual treatment of a speech by a friendly visiting head of state, the Chinese press deleted all the words after "escalate" in their reports of this speech.[103]

It should be noted that the absence of agreement on many issues did not prevent the Chinese media from representing Pakistan as an ally in the struggle against imperialism. This was done in several ways. The Chinese press gave great coverage to any signs of America's displeasure at Pakistan's friendship with China.[104] On other occasions long polemics against the U.S. were inserted in the middle of factual accounts of Sino-Pakistani meetings, thus giving the false impression that China and Pakistan were united in their opposition to "U.S. imperialism."[105] It is possible that the Chinese were to some extent embarrassed by the coldly pragmatic nature of their relationship with Pakistan. At any rate their treatment of it in the press showed signs of a desire to reconcile the relationship with their ideology, or to present it in such a way that it appeared to accord with doctrine. The fact that several of the discussions were described as "frank" might also indicate that disagreements over international issues were a source of friction.

Second, there is the question of the extent of China's involvement with Communists and insurrectionists in East Pakistan. During the Cultural Revolution, allegations were made on several occasions that China was involved in aiding a breakaway movement in East Pakistan.[106] After 1970, China's opposition to Mujibur Rahman's group in Bangladesh was explained by some observers by the assertion that Peking still backed the

102. Throughout 1965 China called for a "fight to the end" in Vietnam.

103. For the Chinese version of the speech, see NCNA, 2 March 1963.

104. See, for example, *Peking Review*, 1 March 1963 and 10 May 1963, and NCNA, 19 July 1965.

105. For example, a *People's Daily* editorial in March 1965 which, after declaring that the views of China and Pakistan "concur in such fundamental issues as opposition to imperialism and big nation chauvinism, strengthening of Afro-Asian solidarity, and safeguarding of world peace," suddenly launched into an attack on American policies in Vietnam before returning to the subject of Sino-Pakistani relations (NCNA, 9 March 1965).

106. For such reports, see NCNA, 24 January 1967, and New Delhi Radio, 21 November 1969.

secessionists, but only the most radical among their number in the hope of seeing them win power after a people's war.[107]

It should be noted first that the source of these rumours was highly suspect, since most of them emanated from New Delhi and Moscow—indeed Moscow at first opposed the East Pakistan secessionist movement on the grounds that the whole affair was a Chinese plot.[108] Second, on some occasions the evidence linking China with East Pakistan's revolutionary movements has been very circumstantial. For example, the majority of twenty-eight junior army officers who were arrested in East Pakistan in 1968 for plotting a secessionist coup were graduates of a Chinese-run guerrilla school operating in East Pakistan.[109] However, the school had been set up jointly by China and Pakistan to train guerrillas for action in India, and there is no reason to suspect that Peking intended to use it for any other purpose. Third, although there was a Peking-oriented Communist party in East Pakistan, it was very small and insignificant. Moreover, when the leaders of this party began to back the secessionist movement, they received no support from Peking.[110]

Even those normally revealing sources of information about the private opinions of Chinese leaders, Red Guard wall posters and other publications, confirmed the unique position held by Pakistan in Peking's perspective. A speech by Yao Wen-yuan in 1968 to the Shanghai Revolutionary Committee explained China's foreign policy in "unity and struggle" terms, but, in accordance with united front precepts, cautioned against treating all "national bourgeois" regimes in the same way. Three categories of countries were to be distinguished. The most "reactionary," including India, Indonesia, and Burma, were the principal targets of "struggle." In the middle were countries like Cambodia and Nepal. On Cambodia, Yao stated that Prince Sihanouk had "repeatedly tried to blackmail China by threatening to go over into the imperialist camp. Let us face the reality; he is a reactionary through and through. We must fight against the reactionary regime in Cambodia, *but we must never forget that the situation in that country is different from the situation in India, Burma, and Indonesia*" [emphasis added]. Similarly, the king of Nepal was described as an "insignificant reactionary" who had tried to be friendly with China, but although Yao

107. George, "Peking's Pre-War Message."
108. Clark, "Soviet Policy," p. 101.
109. *Japan Times*, 9 March 1968.
110. *Far Eastern Economic Review*, 17 April 1971.

maintained "We have to intensify our political fight against the monarch in Nepal," he added "but that fight must be very strictly controlled." Finally, in a class of its own stood Pakistan. Although Yao asserted "We must never forget he [Ayub Khan] is a genuine bourgeois," there was no call for any kind of "struggle" against Pakistan.[111]

The only significant way in which ideology may have affected China's relations with Pakistan after 1960 is that it might have inhibited Peking from proceeding too rapidly towards an informal alliance with Pakistan after the Sino-Indian War. As has been seen, it was not until 1964 that China came down on Pakistan's side over the Kashmir question, and in this respect Peking showed considerably more reluctance than the Soviet Union, which had backed India's claim to Kashmir since 1955.[112] Ideology might have to some extent restrained China from cementing a relationship with what appeared to be its "natural ally." However, it is equally possible that Peking did not wish to force India into a closer alignment with either Moscow or Washington.

CONCLUSION

If the Sino-Pakistani relationship, by virtue of China's support for Pakistan during a war, comes the nearest of the four case studies to the traditional notion of an alliance, it is therefore not surprising that it should derive its rationale from the traditional moulder of alliances: the international system. The concept of "system" denotes a relationship between two or more units in which an action by one will cause a reaction by the others. In the present case three such sets of relationships may be distinguished: the triangular great power system; the essentially bipolar system comprising India and Pakistan; and what may be termed a "geopolitical" or "pivotal" system, involving India, Pakistan, the Soviet Union, and China, all of whom have vital interests centring on the northwestern area of the sub-continent.[113]

The three systems are interlocked to such an extent that an action deriving its logic from one system will tend to have an effect on another. In a

111. *Times of India*, 17 May 1968.
112. Clark, "Soviet Policy," p. 46.
113. For a discussion of the geopolitical importance of Pakistan, see A. Tayyeb, *Pakistan: A Political Geography* (London, 1966), pp. 217–220.

typical chain of events on the subcontinent, a great power might seek to improve its relations with a local power in the belief that in so doing it is promoting its interests against those of another major power. However, to the local powers this action would be seen in the light of their rivalry with each other, and one would attempt to counter the other's advantage by moving closer to another major power. This in turn would cause a reaction by both the two great powers and the other subcontinental state. This sequence has been repeated many times. The "geopolitical " system has been an added complication, particularly for China and India, whose hostilities have derived from the quite separate conflict centring on the northwestern frontier. Their conflict has of course had repercussions on the other two systems.

All three major powers have at different times attempted to break out of this vicious circle by seeking a balanced relationship with both local powers or attempting to bring them closer together. On all occasions such moves have failed, in the one case because neither India nor Pakistan has ever been able to see a "balanced" relationship as anything but unbalanced in favour of their rival, in the other because the gulf between them has been too wide.

Any account of the changing alignments of the major powers must therefore be a history of the interactions among the three systems. For China no less than the two superpowers, all three systems have shaped her policies. Thus, while the geopolitical conflict between China and India during the 1960s was one of the factors causing China to gravitate towards Pakistan, it was not the sole factor. For China the security of Tibet and Sinkiang has been the most constant influence on its foreign policy. However, this strategic factor has not been immune from the effects of China's membership of the other two systems. In December 1971, for example, it was China's hostility towards the Soviet Union rather than towards India which caused China to range itself solidly behind Pakistan. Also in the Kashmir crisis China was in part attempting to establish her equality with the two superpowers, who were suspected of "colluding and conspiring" against her. Moreover, the bipolar system of India and Pakistan has in general been the dominant system, in the sense that all three major powers have at times been led into situations they might have preferred to avoid by the intensity and dynamics of the Indo-Pakistani hostility.

China was, in part, led into an alliance with Pakistan in 1963. Once there, Chinese policy revolved around a principle that is inseparable from both alliances and international systems: the balance of power. The aim was the classic one of preventing the dominance of a single power on the subcontinent—in this case either India or the Soviet Union.

As this analysis may suggest, the Sino-Pakistani relationship, in addition to being more like a traditional alliance than any of the other case studies, is also closest to the alliance model. China's subcontinental policy in general may be depicted in terms of a threat to China's security producing a reaction by Peking that was aimed at obtaining a more favourable regional balance of power, with China's reaction itself being conditioned by "imperatives and constraints arising out of China's geopolitical location" (Propositions One to Five, alliance model). China had no long-term strategy but was prepared to adjust pragmatically to such developments as a more conciliatory Indian posture (Proposition Four). Similarly the propositions relating to "specific alliances" also fit this relationship quite closely. China's primary objective in forming the alliance was to increase its military and diplomatic power vis-à-vis an enemy (or in this case, enemies) (Proposition Six). China's overriding criterion was that Pakistan and China shared a common perception of threat (Proposition Seven). China did not interfere in its ally's internal affairs (Proposition Eight), and the alliance was fundamentally shaped by "regional and global balance of power considerations" (Proposition Nine).

CHAPTER SIX

China and Cambodia

Apart from Indonesia and Pakistan, Cambodia during the Sihanouk era is the only other non-Communist country to have received both military aid and some kind of verbal commitment to its defence from China. Several accounts of the relationship between the two countries from Cambodia's perspective have already been published, and there is a high degree of consensus among these as to the chief considerations which motivated Prince Sihanouk in his policy towards China.[1] These may be briefly listed as follows:

1. Sihanouk was convinced that his country faced the serious threat of being swallowed up by one of its traditional adversaries, Thailand and Vietnam. In his opinion only a guarantee of its security from a great power—or preferably from all the great powers—would enable Cambodia to retain its independence. Failing this, he hoped to try to balance the conflicting demands of the major powers against one another and to use them to keep Cambodia's neighbours in check.

2. America's growing involvement in Vietnam in the early 1960s served to strengthen his belief in the necessity of an understanding with China. This was so for four reasons. First, he thought it probable that America would not prove able to achieve victory in a protracted internal war in Vietnam. As early as May 1963, he predicted in an interview, "The Americans can keep things going as they are now in Vietnam for many

1. M. Gurtov, "The Politics of Survival" (University of California, Ph.D. thesis, 1970); M. Leifer, *Cambodia, the Search for Security* (London, 1967); "Cambodia and China," in A. M. Halpern (ed.) *Policies toward China* (New York, 1965), pp. 329–347; R. M. Smith, *Cambodia's Foreign Policy* (New York, 1965).

2. *New York Times*, 31 May 1963.

years. But in the end America will get tired of the endless war and withdraw, leaving the field open for the Vietcong."[2] Second, he believed a Communist victory in Vietnam to be inevitable and thought that only Peking's influence with Hanoi might be able to save Cambodia from the fate which, in his opinion, would await it at the hands of a united, Communist Vietnam. Third, he wished to keep Cambodia out of the war as far as possible. And, fourth, he thought it unlikely that in a war situation the United States would act against the interests of its allies, South Vietnam and Thailand.

3. Although Cambodia's foreign policy did have the rational basis outlined here, it was also affected by a number of factors relating to Sihanouk's personality. His excitability and impulsiveness often led him to take decisions and adopt postures that he had cause to regret later. Most of these actions tended to be directed against the West, since he was convinced that all Westerners—with the partial exception of the French—had a contemptuous and racialistic attitude towards Cambodia in general and himself in particular.[3] His sensitivity to alleged insults—on one occasion he wrote a letter to all Western newspapers demanding that they stop referring to Cambodia as "tiny"[4]—was a major factor in several specific decisions which had the effect of shifting Cambodia away from the U.S. and towards China. Conversely China, which had the advantage of being Asian, was careful to avoid giving offence to Sihanouk. His speeches are full of references to China's respect for Cambodia, to the fact that it treated small states as equals, and to its understanding of Cambodia's problems. The Cambodian leftist Chau Seng, who was a keen advocate of friendship with China within Sihanouk's united front political party, Sangkum, showed his awareness of this factor when he said in an interview, "We are good friends with China because they do not give us advice. They are very sensible because they know that the Prince is very sensitive and if we receive an order from abroad, he does just the opposite."[5]

3. See, for example, his "memoirs," where he writes of the Western accounts of the 1970 coup in Cambodia: "Many of the articles and books by Western writers have one thing in common: patronizing overtones of 'West knows best.' Asians have grown understandably sensitive to assumptions of Caucasian superiority." N. Sihanouk and W. Burchett, *My War with the C.I.A.* (Harmondsworth, 1973), p. 19.

4. *Philippine Herald*, 9 December 1965.

5. *New York Times*, 15 October 1965.

If, for Sihanouk, an accommodation with China was "synonymous with Cambodia's survival,"[6] China clearly had less at stake and her underlying motives are less immediately apparent.

1954–1963

The overriding Chinese concern which emerged during the 1954 Geneva conference was to prevent the formation of a U.S.-dominated alliance in Indochina and also the establishment of U.S. bases there. In order to achieve this, Chou En-lai had been prepared to give way on China's position with regard to Cambodia to the extent of putting pressure on the Vietminh and its Cambodian allies to moderate their demands for Communist power in Cambodia, on the assurance of Anthony Eden and Pierre Mendès-France that Cambodia and Laos would remain neutral.[7] However, by a show of intransigence toward the end of the conference, the Cambodian delegation had been able to gain more than this private deal among the great powers had arranged, in particular the right to join an alliance and accept bases if Cambodia's security was threatened.[8] Notwithstanding this, Chou En-lai, in his final statement at the conference, made it clear that nothing had changed so far as China was concerned: "We note that after the armistice the three states of Indochina will refrain from joining any military alliance, and that the establishment of military bases on their respective territories by any foreign country will not be allowed."[9]

This explains Peking's anger when the SEATO treaty extended protection to Cambodia, Laos, and South Vietnam by means of a protocol in September 1954. A Chinese government statement of 10 September 1954 said, "Responsible officials of the British and French governments on a number of occasions affirmed at Geneva that the Indochinese states must not participate in any military alignment. Now their representatives have affixed their signatures to this protocol in direct contravention to their promise at Geneva."[10]

6. Leifer, *Cambodia*, p. 190.
7. See A. Eden, *Full Circle* (London 1960), pp. 107–145, and the same author's *Towards Peace in Indochina* (London, 1966), p. 4.
8. Smith, *Cambodia's Foreign Policy*, pp. 52–86.
9. NCNA, 21 July 1954.
10. NCNA, 10 September 1954.

Chou En-lai took the opportunity of the 1955 Bandung conference to explain to Prince Sihanouk China's position. On Sihanouk's account,

> Last April Mr. Chou En-lai asked me in Bandung, Do you plan to grant bases or to sign an alliance with the U.S.? I replied that Cambodia would never compromise with its independence. Mr. Chou En-lai replied that he was quite satisfied with this and recognised that Cambodia had a right to organise her national defence and call on foreign instructors.[11]

Sihanouk, however, was under strong pressure from the U.S.A. as well as China and, in the circumstances of American predominance in the mid-1950s, felt it more necessary to make concessions to Washington than to Peking. Hence, one month after Bandung, Sihanouk, in a move which might have been designed to test the limits of Chinese tolerance of Cambodia's "right to organise her national defence," signed an agreement with Washington whereby the U.S. became the exclusive supplier of military aid to Cambodia.

On this occasion it had not been perfidious imperialism which had "deceived" China but a state which only existed in its monarchial form because of China's forbearance at Geneva, and Peking's anger was unmistakeable. The Chinese press in attacking the agreement, which it described as a "military pact," implied that Cambodia had been tricked into signing an agreement that might entail far more than military aid: "Cambodia should be able to see as clearly as others that what the U.S. calls military aid is to pull the 'aided' country into its aggressive military alliances." It spelt out precisely its objections to the agreement, which were a clause stipulating that Cambodia should contribute to the defence "of the free world" and the fact that the agreement permitted the U.S. to transport military supplies across Cambodia. It asserted that these clauses contravened the Geneva agreements and Sihanouk's own promise at Bandung and ended with a vague warning about the possibility of reprisals from leftist forces in Cambodia: "It is justifiable for the people of Cambodia to condemn this agreement." However, Sihanouk was also assured that China and North Vietnam were willing to "observe the principles of coexistence with Cambodia."[12]

Sihanouk was sufficiently alarmed by China's reaction to reiterate on several occasions during 1955 Cambodia's determination to remain neutral.

11. *The Hindu*, 13 July 1955.
12. All quotations from NCNA, 24 June 1955.

Peking took note of these pledges, and when Sihanouk visited China in February 1956 Chou En-lai publicly reminded him of them.[13] At the same time as, and partly in reaction to his visit, South Vietnam and Thailand closed their frontiers with Cambodia, thus imposing an economic blockade on the country. In response to this, but also to make amends for his "military pact" with the U.S., Sihanouk signed a friendship treaty with China.[14] Shortly after his return to Phnom Penh, the United States stopped its economic aid to Cambodia, allegedly because of corruption in the handling of the funds.[15] Sihanouk, however, was convinced that this was evidence of America's complicity in the "plot" against his country by Saigon and Bangkok. In one of several dramatic moves in response to this—which included Sihanouk's resignation as premier—a four-man economic mission was sent to China on 6 April.[16] On 24 April a trade agreement between the two countries was signed, and Peking also promised to give Cambodia economic aid—the first aid agreement between China and a non-Communist country.[17]

Peking's reaction to Cambodia's military aid agreement with the U.S. had shown that its notion of Cambodian neutrality was somewhat stricter than the conventional legal understanding of the term. Specifically, in spite of the promise which Sihanouk claimed to have received from Chou En-lai at Bandung, Cambodia's "right to organise her national defence" did not include the right to become solely dependent on the U.S. for military supplies nor to permit any significant American military presence. Peking's response to Phnom Penh's rift with Washington in 1956 suggested another, equally understandable, qualification to China's acceptance of Cambodian neutrality—that its preference was for a Cambodian foreign policy that was inclined towards China and antagonistic towards the U.S. This emerged clearly from Chinese press commentary on Cambodia during April. On 7 April, *People's Daily* described the Sino-Cambodian relationship in the customary way as one embodying the principles of peaceful coexistence and proving China's respect for Cambodian neutrality.[18] Three weeks later, after the signing of the trade and aid agreement, *People's Daily* saw a new

13. NCNA, 14 February 1956.
14. NCNA, 19 February 1956.
15. For the details of this affair, see Leifer, *Cambodia*, pp. 76–78.
16. NCNA, 9 April 1956.
17. NCNA, 24 April 1956.
18. NCNA, 11 April 1956.
19. NCNA, 2 May 1956.

basis to the relationship in both trade and common opposition to imperialism: "The two countries have materials that supplement each other's needs, and what is more important, both oppose colonialism and stand for national independence and the prosperity of the domestic economy."[19]

It should also be observed that Sihanouk had responded to a threat from Cambodia's traditional adversaries by seeking, and receiving in the form of the friendship treaty, some kind of counterbalancing gesture from China. This was very far from being an alliance commitment to Cambodia by China, but since Peking must have been well aware of the construction which Sihanouk hoped Cambodia's neighbours would place upon the treaty, this suggested that China might not be reluctant to assume the role of Cambodia's protector under certain conditions.

Such was not Sihanouk's intention in the 1950s when he still hoped to play a balancing game between the United States and China: "What choice have we but to try to maintain an equal balance between the 'blocs'? . . . By practising a genuine neutrality we have a chance of not bringing down a storm on our heads."[20] As one facet of Cambodia's "balancing" policy, Phnom Penh continued not to recognise the People's Republic of China even after the signing of the Sino-Cambodian friendship treaty. This was clearly aimed at appeasing American sensibilities. When Cambodia eventually did recognise China on 22 July 1958, Sihanouk was once again using a pro-China gesture as a weapon against Cambodia's local adversaries. In June 1958 a battalion of South Vietnamese troops had crossed the de facto boundary with Cambodia and set up new border markers, protected by a minefield.[21] In July, Sihanouk went to Bangkok on a fruitless mission to resolve another border issue with Thailand.[22] He was later to explain that the failure of the International Control Commission for Indochina to act against the South Vietnamese incursions had prompted him to take the step of recognising China.[23]

On Peking's side, the 1956 shift away from an emphasis solely upon Cambodian neutrality and peaceful coexistence was still apparent in 1958. Several Chinese statements explicitly linked what was described as

20. Norodom Sihanouk, "Cambodia Neutral: The Dictates of Necessity," *Foreign Affairs*, July 1958, p. 585.

21. *New York Times*, 31 January 1959.

22. This involved a dispute over the ownership of the Khmer temple of Prah Vihar. For the details, see L. P. Singh, "The Thai-Cambodian Temple Dispute," *Asian Survey*, October 1962.

23. *Agence Khmer Presse*, 2 November 1961.

"Cambodia's support for China in international affairs" to China's economic aid and diplomatic support for Cambodia against "foreign interference."[24] In fact the only significant way in which Cambodia "supported" China in the 1958–1960 period was by changing its vote from ab-
stention to opposition on the annual U.N. resolution calling for postpone-
ment of discussion of the admission of China question.[25] This suggests
that Peking was prepared to give Cambodia aid, friendship, and some support against its enemies in return for a relatively cheap diplomatic quid pro
quo on Cambodia's part.

However, there were very definite limits to China's support for Cambodia, as became clear during Chou En-lai's visit there in May 1960. In a
speech on 6 May, Chou declared that Cambodia in its "struggle to defend
national independence" could count on the "unfailing support" of China.[26]
This was vague enough—containing, for example, no reference to Cambodia's "territorial integrity"—but Chou's reply to a question at a subsequent
press conference, which asked him to expand upon this statement, was a
masterpiece of equivocation:

> If the kingdom of Cambodia is aggressed upon from whichever direction,
> the Chinese people . . . will stand on the side of the Royal Cambodian
> government. As to the kind of support, undoubtedly moral and political
> support, as there has always been. As to support in other aspects, we will
> take into consideration the needs of the Royal Cambodian government, the
> possibilities at our disposal, and the conditions prevailing at the time.[27]

It seems clear that one reason for Chou's guarded attitude was Cambodia's
unwillingness to take a more "positive" stand in international affairs—in
other words, one that involved opposition to the United States. The joint
communiqué issued after Chou's visit indicated some disagreement
between the two sides: "In the talks, both sides *exchanged views extensively* on questions relating to the two countries and current international questions in general. The talks were held in an atmosphere of
sincerity and frankness" [emphasis added].[28]

24. See, for example, speeches by the Chinese ambassador to Cambodia,
NCNA, 21 November 1958, and Ch'en Yi, NCNA, 7 March 1959, and a message
sent to Sihanouk by Chou En-lai, NCNA, 8 November 1960.

25. See Halpern, *Policies toward China*, pp. 503–507, for details of U.N.
voting on the China question from 1950 to 1965.

26. NCNA, 6 May 1960.

27. NCNA, 11 May 1960.

28. NCNA, 8 May 1960.

Until 1960 there had been two distinct phases in the Sino-Cambodian relationship, both deriving their character primarily from the perceptions and anxieties of the smaller state. In the first phase, at Geneva and for a year afterwards, Sihanouk had attempted to ensure Cambodia's neutrality and independence by basing Cambodia's foreign policy on an informal acceptance of American predominance in the region. In the second he had attempted to accommodate Chinese pressure but not to a point where he upset Cambodia's relationship with Washington. As the situation in Laos and Vietnam steadily worsened, a third phase developed, lasting roughly from 1960 to November 1963, with, once again, Cambodia's concerns and preoccupations, rather than China's interests, determining the course of the relationship.

During this period, Sihanouk attempted to reconcile two conflicting objectives. On the one hand, he was now convinced that *in the long term* China would be the predominant power in Asia as a whole, while a united Communist Vietnam would dominate Indochina.[29] On the other hand, America remained *in the short term* still very much the dominant power in Asia. Hence, Sihanouk believed that he needed to provide for Cambodia's long-term survival by ingratiating Cambodia further with China in order to earn China's good will both for its own sake and because Peking might be prepared to restrain Vietnam if it felt that China's interests were better served by Cambodia remaining independent. However, in the short term Sihanouk was unwilling to adopt an anti-American posture, which emerged during 1960–1963 as Peking's principal requirement in return for a stronger commitment on its part to Cambodia's survival.

The pattern of relations between the two countries during this period is best interpreted as a subtle diplomatic tug of war, with each state exerting pressure on the other in an effort to persuade it to shift towards the required policy stance but with neither conceding the other's essential demands. Sihanouk made it clear that he would like a stronger statement of support from China than had been given by Chou En-lai in 1960 but refused to make any significant anti-American gesture in return. Equally, Peking would not give Sihanouk what he desired without such a gesture.

Through 1960, Sihanouk made several noncontroversial moves aimed at winning China's favour. These included sending three sons to be educated in Chinese schools, establishing a Cambodia-China Friendship Society, and

29. See his press conference, Phnom Penh, March 1961, cited in Smith, *Cambodia's Foreign Policy*, p. 116.

supporting Chou En-lai's proposal for a "zone of peace" in Indochina.[30] At
the end of the year Sihanouk visited China again, at a time when Saigon
was intensifying its claim to certain Cambodian islands, in the hope that
Peking would issue a strongly worded statement of support. However, on
the day of his arrival a *People's Daily* editorial indirectly called upon
Sihanouk to take a more positive stand against the U.S. It praised Sihanouk
for having observed the five principles of peaceful coexistence but also for
having "maintained a firm attitude in dealing with various kinds of imperialist obstruction." It then added that because imperialism was "intensifying its subversion," "closer unity" was necessary.[31]

During the visit Sihanouk was unable to secure a more definite Chinese
commitment to Cambodia's survival, while Peking did not obtain a more
"anti-imperialist" posture from Sihanouk. Each side's statements attributed
to the other more "support" than was actually given, with the Chinese
speeches repeatedly associating Cambodia with attacks on the U.S. and
Sihanouk thanking China for its great help against aggression. Conversely,
each side ignored the other's indirect requests—Sihanouk did not mention
the U.S. while the Chinese continued to give only vague statements of support to Cambodia. Typical of the latter was Liu Shao-Ch'i's speech on 16
December, when he promised that "the Chinese people will be the most
faithful friends of the Cambodian people, whether in our respective causes of
safeguarding our national independence or in our common cause of
defending world peace."[32]

Shortly after Sihanouk's visit a *People's Daily* editorial entitled "The
Basis of the Mutual Friendly Relations between China and Cambodia" spelt
out the reason why the present basis of the relationship—peaceful coexistence and Cambodian neutrality—was not sufficient to earn Cambodia a
stronger commitment from China. China, it declared, wished to conduct
relations with non-Communist states on the basis of peaceful coexistence,
but it also cooperated with Third World countries "in the struggle for world
peace and against imperialist aggression." Moreover the second consideration was of more immediate importance since it was not yet possible
for peaceful coexistence to be the basis of all international relations because
"imperialism headed by the United States" was attempting to "sabotage
and obstruct" its realisation.[33]

30. NCNA, 13 July 1960, 13 December 1960, and 21 December 1960.
31. Quotations from NCNA, 15 December 1960.
32. NCNA, 16 December 1960.
33. NCNA, 22 December 1960.

During 1961–1962 Sihanouk continued to seek a more solid statement of support from China and to make marginal adjustments to the wording of Cambodian foreign policy statements in vain attempts to secure such a statement. On several occasions he sent messages expressing his gratitude for China's "resolute support" for Cambodia but still felt unable to align Cambodia with China on questions other than those relating to China's "legitimate rights."[34] The Chinese replies to his letters display an equally consistent pattern: China's support was stated in far less strong and specific terms than Sihanouk himself used, and Sihanouk was repeatedly reminded that, in China's view, the greatest threat to Cambodia's security was the U.S. For example, although Chou En-lai supported Sihanouk's call in 1962 for an international conference to guarantee Cambodia's neutrality, the greater part of his letter of reply to Sihanouk was devoted to an attack on the U.S.[35]

It should be stressed that what Sihanouk was really interested in—and here there are some similarities with Pakistani objectives—was not an alliance with China but a strongly worded declaration of China's support for Cambodia's continuing existence. This, he hoped, would serve three purposes: he could use it as a bargaining counter with Thailand and South Vietnam; he could brandish it in the face of the Americans in order to induce them to take more interest in Cambodia's problems; moreover, it would also serve notice on Hanoi of China's interest in the integrity and survival of Cambodia. As has been seen, even without such a declaration he had been able to derive considerable mileage from his relationship with Peking, and continued to do so in 1962. In August he disclosed to the newly appointed U.S. ambassador to Cambodia that China had offered to supply Cambodia with small arms and shortly afterwards, to drive the point home, wrote to fourteen countries demanding a conference to be held on Cambodian neutrality and suggesting that, if it were not held, Cambodia might have to take "very important decisions to defend its existence."[36] This vague hint at the possibility of closer ties with China was followed up by a public threat from Sihanouk in September to ask China to send into Cambodia enough forces to "discourage aggression" if no other countries would guarantee Cambodia's borders.[37] A month later he declared that he

34. See, for example, NCNA, 12 November 1961, 20 July 1962, and 18 November 1962.
35. Text of letter in *Peking Review*, 7 September 1962.
36. *Observer*, 2 September 1962.
37. *New York Times*, 4 September 1962.

had received a formal assurance from Peking that China would support Cambodia under all circumstances and at the same time threatened to "renounce" American aid.[38] However, such threats lost much of their credibility without a clearcut statement from Peking to sustain them.

An additional complication reappeared in 1961: The Vietminh was found to have been involved in assisting leftist groups in Cambodia in covert operations against Sihanouk.[39] Charges were also laid by Saigon in March and November 1961 that North Vietnamese regulars had established bases in Cambodia with a garrison strength of 6,000.[40] To Sihanouk, who tended to see political relationships essentially in terms of overlords and clients, the Vietminh was clearly controlled by Hanoi, while North Vietnam itself was dominated by China. So the importance of good relations with China—which might, in Sihanouk's view, be able to induce its "clients" to stop interfering in Cambodian affairs—was increased rather than diminished as a result of the Vietnamese Communist incursions.

However, any private efforts to persuade China to admonish its "clients" were unsuccessful during 1962, which witnessed a decline in the number of "friendship" delegations compared with the last few years. It is probable that Sihanouk raised the question of incursions by the Vietnamese Communists during his visit to China in February 1963. It may have been this that *Realités Cambodgiennes* was referring to when it editorialised after the visit, ". . . some [trifling] misunderstandings, which have been allowed to develop between the two governments in the course of the last few years, have been cleared up."[41] However, Sihanouk made little progress in his attempt to obtain a definite statement from Peking with respect to assistance against Thai or Vietnamese aggression. Speeches by Liu Shao-ch'i and Peng Chen said nothing on the subject of Cambodia's "territorial integrity" and made only the usual vague references to support for Cambodia's "sovereignty and independence."[42] Similarly Peking obtained little from

38. NCNA, 2 November 1962. The text of this "assurance" was not released, and it is unlikely that it amounted to anything more than the previous vague promises.

39. Smith, *Cambodia's Foreign Policy*, pp. 120–121.

40. International Documentation and Information Centre, *Cambodia: Problems of Neutrality and Independence* (The Hague, 1970), p. 7.

41. *Realités Cambodgiennes*, 1 March 1963.

42. Liu Shao-ch'i, NCNA, 12 February 1963, and Peng Chen, NCNA, 14 February 1963.

Sihanouk. In one speech he exaggerated, as usual, China's assistance and in-dicated that Cambodia had a somewhat different understanding of the identity of the "imperialists" from that of China: "We will never forget that it was China's formal declarations of support and warnings which have checked the warmongers and *imperialists of Saigon and Bangkok, who know the value of China's words* and China's determination" [emphasis added]."[43] The joint communiqué issued after the visit contained only the usual references to Cambodia's support for China's claim to Taiwan and a U.N. seat as well as a very restrained statement on Laos.[44]

A slight change in China's position occurred at the end of Liu Shao-ch'i's visit to Cambodia in May 1963. This visit took place just after Hanoi had renounced its claims to the island of Phu Quoc, which Cambodia had for some time been disputing with Saigon.[45] Sihanouk may have believed that the North Vietnamese statement had been a result of Chinese pressure. Whether or not this was the case, it is significant that the joint communiqué on this occasion contained, for the first time, a specific statement of China's support for Cambodia's "territorial integrity."[46] This suggests that one factor that had prevented Peking from publicly supporting Cambodia's ter-ritorial integrity had been the North Vietnamese claim to the island.

Sihanouk's adoption in August of China's position on the nuclear test ban treaty may have been partly intended as an expression of gratitude for China's apparent help against Hanoi. However, it was also designed to indicate to Peking that Sihanouk believed he had gone far enough along the path of "positive" neutrality to earn the long-sought commitment from China to Cambodia's defence. In a speech on 22 September Sihanouk directly related Cambodia's support for China on the Moscow treaty issue to the hoped-for guarantee from China and argued,

> We prefer to be with China alone than with a multitude of countries who, in case of danger, would leave us in the cold. *China's friendship is of vital importance to us.* It is certain that without China's determination to come to our aid in case of aggression, the troops of Ngo Dinh Diem and Sarit would have attacked us long ago. Our international policy is based on neutrality, but should we be obliged one day to choose between China and the others, we would, without hesitation, choose to be on the

43. NCNA, 14 February 1963.
44. NCNA, 27 February 1963.
45. Smith, *Cambodia's Foreign Policy*, p. 121.
46. NCNA, 5 May 1963.

side of the PRC, for *she alone would take the trouble to fight* [emphasis added].[47]

Nevertheless, Peking remained unmoved by Cambodia's support over the Moscow treaty. Shortly after declaring his stand on this issue, Sihanouk tried to ascertain how much extra support this had earned him from Peking by handing two notes concerning South Vietnamese "military provocations" to the Chinese Foreign Ministry. However Peking, which waited two weeks before replying to these notes and a further eleven days before publicising them, merely reiterated its previous position:

> The struggle of the Royal government and people of Cambodia against foreign aggression and for the defence of national independence and state sovereignty is a just struggle and is not conducted in isolation. The Chinese government hereby declares once again that the Chinese government and people will, as always, resolutely support the Royal government and people of Cambodia in their just struggle.[48]

On 12 November 1963 Sihanouk renounced all American economic and military aid in an attempt to pressure the U.S. into agreeing to his call for an international conference on Cambodian neutrality. For a week it was unclear whether he intended to match his words with action, since within two days of his original statement he had begun to qualify his stand.[49] However, on 19 November he reiterated his demand for a total cessation of American aid, this time using the pretext of alleged U.S. backing for the anti-Sihanouk Khmer Serai (Free Khmer).[50] Peking, which had remained silent during Sihanouk's earlier vacillations, acted quickly before he could change his mind again. On 21 November it issued a statement that declared China's support for Cambodia in by far the strongest language used to date:

> The Chinese government solemnly declares that if the Kingdom of Cambodia, which has persevered in its policy of peace and neutrality, should encounter armed invasion instigated by the U.S. and its vassals, the Chinese government and people will firmly side with the Kingdom of Cambodia and give it our all-out support. U.S. imperialism must bear all the consequences arising therefrom.[51]

47. NCNA, 22 September 1963.
48. *Peking Review*, 27 September 1963.
49. *New York Herald Tribune*, 15 November 1963; *New York Times*, 17 November 1963.
50. *New York Times*, 20 November 1963.
51. NCNA, 21 November 1963.

Sihanouk had at last obtained his strong statement from China but only at the price which Peking had all along stipulated. There can be no question that Peking made this statement in response to Sihanouk's anti-American gesture. The reasoning behind China's action seems clear enough. There was little prospect of the "invasion" to which the statement referred actually taking place—not, at least, in response to Sihanouk's curtailment of American aid—so it must be assumed that Peking's motives, like Sihanouk's, revolved around longer term political-diplomatic considerations. Sihanouk had shown, both on this and other occasions, that he fitted very well the Maoist conception of a "national bourgeois" leader who was "vacillating by nature." Hence, if his actions after renouncing American aid were going to run true to form, it was likely that he would seek to restore Cambodia's former position of equidistance from Washington and Peking by using China's statement as a diplomatic weapon to extract a stronger commitment to Cambodian neutrality from Washington. However, the timing of Peking's statement made it appear that Sihanouk had been acting in collusion with Peking, which would naturally make it more difficult for Sihanouk to restore Cambodia's relationship with the U.S. Moreover, the statement had, in effect, welcomed Sihanouk as a full-fledged member of the anti-imperialist united front with the clear implication that China's understanding was that the Sino-Cambodian relationship was now based on common opposition to the U.S. rather than its former basis of peaceful coexistence and Cambodian neutrality. Hence, Peking's message to Sihanouk seems to have been that any move to improve relations with the U.S. was likely to earn China's displeasure.

UNITY AND STRUGGLE, 1964–1969

If the preceding interpretation of Chinese motivation is correct, Peking's assessment of Sihanouk was a perceptive one. Peking may have remembered that shortly after Cambodia recognised China in 1958, Sihanouk had made a series of diplomatic moves and statements clearly aimed at demonstrating that he had not become aligned with China.[52] This was a typical example of his foreign policy technique of seeking to balance great power influences against each other and appealing to their rivalry with each

52. For example, in September 1958 he paid a two-month visit to the U.S., saying on his return that the U.S.-Cambodian relationship was "steadily becoming closer" (*New York Times*, 27 October 1958).

other as a means of maintaining their interest in Cambodia's problems. The same intentions were evident in his manoeuvres following his renunciation of American aid in November 1963. On the day after Peking came out with its declaration of support, the Cambodian ambassador in Washington asserted that Cambodia had no intention of asking China for military aid.[53] Sihanouk himself made a number of threats over the next three months that Cambodia might sign a formal alliance treaty with China but always coupled these with the demand for an international conference on Cambodian neutrality.[54] Moreover, in January 1964 he made several gestures which seemed to be intended to convince the U.S. not to take his threats too seriously. For example, he postponed his 15 January deadline for the U.S. to remove its personnel and said that he hoped Filipino mediation between Cambodia and the U.S. would succeed.[55] He also complained that the U.S. had cut off its aid too quickly after he had demanded that it be terminated and denied that he was placing Cambodia under Peking's influence.[56] In February he suggested that if the U.S. was unwilling to attend an international conference on Cambodia, it might consider setting up border posts along the Vietnam-Cambodian border—a move which would have hurt the Vietnamese Communists more than Saigon.[57] Even as late as March, Sihanouk was reported to have criticised North Vietnamese policies and to be renewing contacts with Saigon on the grounds that Cambodia would seek friendly relations with whichever of the two Vietnams was "less demanding with respect to our country."[58]

However, on this occasion, as Peking may have calculated, Sihanouk had overplayed his hand. Washington, whose understanding of Sihanouk's problems and situation was less than Peking's, plainly regarded his behaviour as irrational and could see no reason to give him a diplomatic "victory" by meeting his demands. With implicit pressure from China as well, Sihanouk had little option but to try as best as possible to play the part of an anti-imperialist friend of China. The pattern of Sino-Cambodian relations over the 1964–1966 period was in one sense similar to that which had prevailed in the earlier period. Sihanouk from time to time pressed Peking to reiterate its pledge of support for Cambodia; Peking required in return further evidence of Cambodia's "anti-imperialist" credentials. There were, however, two significant differences: The game was played against a background of rapidly worsening conflict in Vietnam, and Sihanouk was working from a much weaker position. In the earlier period he had wanted a

53. *Daily Telegraph*, 22 November 1963.

strong statement of support from China mainly as one of several bargaining counters with both Washington and his regional adversaries—including Hanoi. Now his capacity to steer a precarious course between China and the U.S. was greatly restricted, while at the same time Cambodia's need of great power guarantees of its security grew more urgent daily. Thus circumstances combined to increase Cambodia's dependence on China for economic and military aid—now no longer available from the U.S.—and for protection from the vicissitudes of regional conflicts.

Over the 1964–1966 period, Cambodia found itself supporting more and more Chinese policy positions on international issues. Often this support was offered gratuitously as part of Sihanouk's campaign to win Peking's approval, but sometimes Chinese pressure appears to have been applied. Cambodia sought to win Peking's approval by adapting its policies in what were believed to be directions acceptable to Peking. This process of adaptation affected three different dimensions of policy making:

1. The language and style of both domestic politics and foreign policy.
2. The substance of Cambodia's policy on various international issues.
3. Cambodia's attitude towards the Vietnamese war.

There are many examples of the first of these dimensions. For example, Sihanouk made the best of the end of American aid by declaring that Cambodia would become a shining example of "self-reliance" in Asia, a stand which won him the approval of Peking.[59] Many other concepts and expressions which originated in China began to appear. An appeal from the Cambodian Assembly to "parliamentarians of the world" to support Cambodia's "struggle" and condemn the U.S. illustrates well the extent to which Chinese Communist jargon had been adopted in Cambodia. It read in part,

> The Khmer people, long tempered in the anti-colonialist struggle and guided by their leader, are more resolute than ever in opposing imperialism and its lackeys, in order to defend their national independence

54. See the *Straits Times*, 29 December 1963; *The Nation*, 11 February 1964; *New York Times*, 13 February 1964.

55. *New York Times*, 11 and 15 January 1964.

56. *New York Times*, 17 January 1964.

57. *The Nation*, 11 February 1964.

58. *New York Herald Tribune*, 17 March 1964.

59. See, for example, a message sent by Sihanouk to Chou En-lai and Liu Shao-ch'i, NCNA, 9 November 1964.

and territorial integrity won at great cost. This struggle is undoubtedly part of the national liberation movement now being carried out by the peoples of the world.[60]

Even the unlikely figure of Lon Nol was quoted as saying during a visit to China, "In order to fight resolutely against the bullying, insults, intimidation, and aggression of U.S. imperialism and its lackeys, the people and armed forces of Cambodia, under the wise leadership of our respected leader, are more determined than ever to carry the struggle to the end, no matter what difficulties we will encounter."[61]

Although the Chinese press was always ready to print material of this kind, it is difficult to say whether this example of Cambodia's deference to China carried much weight with the Peking government. Cambodia's position on international issues was another matter, and it is in this area the pressure from Peking was most apparent. At first Sihanouk seemed to hope that the adoption of some of the language and style of Chinese commentaries of foreign affairs would be sufficient to establish his credentials as an anti-imperialist ally of China. For example, his comment on returning from the Philippines, "We must encourage the Philippine patriots in the difficult task of liberating their country from foreign interference,"[62] hardly counts as evidence that Cambodia had undertaken a concrete commitment to aiding the national liberation movement in the Philippines. Nor did the declaration of one Cambodian newspaper (*Meataphum*) that Cambodia would "never coexist peacefully with imperialism"[63] reflect any real change in substance in Cambodia's foreign policy, although it was one of many such Cambodian articles on foreign policy that was quoted in the Chinese press.

Often, however, Sihanouk's desire to accommodate China led him to take up positions that appeared to provide little benefit to Cambodia or were positively harmful to Cambodia's interests. This happened most frequently in matters relating to Vietnam, but it also affected other aspects of Cambodian policy. For instance, in one speech during a visit to China in 1965 he offended the Soviet Union by appearing to agree with Peking's line on the insincerity of Soviet support for the Vietnamese Communists.[64] On this

60. NCNA, 23 March 1964.
61. NCNA, 26 November 1965.
62. *Observer Foreign News Service*, 25 February 1964.
63. NCNA, 19 August 1964.
64. For the details, see *Far Eastern Economic Review*, 25 November 1965, pp. 369–371.

occasion Moscow made matters worse by treating the ever-sensitive Sihanouk in what he described as a "humiliating" fashion.[65] However, the initial move was Sihanouk's, and it is possible that he made it in response to pressure from Peking. In Sihanouk's own statement on this incident, he appeared to suggest that Peking had urged him to reject Soviet economic aid. This is the implication of the following "advice," which according to Sihanouk was sent by Mao and Liu Shao-ch'i:

> It is not a good solution to rely on foreign aid and loans. . . . If people want to remain free, it is infinitely preferable to forge ahead by their own means and their own efforts.
>
> China, which had once been a "recipient" of Soviet aid, finally adopted this latter solution. We hope that your country, Cambodia, will have only commercial relations with foreign countries as soon as possible.[66]

It is difficult to see how Cambodia might have benefited from giving up Soviet aid, especially since its aid from China had tended to demonstrate China's inexperience in this field.[67]

However, it was mainly in connection with events in Vietnam that Sihanouk found himself following a course that did not always serve Cambodia's interests. Sihanouk's concern remained constant throughout the Vietnam war: to prevent it from spreading to Cambodia itself. His greatest hope was for an international conference to guarantee Cambodia's neutrality, but failing this he had resorted to a series of ad hoc measures, of which seeking a proclamation of support from Peking was one. However, Cambodia's alignment with China made it difficult for him to observe a neutral stand on the war itself, and from 1964 he tended to give verbal support to the Vietnamese Communists. This in turn compromised his campaign for neutralisation of Cambodia. Moreover it won him few benefits from the Communist side. In December 1964 officials from Hanoi, Phnom Penh, and the South Vietnamese NLF had met in Peking, at Sihanouk's request, to discuss a treaty that would guarantee Cambodia's frontiers but

65. Interview with Sihanouk, *Far Eastern Economic Review*, 9 December 1965, p. 456.

66. *Peking Review*, 22 October 1965.

67. According to one report, Cambodia by the end of 1964 had received from China a paper factory and a sugar refinery, both with the wrong sort of machinery, a cement works on a site thirty miles away from the nearest water, and a plywood factory that used glue which came unstuck (*Observer Foreign News Service*, 17 November 1964).

talks had broken down, ostensibly because of differences between Hanoi and the NLF.[68] It is possible that an additional factor may have been Vietnamese doubts about simultaneous talks being held in New Delhi with a view to improving U.S.-Cambodian relations.

Two further illustrations of the way in which Sihanouk's deference to China's wishes restricted his freedom of action with regard to Cambodia's security problems might be noted. In September 1964 a Security Council report recommended that a U.N. presence be established along the Cambodia-South Vietnam border. This would have gone some way towards meeting Sihanouk's wishes, but he rejected it on the grounds that the report also suggested that Cambodia re-establish diplomatic relations with Saigon.[69] Sihanouk had indicated his willingness to improve relations with Saigon earlier in the year but by September—after the Tonkin Gulf incident—such a move would have earned him the displeasure of Peking. In 1965 he was obliged to abandon his cherished aim of having Cambodian neutralisation guaranteed by an international conference because the Chinese and North Vietnamese were opposed to Saigon's representation and also believed that the conference might turn to discussing a negotiated settlement in Vietnam, in which they were no longer interested.[70]

It should be emphasised that Sihanouk's decisions were often taken independently of any specific "advice" from Peking. However, he consistently shaped his policies with a view to the likely reaction of China, and sometimes Peking did apply both indirect and direct pressure on Sihanouk. The indirect pressure took several forms. First was the familiar gambit of not giving Cambodia as firm support in public declarations as Sihanouk would have liked. On several occasions Chinese reaffirmations of support for Cambodia contained statements such as, "There is no doubt that the aggressive schemes of U.S. imperialism will be completely smashed by the Cambodian people," or "We are convinced that final victory will certainly belong to the heroic and unyielding Cambodian people."[71] This stress on the "heroic" role to be played by Cambodia in resisting "U.S. imperialism" would seem to imply some limitation to China's commitment of "all-out support."[72] Second, China often linked its pledges of support to Cambodia

68. *New York Times*, 6 January 1965.

69. *New York Times*, 13 September 1964.

70. *Australian*, 29 April 1965.

71. NCNA, 15 September and 2 November 1964.

72. See also Gurtov's discussion of the limited nature of the Chinese commitment, "Politics of Survival," p. 123.

with a reference to Cambodia's reciprocal support in international affairs, and sometimes specifically to Cambodia's attitude to the Vietnam war. For example, in August 1965 the *People's Daily* pledged "resolute support" for Cambodia's "just struggle" and immediately afterwards praised Cambodia's "courage" in censuring U.S. policy in Vietnam.[73] Similarly Ch'en Yi linked China's support for Cambodia with Cambodia's "profound sympathy" for the Vietnamese Communists.[74] Third, Peking would sometimes lay down a line on an issue that was contrary to a known position taken by Sihanouk. For example, Chou En-lai sent a message to the 1965 Indochinese People's Conference insisting that American forces must be withdrawn from South Vietnam before any international agreement could be reached on Indochina. This caused Sihanouk to cancel his own planned address to the conference, in which he had adopted a more conciliatory posture towards the U.S.[75]

Peking also used more direct pressure on Sihanouk. On at least two occasions after Cambodia had broken off its diplomatic relations with the U.S. in May 1965, Sihanouk was warned that any move towards a resumption of relations would damage Sino-Cambodian relations. In October 1965, Sihanouk himself informed a delegation departing for China to seek military aid that he had been told by Ch'en Yi that if Cambodia changed its attitude towards China or assumed a more friendly posture towards the U.S., this would harm its relations with China.[76] In August 1966, following reports that Averell Harriman was to go to Cambodia to discuss a resumption of relations, a Chinese Foreign Ministry statement flatly informed Sihanouk that the U.S. was not to be trusted and "reminded" him that China was "the most trustworthy friend of the Cambodian people."[77] China also objected to a Cambodian proposal for enlarging the International Control Commission (ICC) in Cambodia. This time *Realités Cambodgiennes* chose to take issue with Peking. It stated pointedly that "thanks to the authority and honesty of its Indian president" the ICC had always conducted itself in a correct fashion—thus directly refuting Peking's claim that the ICC was an "agent of U.S. imperialism." It also said that, while Cambodia was against American *imperialism*, it was not anti-American.[78]

In 1967 three distinct factors contributed to the worsening of Sino-

73. NCNA, 15 August 1965.
74. NCNA, 19 December 1965
75. Gurtov, "Politics of Survival," p. 123.
76. *Phnom Penh Radio*, 21 October 1965.
77. *Japan Times*, 9 August 1966.
78. *Realités Cambodgiennes*, 19 August 1966.

Cambodian relations. One was the Cultural Revolution and its overflow into Cambodian domestic politics. The second concerned the developing internal war in Cambodia. The third was a continuation of an earlier trend: Peking's disapproval of the tendency of Cambodian foreign policy to "vacillate." The first evidence of Sino-Cambodian frictions appeared in August 1966, as has already been discussed. This is consistent with Cambodian claims in September 1967 that the decline in relations between the two countries dated back to "the middle of last year"[79] and indicates that the Cultural Revolution was the culminating factor in, rather than the sole cause of, the decline.

However, the Cultural Revolution did manifest itself in Cambodia in several ways and through several different agencies: the Overseas Chinese, the Chinese embassy, the Khmer-Chinese Friendship Association (KCFA), the five Chinese language newspapers, and Chinese instructors working with the Cambodian army. The actual incidents, however, were irritating to Cambodian sensibilities, but relatively trivial: Overseas Chinese demonstrations outside the Soviet embassy and elsewhere,[80] the distribution of Mao badges among the Cambodian army,[81] and Cultural Revolution propaganda by the Chinese language newspapers.

At first Sihanouk attempted to place all the blame for these incidents on "Sino-Khmer" elements, rather than Peking. In May, for example, he declared that China's conduct had been irreproachable and that China remained the "cornerstone" of Cambodia's foreign policy.[82] It is possible that he may have genuinely believed that Peking was not responsible for the incidents, especially since China's economic aid programme did not seem to have been affected.[83] However, this confidence was shaken when he sent his foreign minister, Phurissara, to Peking in August—significantly the month when ultra-leftist influence in the foreign ministry was at its height—to ascertain Peking's official position. Phurissara was treated coolly and informed that Peking upheld the right of Overseas Chinese in Cambodia to engage in pro-Mao demonstrations.[84] It was this which prompted Sihanouk to embark upon a series of moves in September which seem to

79. *Realités Cambodgiennes*, 22 September 1967.
80. *Realités Cambodgiennes*, 3 February 1967.
81. *Realités Cambodgiennes*, 26 May 1967.
82. Ibid.
83. Gurtov, "Politics of Survival," p. 147.
84. Ibid., pp. 219–220.

have been partly designed to force Peking's hand.[85] In the event, Chou En-lai prevented the crisis from developing too far by sending a message to Sihanouk reassuring him that China wanted to preserve the traditional friendship between the two countries. This caused Sihanouk to cancel a previous order cutting down the size of Cambodia's embassy in Peking.[86] A *Realités Cambodgiennes* editorial, aptly entitled "La fin des illusions," stated that Cambodia, too, wished to maintain a close friendship but not at too great a cost.[87]

Although the Chinese groups and organisations in Phnom Penh all acted to some extent independently of Peking during 1967, their behaviour was also a reflection of an official disapproval of Cambodian policies unrelated to the Cultural Revolution. Essentially Sihanouk may have appeared to Peking in 1966–1967 to be considering moves which would have broken the unspoken agreement between the two countries concerning the limitations Cambodia had accepted on its freedom in international affairs in return for China's support. An article in the *Far Eastern Economic Review* in June took the view that the difficulties between the two countries "coincided with a trend in Cambodian foreign policy which is seeking contacts with the West, while continuing to condemn American policy."[88] It cited as evidence of this the visits to Cambodia of an American senator, the Australian prime minister, and the West German and Israeli foreign ministers. Sihanouk himself wrote to the same journal to deny any such trend stating, "I doubt if China has been affected by this [the visits of Westerners]." However, his next sentence contained what might have been intended as a hidden barb for Peking: "She knows in any case extremely well that I am an independent neutral who accepts neither reproaches nor even 'advice' from friends."[89]

What might have been even worse than pro-Western gestures from China's perspective was an attempt by Sihanouk to use the Sino-Soviet antagonism to pressure China into recognising Cambodia's frontiers. In spite of several years of negotiations with the Vietnamese Communists,

85. Abolishing the KCFA (1 September), dismissing two leftist members of his cabinet (11 September), and announcing that Cambodian embassy representation in China would be cut to one person.

86. *London Times*, 19 September 1967.

87. *Realités Cambodgiennes*, 22 September 1967.

88. *Far Eastern Economic Review*, 15 June 1967, p. 627.

89. *Far Eastern Economic Review*, 27 July 1967, p. 192.

Cambodia had been unable to obtain from them recognition of her borders. In May 1967 Sihanouk decided to force the issue by demanding that all countries clarify their positions on this question.[90] However, the country on which Cambodia concentrated its efforts in order to achieve an initial diplomatic breakthrough was the Soviet Union, and it was not until Moscow formally recognised Cambodia's frontiers that the NLF, Hanoi, and finally China followed suit. Even then, as a mark of its annoyance with Phnom Penh, China at first only went so far as to declare its "respect" for the frontiers, not its "recognition" of them.[91] As Gurtov puts it, "Sihanouk had used the Soviets to bring about a Chinese written promise on the borders that Peking would have preferred not to make."[92]

The third issue which may have stood between Peking and Phnom Penh concerned the internal political situation in Cambodia during 1966–1967. The September 1966 elections in Cambodia had produced a more conservative Assembly, which in turn had led to a conservative cabinet under General Lon Nol.[93] The shift in power away from Cambodia's radicals had inclined them towards less constitutional means of asserting their position, including insurrection in the province of Battambang. Although the resignation of Lon Nol's cabinet in May and the subsequent establishment of a new cabinet which included the leading leftists Chau Seng and So Nem had led to an easing of the situation in Battambang, this proved to be short-lived. Both Chau Seng and So Nem were dismissed by Sihanouk after they published in the newspaper edited by them the text of a telegram from the Peking Chinese-Khmer Friendship Association to its Phnom Penh counterpart, protesting the abolition of the KCFA and criticising "reaction" in Cambodia.[94] This action, combined with leftist criticism that Sihanouk was seeking an improvement of relations with Washington, formed the background against which fresh insurgencies broke out at the end of 1967.[95] The insurrection grew in size during 1968–1969 and received a

90. See Gurtov, "Politics of Survival," pp. 244–247, for a detailed account.
91. See NCNA, 13 June 1967, for the text. *Realités Cambodgiennes* (23 June 1967), remarked somewhat acidly: "One can only respect that whose existence one recognizes."
92. Gurtov, "Politics of Survival," p. 146.
93. M. Leifer, "Rebellion or Subversion in Cambodia," *Current History*, February 1969, p. 89.
94. *Japan Times*, 16 September 1967; *Far Eastern Economic Review*, 21 September 1967.
95. Leifer, "Rebellion or Subversion," pp. 91–93.

considerable stimulus when Sihanouk himself joined the rebels following his overthrow in 1970.

The question of foreign involvement in the uprisings is a matter of debate. Girling argues that the "Vietnamese were careful not to antagonize Sihanouk by direct support of the Cambodian rebels."[96] The internal origins of the rebellion are also stressed by Osborne.[97] Against this is the persistent claim of the governments of both Sihanouk and, after 1970, Lon Nol that the rebellion was incited by outside forces. In 1967 Sihanouk did not publicly link China with the insurrection, although he claimed on one occasion that Cambodian leftists were plotting to turn Cambodia into a dependency of China.[98] He did, however, accuse North Vietnam of supporting the Battambang insurgency.[99] In 1968 he explicitly linked China with the revolt for the first time: "This war has been imposed on us because I have not agreed to become the ally or satellite of China, the NLF, and the DRVN."[100] He specifically charged that Cambodia was being "punished" for receiving a U.S. mission under Chester Bowles which went to Cambodia in January 1968 to discuss the issue of American "hot pursuit" of Vietnamese Communist troops escaping into Cambodia. In further speeches on this matter he tended not to refer to the Communist countries by name but to "Asian communism" as the originator of the insurrections. In March, however, he charged that China was resuming its propaganda against his regime.[101] After this, although verbal attacks on the Vietnamese Communists increased in intensity, China was no longer accused of complicity. Yao Wen-yuan's caustic private remarks on Sihanouk in 1968 (cited in Chapter 5) did not escape Sihanouk's eagle eye, but *Realités Cambodgiennes* merely noted mildly that they suggested "a curious conception of peaceful coexistence."[102]

It is not difficult to believe that the Vietnamese Communists—who by this time had troops stationed semipermanently in Cambodia—had, at the very least, some links with the Cambodian rebels. It also appears possible, albeit

96. J. L. S. Girling, "The Resistance in Cambodia," *Asian Survey*, July 1972, pp. 557–558.

97. M. Osborne, *Politics and Power in Cambodia* (Camberwell, Victoria, 1973), pp. 96–107.

98. *Washington Post*, 6 August 1967.

99. *Japan Times*, 6 June 1967.

100. *Realités Cambodgiennes*, 3 February 1968.

101. *Realités Cambodgiennes*, 1 March and 8 March 1968.

102. *Realités Cambodgiennes*, 18 May 1968.

from purely circumstantial evidence, that there was some connection between "pro-Western" moves by Sihanouk and the onset of the rebellion.
However, the question of China's complicity needs to be carefully defined.
"Initiation" or "control" of the revolts is one matter, "support" is quite a
different affair. There were by 1967 enough Cambodian opponents of
Sihanouk's domestic *and* foreign policies to render absurd his claims that
the insurrection was entirely created by external forces. Whether China
privately supported the rebellion in some way is more difficult. Certainly,
and unsurprisingly, there is not a single Chinese document which establishes
definitely that support of any kind was forthcoming from China. It is clear,
however, that Peking had some doubts about the course of Cambodia's
foreign policy in 1968–1969, and here I must return briefly to an account of
Sino-Cambodian relations in this period.

The Sino-Cambodian relationship had appeared to be restored to its old
basis at the end of 1967, when border incidents involving U.S. troops in
Vietnam led Phnom Penh to declare on 26 December that should the U.S.
invade, Cambodia would "immediately appeal to the friendly powers for
direct assistance." Peking, no doubt pleased to be able to return to the
familiar and time-honoured rituals, responded with a firm statement that

> . . . the Chinese government and people resolutely support this just stand
> of the Royal Cambodian government. . . . The Chinese government is
> closely watching the developments and hereby states that if U.S. im-
> perialism dares to launch a war of aggression against Cambodia, the
> Chinese government and people will definitely not look on with folded
> arms and . . . will certainly adopt every necessary and effective measure to
> support the Cambodian people.[103]

However, shortly after this, in negotiations with Chester Bowles, Sihanouk
appeared to go some way towards conceding the American right of "hot
pursuit."[104] This fresh evidence of Sihanouk's perfidy, together with the
renewal of violence in Battambang, caused relations to sour for some
months, as mentioned earlier.

One indication of the relatively low level of Sino-Cambodian relations in
1968–1969 is the fact that in *Peking Review* during 1968 there were only
three articles on Cambodia, and only two in 1969. Four of these, including
the one just cited, were written in response to Cambodian denunciations of

103. NCNA, 4 January 1968.
104. Gurtov, "Politics of Survival," pp. 235–236.

U.S. military incursions and contained statements of support for Cambodia. It is instructive to compare them. The second appeared in April 1968, following an April 15 statement by Phnom Penh condemning an intrusion by a U.S. aircraft. This time Cambodia received, in the form of a "Commentator" article, a much shorter and more lukewarm expression of China's support than it had in January: "Should U.S. imperialism dare to extend its war of aggression to Cambodia, the Chinese people will resolutely stand by the Cambodian people and give them powerful backing."[105] Following a similar incident in June, and again after waiting some days for a Cambodian denunciation, Peking issued an even weaker statement: "The Chinese government affirms that the Chinese government and people will, as always, firmly support the Royal Government of Cambodia and the Cambodian people in their just struggle against U.S. imperialist aggression."[106]

The most interesting statement was made in November 1969. In the intervening period Sihanouk had, in December 1968, ordered the army to increase its pressure on the Vietnamese Communists operating in Cambodia[107] and in June 1969 had resumed relations with the United States. China's displeasure was made apparent, in the usual oblique fashion, in its November 1969 note. The note followed a written protest by Sihanouk against American incursions, and after giving its "firm support to this just statement of Samdech Sihanouk," it proceeded: "The Chinese government and people firmly support the Cambodian people in their just struggle against U.S. imperialist aggression and firmly believe that the aggressive activities of U.S. imperialism against the Indochinese countries will definitely meet with thorough defeat in the face of the Indochinese people's close unity and resolute resistance."[108] The three points to note in this statement are its nonuse of Sihanouk's royal title, the reference to support for the "Cambodian people" rather than the "government and people," and the clear implication that defeat of the U.S. was the responsibility of the "Indochinese people."

To return to the question of China's support for the insurrection. It is clear that Sihanouk's moves against the Vietnamese Communists and towards Washington in 1968–1969 had caused Peking to rethink its attitude towards Cambodia and to refuse to give any further pledges as strong as

105. *Peking Review*, 26 April 1968, p. 27.
106. *Peking Review*, 19 July 1968, p. 6.
107. *Washington Post*, 3 February 1970.
108. *Peking Review*, 5 December 1969.

those in 1963–1966 and January 1968. It is not unreasonable to suppose that, as its hopes for Sihanouk faded, so it tended to look more to the leftist forces in Cambodia. The reference to "the Cambodian people" in the last statement may have been an indication of this. However, it is still difficult to establish that Peking had any direct links with the rebels. The complex and unfathomable set of relationships among Peking, Hanoi, and the NLF must also be considered. If, for example, the NLF had a close relationship with the Cambodian guerrillas, did this automatically mean that support for the guerrillas became part of the policy of Hanoi and Peking? Sihanouk had hoped that Peking would be able to influence its Vietnamese clients. It is impossible to tell whether Peking had proved unwilling or simply unable to do this.

Some light on Peking's attitude to Cambodia is cast by its reaction to events in 1970. Sihanouk was overthrown on 18 March, but it was not until 5 May that Peking formally severed relations with the Lon Nol government. Lon Nol later revealed that China had broken off relations with his government only after he had turned down Peking's request to aid the Vietnamese Communists. He had apparently been informed that Peking considered the fall of Sihanouk to be an internal matter and would recognise Lon Nol's government if he met three specific conditions: permitting the shipment of arms through Cambodia; maintaining sanctuaries for Vietnamese Communist troops, and assisting them in their war propaganda.[109] Lon Nol's account is supported by the time gap between the coup and China's recognition of Sihanouk's government in exile as well as by Peking's lack of trust in Sihanouk—who had spent the first two months of 1970 informing anyone who would listen that the U.S. had to remain in Indochina or Cambodia would become a satellite of China.[110] Thus Peking had been faced with two alternative policies after the coup: to accept what appeared to be a golden opportunity to intensify the "people's war" in Cambodia or to seek to re-establish a relationship with the Cambodian government on a new basis. The fact that Peking initially chose the latter seems to suggest that it did not have very extensive contacts with the Cambodian guerrillas, and that a "people's war" in Cambodia did not take precedence over the utility of Cambodia for the Vietnam war.

109. *Guardian*, 12 May 1970.
110. *International Herald Tribune*, 28 February 1970.

CONCLUSION

The pattern of Sino-Cambodian relations was different again from those outlined in both previous case studies. Cambodia received a strong verbal commitment from China, but, unlike the Pakistan case, this was intended to serve purposes other than those associated with a conventional alliance commitment. Similarly, Peking did not display much interest in the revolutionary prospects of Cambodia. Although it eventually supported a "people's war" in Cambodia, it did so only after ascertaining that the new Cambodian government of Lon Nol was not prepared to tolerate Vietnamese Communist incursions to the same extent as had Sihanouk.

A further point may be noted. Cambodia's foreign policy went through four phases in the period under consideration. The first was one of formal neutrality during which Phnom Penh was, if anything, somewhat more inclined towards the U.S. than the other major powers. During the second period, beginning in 1956, Phnom Penh sought a more balanced position between the U.S. and China by adjusting its foreign policy to take more account of such basic Chinese interests as U.N representation. In the third, beginning in 1963, Cambodia adopted a more assertive posture of opposition to "American imperialism," while in the fourth, Phnom Penh acquiesced in Vietnamese Communist use of Cambodian territory. Hence each change involved a further accommodation by Cambodia of Chinese interests. However, although Peking exerted some pressure on Sihanouk throughout the period, this mostly took the form of persuasion and economic aid until 1965–1966 when, by Sihanouk's account at least, a menacing undertone began to appear in China's "advice" to him. In fact many of the key shifts in position were made by Sihanouk without much apparent pressure from Peking. This was particularly the case of Sihanouk's most important move, the renunciation of American aid in 1963, when Peking seems to have merely capitalised on Sihanouk's purely gratuitous adoption of an anti-American position.

In view of the apparent uniqueness of the Sino-Cambodian relationship, is it possible to fit it into either the alliance or united front categories? Cambodia is the only state in the world to have gone through a progressively closer relationship with China and ended up with a Communist (or quasi-Communist) government. Unfortunately for this study, however, this was, as has been demonstrated, an entirely fortuitous development rather than the result of a classic, long-term united front policy by China towards Cambodia. Indeed, the Lon Nol coup d'état had occurred in part because of growing discontent in Cambodia over Sihanouk's acquiescence in the Vietnamese Communist incursions. Since Chinese pressure had been partly responsible for this policy of Sihanouk's, it could equally be argued that one effect of China's policy towards Cambodia had been to bring into existence a right-wing, anti-Chinese dictatorship there.

Peking was indifferent to the internal political situation in Cambodia so long as Phnom Penh adhered to an acceptable foreign policy line. The only significant sense in which the united front model might be thought to fit this relationship is to be found in Peking's progressive upgrading of what was "acceptable." At Geneva, neutrality had been enough. Later an "anti-imperialist" stance had been required, then (according to Sihanouk) a rift with Moscow and support for the Vietnamese Communists. Moreover, especially in the 1963–1968 period, Peking employed several varieties of "struggle" against Sihanouk in an attempt to ensure his compliance. At first glance this looks like a "unity and struggle" strategy towards a united front partner with the aim of the gradual radicalization of the partner. However, here again appearances are deceptive. While some of the *tactics* ("material benefits," "education and criticism") which Peking used in its relations with Phnom Penh may be equated to united front tactics, they were not part of an overall united front *strategy*. At least in the post-1963 period, China's increasing pressure on Sihanouk was largely a response to the developing situation in Vietnam rather than part of a long-term strategy towards Cambodia itself. However, it is possible that China's move in the late 1950s away from an acceptance of Cambodian neutrality and a "peaceful coexistence" relationship was related to the more general shift in China's policy at this time, as discussed in Chapter 3. Hence, some connection between the united front doctrine and China's policy towards Cambodia is discernible in that single instance.

Although China's policy seems to have been guided mainly by strategic considerations relating to the importance of Indochina for China's security, the alliance model provides only a partial explanation of Peking's objectives. The first five propositions in the alliance model, which set out the broad geopolitical and security factors that are the basis of the model, are all applicable to this case. Peking's consistent concern from 1954 was that Cambodia avoid any entanglement with the U.S. that might involve a threat to China's security. Apart from this Peking made few demands of Cambodia until the situation in Vietnam began to worsen, and then too China's behaviour was largely determined by the strategic importance of Cambodia for the prosecution of the war by the Vietnamese Communists. However, Propositions Six to Nine of the alliance model do not entirely fit the Cambodian case, mainly because the two states did not share the same threat perception (Proposition Seven). Cambodia's adversaries were seen by Sihanouk to be *both* Vietnams and Thailand, while China's were the U.S.A. and the Soviet Union.

Although never quite a conventional alliance up to the time of Sihanouk's overthrow, the Sino-Cambodian relationship took on more of the characteristics of an alliance with the victory of the Khmer Rouge. Fraternal solidarity is unlikely to replace the traditional Cambodian antipathy towards Vietnamese of any colour, and if Thailand continues to pursue a policy of placating its Indochinese neighbours the only conceivable threats to Cambodia are Vietnam and China itself. Rather than see a powerful Communist Indochina united under Hanoi, which could, in alliance with the Soviet Union, constitute a major threat to China, Peking may well prefer to back Cambodian independence against Vietnam. Since all the actors in this scenario would share, at least in some respects, a common ideology, it would be even harder to find evidence of the influence of ideology on China's policy in Indochina in the contemporary situation than it has been for the 1954–1970 period.

CHAPTER SEVEN

China, Tanzania, and the African Revolution

Unlike the three Asian states that have been considered in case studies, Tanzania did not receive from China a verbal commitment of support against aggression. Nonetheless the relationship between the two states has been close enough for one author to term it a "partial informal alliance."[1] Tanzania was one of only nine non-Communist recipients of military aid from China in the period up to 1970.[2] China's commitment to build the Tan-Zam railway—an undertaking eagerly sought by Peking, as will be seen—put Tanzania in a special category because of the size and possible implications of the project and because it made Tanzania the second largest non-Communist recipient of Chinese economic aid.[3] Hence, although it does not really fit the definition of "alliance" given in Chapter 2, Tanzania may be counted as one of the four non-Communist developing nations that have been most closely associated with China. While China's immediate security and strategic interests obviously enter more forcefully into the picture in her relations with states such as Pakistan or Cambodia, it is still

1. G. T. Yu, *China and Tanzania: A Study in Cooperative Interaction* (Berkeley, 1970), p. 13.

2. Others being Pakistan, Cambodia, Indonesia, Guinea, Mali, Congo (Brazzaville), Algeria, and Syria. *The Arms Trade with the Third World* (Stockholm, 1971), p. 360.

3. Main recipients of Chinese aid up to 1970 in order of magnitude:

Pakistan	$309 million	Indonesia	$122 million
Tanzania	$256 million	Cambodia	$ 92 million
Zambia	$217 million		

Source: *China's Aid to the Third World* (British Foreign Office, May 1972), p. 32.

possible to ask what part has been played by broad strategic/diplomatic considerations in China's policy towards Tanzania.

The principal interest of the relationship is to be found in what it may reveal about the united front doctrine and China's foreign policy. Particularly in the early 1960s Peking's public and private statements on Africa suggest a considerable interest in the prospects for revolution in Africa. Since China established closer relations with Tanzania than any other African state, the question clearly arises of whether Peking viewed this relationship from the "dual policy" perspective of the united front doctrine. The remainder of this chapter considers first China's policies and objectives in Africa as a whole, and second, against this background, China's policy towards Tanzania.

CHINA AND AFRICA

Secret PLA documents captured in 1961 suggest that China's interest in Africa was focussed on the long-range revolutionary possibilities there.[4] Africa, it was stated, was important because it was "now the centre of the anticolonialist struggle and the centre for East and West to fight for the control of an intermediate zone, so that it has become a key point of world interest." Moreover Africa was, in the words that Mao had once used to describe China, "poor and blank" and thus susceptible to the "correct" influences:

> Africa is now like a huge political exhibition, where a hundred flowers are truly blooming, waiting there for anybody to pick. But everything must go through the experience of facts. History and realistic life can help the Africans to take the road of healthy development. We must tell them about the Chinese revolutionary experience in order to reveal the true nature of both new and old colonialism.

However, Africa was not ready for a rapid transition to socialism; this would come later following the building up of Marxist forces via a united front against imperialism:

> The important part of its activities lies in the national revolution and in making the united front spread everywhere on the continent. *According to the analysis of Marxism it is to be confirmed that the embryo of national revolution in these countries will become a genuine people's*

4. The following quotations from PLA documents cited in J. Chester Cheng, *The Politics of the Chinese Red Army* (Stanford, 1966), pp. 484–485.

revolution, give rise to Marxists, form political parties of proletariats and go towards the Socialist Revolution [emphasis added].

China's policy, which was cast in domino theory terms, was therefore to be based on a long-term perspective:

> Among the independent countries in Africa, if only one or two of them complete a real national revolution, solving their own problem of resisting imperialism and reaching an internal solution of a democratic national revolution, the effect will be very great, the time ripe for action, the revolutionary wave will be able to swallow the whole African continent, and the 200 million and more Africans will advance to the forefront of the world. We should take long-range views of this problem.

China's policy towards Africa was seen to follow logically from the basic perception of Africa as in the first, anti-imperialist stage of a two-stage revolutionary process, with the second stage to be that of socialist revolution. China's role was described as one of education and guidance, although it was stressed that the contribution of any external power could be only secondary to that of internal forces.

This document should not necessarily be taken at its face value, that is, as establishing that China's policy in Africa was based on long-term revolutionary prospects and a united front strategy. Internal documents have their own propaganda purposes and a heavy emphasis in them on revolutionary goals does not prove that those goals motivated policy decisions. Hence, it is necessary to examine China's actual behaviour to ascertain whether there has been any correspondence between it and the ideological formulations outlined here.

China's first substantial initiative in Africa was to offer economic aid and "volunteers" to Egypt during the Suez crisis.[5] It was only after Suez that China's Foreign Ministry set up a department dealing with African and Middle Eastern affairs—clearly a response to the emergence of an unexpected "antagonistic contradiction" with imperialism. Developments in Algeria played an even greater part in stimulating China's interest in Africa since they were seen as both anti-imperialist and revolutionary. Moreover the Algerian revolution took a form which seemed to Peking to have some of the characteristics of China's own revolution. Chou En-lai, visiting Algeria in December 1963, praised the Algerian FLN for its exemplary con-

5. H. M. Kerr, "The Middle East and China," in A. M. Halpern (ed.), *Policies towards China: Views from Six Continents* (New York, 1965), p. 439.

duct of the revolutionary struggle, singling out its "reliance on the masses," its formation of a "broad united front," its adoption of armed struggle, its use of the countryside as a base area, and its "correct revolutionary leadership."[6] Following its official recognition of the Algerian FLN in September 1958, Peking's attention came to be focussed increasingly on countries in Africa which were thought to have similar conditions—and revolutionary prospects—to those of Algeria, such as Cameroon, Kenya, and the Congo.[7] Peking's contacts were at this stage primarily with liberation movements in Africa, and its message to such movements was consistent: They should follow the course charted by the FLN.[8]

During the early 1960s Peking sought to encourage four tendencies in Africa: anti-imperialism, support for African national liberation movements, the pursuit of self-reliance, and efforts towards Afro-Asian solidarity.[9] Here again the central conception which seemed to be guiding China's policy in Africa was of a broad united front directed externally against imperialism and internally towards promoting a revolutionary upsurge. The African united front was also seen as reinforcing a worldwide revolutionary trend: "The African people's anti-imperialist struggle is inseparable from that of the Asian and Latin American peoples. Their formation of a broader anti-imperialist united front in the struggle will inevitably promote a greater upsurge of the national liberation movements in the three continents."[10]

Chou En-lai's tour of Africa in 1963–1964 had as one of its objectives the promulgation of these views.[11] Chou made it clear that China placed Africa in a special category by offering the African states a new version of the five principles of peaceful coexistence. The original five principles had stressed nonaggression, equality, noninterference, and mutuality as the basis of relations among states with different social systems. The new five principles, which were said to guide China's relations with African and Arab countries

6. *Peking Review*, 3 January 1964, p. 32.

7. M. A. El-Khawas, "China's Changing Policies in Africa," *Africa Today*, November 1973.

8. B. D. Larkin, *China and Africa* (Berkeley, 1971), p. 27.

9. See Liu Ning-yi's proposals at the AAPSO conference at Moshi in 1963 (NCNA, 14 February 1963).

10. NCNA, 15 April 1963.

11. Others being to obtain diplomatic recognition and make known China's line on the Sino-Indian dispute.

and were described as a "creative development" of the old five,[12] read as follows:

1. China supports the African and Arab peoples in their struggle to oppose imperialism and old and new colonialism and to win and safeguard national independence.

2. It supports the pursuance of a policy of peace, neutrality and nonalignment by the governments of the African and Arab countries.

3. It supports the desire of the African and Arab peoples to achieve unity and solidarity in the manner of their own choice.

4. It supports the African and Arab countries in their efforts to settle their disputes through peaceful negotiations.

5. It holds that the sovereignty of the African and Arab countries should be respected by all other countries and that encroachment and interference from any quarter should be opposed.[13]

The new element in these five principles was their emphasis on African unity against imperialism. Chapter 3 has described how Peking after 1957 shifted away from its Bandung position of acceptance of Afro-Asian neutrality and towards an insistence that Afro-Asian countries adopt a "positive" foreign policy. The new five principles for Africa provide one of the clearest illustrations of this tendency.

Another way in which Peking's ideological formulations on Africa were reflected in actual policy decisions is to be found in Peking's backing with finance and other forms of support leftist individuals and parties in various African countries. It should be added that the extent of Chinese "subversion" in Africa in the 1960s has often been grossly exaggerated. Sometimes, as in Ghana, charges of "subversion" followed the overthrow of a government that had been friendly towards China. Elsewhere alarm was caused by the appearance of pamphlets, allegedly published in China or Albania, which called for revolution against "national bourgeois" governments in Africa. One such document, "Revolution in Africa," was claimed by Peking to be a forgery in 1965, as was another, "New Diplomats Will Bring the Great Proletarian Cultural Revolution to Africa," in 1967.[14] Nonetheless it seems clear that during the period 1960–1965 Peking did back opposition movements in Kenya, Cameroon, the Congo, Burundi, and elsewhere.[15]

12. NCNA, 6 February 1964.
13. *Peking Review*, 3 April 1964.
14. NCNA, 5 April 1965, and 23 March 1967.
15. See Larkin, *China and Africa*, p. 27.

Revolution was by no means China's only objective in Africa. As elsewhere, Peking wished to persuade African states to cease their diplomatic and other relations with Taiwan.[16] It should be noted that during much of the 1960s, Taiwan not only had relations with more African states than Peking but was at times able to win recognition from states such as Dahomey and the Central African Republic after they had broken off relations with Peking. In one state, the Ivory Coast, Taiwan's economic impact was almost as extensive as that of Peking in Tanzania.[17]

Two additional factors may have impinged upon China's policies: economics and the Sino-Soviet rivalry. A *People's Daily* editorial in 1964 argued that Africa's abundance of raw materials made it a prime target of neocolonialism.[18] While this was ostensibly a straightforward Leninist assertion, it suggests that Peking itself was not blind to the potential economic advantages of friendship with Africa. Although China gave considerable economic aid to African states, it was generally able to expand its trade with Africa as a byproduct of this. Indeed in the case of Ghana, it was estimated that "the net effect of loans and trade agreements negotiated with China by the Nkrumah regime had been the equivalent of an interest-free sterling loan of several million pounds in favour of the Chinese."[19] However, the point should not be overstated: Even if economic considerations have been a factor in China's African policy, Peking's normal practice has been to attempt to make its economic relations with foreign countries serve political ends, rather than the reverse.[20]

The Sino-Soviet rift had an impact in Africa from as early as 1958 when China granted recognition to the Algerian FLN. Moscow could not afford to take this step, which might have adversely affected its relations with Paris and the French and Algerian Communist parties.[21] The possible intention of China's move was to compromise Moscow's claim to be the leading supporter of national liberation movements. The rivalry between the two grew particularly intense in the early 1960s, causing splits in the southern

16. See L. M. S. Slawecki, "The Two Chinas in Africa," *Foreign Affairs*, January 1963.

17. "Two-China War in Black Africa," *U.S. News and World Report*, 14 September 1970.

18. NCNA, 15 April 1964.

19. "China in Africa" (British Foreign Office, 1972), p. 9.

20. For discussion of this, see F. H. Mah, "China's Foreign Trade," in A. Eckstein (ed.), *Economic Trends in Communist China* (Chicago, 1968).

21. W. A. Nielsen, *The Great Powers and Africa* (New York, 1969), pp. 196–197.

African national liberation movements and the various front organisations that they had jointly sponsored.[22]

One dilemma for China's policy in Africa was that, in most cases, Africans who had recently won independence from European colonial masters did not accept Peking's designation of the United States as the leading imperialist power and therefore the chief target of "anti-imperialist struggle." Peking saw as a chief part of its "educational" task the need to "teach" the African states how to "distinguish between enemies and friends," while events in Africa were often analysed by the Chinese in terms of their usefulness in performing this function. For example, the *People's Daily* stated, with reference to the Congo situation in 1964, "The greatest gain of the Congolese people after more than three years of struggle is their ability to distinguish between their enemies and their friends, between their true friends and false friends."[23]

On other occasions Chinese leaders simply asserted that any anti-imperialist struggle was "objectively" directed against the U.S. simply by virtue of the latter's position as "imperialist chieftain."[24] However, it remains the case that, whereas in other areas China's policy of supporting anti-imperialist revolutions coincided with its interest in seeing the U.S. overstretch its resources in as many parts of the world as possible, the two were not so easily reconcilable in Africa, where the U.S. was not heavily involved. Thus, although Chinese leaders frequently tried to represent African revolutions as anti-U.S.,[25] it is necessary to find an explanation of China's interest in Africa other than its desire to confront—or, more precisely, have others confront—the U.S.

Given that anti-imperialist revolutions in Africa tended to be directed against European powers, it does seem that China's interest was in the

22. For further details of the effects of the Sino-Soviet rift on Africa, see W. A. C. Adie, "China, Russia, and the Third World," *China Quarterly*, July–September 1962; R. A. Scalapino, "Sino-Soviet Competition in Africa," *Foreign Affairs*, July 1964; and G. A. Martelli and R. V. Allen, "Sino-Soviet Rivalry and Southern Africa," in C. J. Zablocki (ed.), *Sino-Soviet Rivalry: Implications for U.S. Policy* (New York, 1966).

23. NCNA, 6 May 1964.

24. See, for example, Chou En-lai's speech of 6 June 1965, SCMP 3475.

25. See Liao Cheng-ch'ih's speech in 1966: "The most important task before the African people is to carry the anti-imperialist struggle through to the end so as to achieve complete political and economic independence. This is a protracted, complicated, and life and death struggle. And U.S. imperialism is the most ferocious and dangerous enemy in this struggle" (NCNA, 24 May 1966).

revolutions themselves rather than their imperialist targets, and that the PLA document cited earlier was a relatively accurate representation of official views in Peking. If so Peking's widespread setbacks in Africa during the 1960s may be attributed in part to a misperception of the situation there that was induced largely by ideological preconceptions, specifically by a tendency to assume that in the long term Africa was bound to follow the course of the Chinese revolution and that China's policy should be based on this assumption. Not only did Peking massively overestimate the revolutionary prospects in Africa, but more importantly it underestimated the durability of "national bourgeois" regimes there.

When Peking began to repair its relations with African countries from 1969, a dramatic change of style was noticeable. The "special" five principles for Africa were quietly dropped, with Peking now claiming to base its relations with Africa, as elsewhere, on the five principles of peaceful coexistence. In its attempts to win influence, Peking no longer stressed the example of the Chinese revolution but concentrated rather more than it had in the 1960s on the relevance of Chinese techniques of economic construction.[26] Thus the "eight principles" of foreign aid, which Chou En-lai had advanced at the same time as the "special" five principles, were retained since they included such objectives as the fostering of self-reliance and concentration on low-investment, rapid-yield projects—both key elements of the Chinese economic philosophy.

Since China's relationship with Tanzania was in many ways the cornerstone of China's post-1969 policy in Africa, the question whether this policy involved a basic change in China's long-term perspective and objectives—an "adaptation" of ideology rather than an attempted "reconciliation" of ideology and reality will be considered in the following section.

THE ORIGINS OF THE
SINO-TANZANIAN PARTNERSHIP

Tanganyika and China agreed to establish relations in 1961, and in April 1962 China's ambassador, Ho Ying, arrived in Dar-es-Salaam for a stay that was to last until he was recalled in 1967. China's interests were at this stage centred on North Africa, Ghana, and the Congo, with less attention being

26. "Chinese Aid to Developing Countries: Road and Rail Projects," *China Topics*, 8 March 1972, pp. 1–5.

paid to East Africa. However, the two countries signed a cultural cooperation agreement on 13 December 1962, and trade between them grew rapidly to a point where in 1963 Tanganyika exported to China 42 percent of its total cotton output.[27] There was, however, no special significance in this statistic. Tanganyika had encountered severe economic difficulties in 1962 and was interested in obtaining any possible outlets for its goods.[28] An end of the year review of African affairs in the *People's Daily* entitled "African Revolutionary Storm Gains Momentum in 1963" mentioned Tanganyika in passing on account of its replacement of British expatriate personnel by Africans but devoted most of its attention to more exciting developments elsewhere.[29] China's first aid project to Tanganyika—the dispatch of two paddy growing experts in January 1964—similarly indicated the relatively low level of Sino-Tanganyikan interaction at this time. Indeed, in the same month a Chinese radio broadcast criticized the calling in of British soldiers to quash an army mutiny in Tanganyika and, in what may have been a gesture of disapproval at Tanganyika's apparent dependence on its former colonial masters, Chou En-lai cancelled a scheduled visit to Tanganyika.[30]

China's interest in East Africa was aroused by another development in January: the leftist coup d'état in Zanzibar. By some accounts the coup itself was Chinese inspired. This has never been established and is probably incorrect,[31] but it is true that Peking moved quickly to recognise and grant aid to Zanzibar after the coup and that during 1964 China's presence in Zanzibar grew rapidly. China's most controversial and intriguing venture in Zanzibar was the establishment of a training centre for African revolutionaries on Pemba Island.[32] There is very little reliable information available about the number of Chinese involved in this project or whether, as has been alleged, the centre was used for training guerrillas for operations in places other than the main target—Portuguese Africa.[33]

27. NCNA, 16 February 1965.

28. *East African Standard*, 16 June 1962.

29. NCNA, 30 December 1963.

30. The *New York Times*, 30 January 1964, claimed that the cancellation was at Chinese, not Tanzanian insistence, as was first thought.

31. Larkin, *China and Africa*, p. 74.

32. *Life* magazine interview with John Okello, leader of the Zanzibar coup, 30 March 1965.

33. During the Congo crisis in 1964, it was claimed that the school was used to train guerrillas for operations against the Congo (Elizabethville Radio in French, 20 September 1965).

China's close relations with Tanganyika itself developed essentially as a byproduct of its links with Zanzibar and the necessity of working with Nyerere after Tanganyika and Zanzibar formed a united republic in April 1964. Peking was presented with a situation having enormous potential for embarrassment when the union was announced since many Tanganyikans, possibly including Nyerere himself, did not share the enthusiasm for all things Chinese of Zanzibarian ministers such as Babu and Karume.[34] Thus China's embassy had to tread warily to avoid charges of interference in the domestic politics of Tanzania of the kind which Peking was encountering elsewhere in Africa. In fact in Tanzania the Chinese proceeded cautiously at the start and have been a model of propriety ever since. This may be accounted for in part by lessons drawn from their unfortunate experiences in other parts of Africa and in part by their growing appreciation of Nyerere's domestic and foreign policies—a point which will be elaborated later.

In June 1964 China signed an economic and technical cooperation agreement with Tanzania involving £16 million Chinese aid.[35] A speech by Chou En-lai before the Tanzanian mission which had gone to China to negotiate the agreement indicated China's reasons for this generosity. Tanzania, he stated, "adheres to a policy of peace, neutrality, and nonalignment, actively supports the struggles of the brotherly peoples of East, Central, and Southern Africa for national independence, and devotes itself to strengthening the Asian-African cause of unity against imperialism. All this is playing a positive role in international affairs."[36]

Of the three facets of Tanzania's "positive role" that were singled out, the most specific and probably the most important in Peking's eyes was its assistance to African insurgent movements.[37] It should be noted, however, that Tanzania had undertaken this role long before the Chinese training centre was established on Pemba Island. In May 1963 the OUA had set up a Liberation Committee for Southern Africa with headquarters at Dar-es-Salaam, and Tanzania had become the effective coordinating centre for this liberation movement—a role that Nyerere took seriously.[38] Tanzania's part

34. See Nyerere's comment as late as 1969, "The Chinese will learn that if they want to control us they will get into trouble" (*East African Standard*, 6 May 1969).

35. NCNA, 16 June 1964.

36. NCNA, 8 June 1964.

37. This had also been stressed in the speech made by Tanzanian Vice-President Kawawa (NCNA, 14 June 1964).

38. Larkin, *China and Africa*, pp. 59–60; Yu, *China and Tanzania*, pp. 33–34;

in Afro-Asian solidarity organisations was also appreciated by China. The Chinese press had noted earlier in the year the Tanganyikan delegation's criticism of Soviet tactics at a recent AAPSO meeting.[39] In addition Dar-es-Salaam had agreed to the Chinese proposal for the exclusion of Moscow from the proposed Second Afro-Asian Conference.[40]

The impression in some quarters that Tanzania was rapidly becoming a Chinese client state gathered strength when Nyerere announced in August 1964 that he had invited China to send a team of instructors to train his army.[41] Nyerere's account of the reasons for his request for Chinese military aid suggests, however, that China's role was originally envisaged as an extremely limited one and that Peking had itself insisted on this. China under the agreement was to send seven instructors with four interpreters for a six-month period—the short time being at Peking's own request.[42] According to Nyerere, he had sounded out several countries before China, with China's offer being "the nearest thing to what I wanted."[43] Together with its instructors China sent quantities of mortars, antitank guns, and heavy machineguns, which were displayed at a special public parade in February 1965.[44]

The increase in China's influence in Tanzanian military affairs after 1964 was a largely fortuitous effect of two things. The first was the Tanzanian decision to turn its army into a "people's army" with all troops being obliged to become TANU party members and involve themselves in various nation-building projects.[45] This move did not stem from a desire to emulate the Chinese PLA but from the necessity of establishing political control over the army to prevent a recurrence of the mutiny of January 1964 which

---

T. C. Niblock, "Tanzanian Foreign Policy—An Analysis," *African Review*, September 1971, p. 92.

39. NCNA, 25 March 1964.

40. The joint communiqué issued at the end of the Tanzanian economic mission's visit noted that the two sides accepted the final communiqué of the preparatory meeting for the proposed Second Afro-Asian Conference. Peking was essentially interested in a single clause in this communiqué—that excluding the Soviet Union. Text of the Sino-Tanzanian Joint Communiqué in NCNA, 21 June 1964.

41. *Observer* (London), 30 August 1964.

42. *Keesing's Contemporary Archives*, vol. 15, p. 20754.

43. *Times* (London), 1 September 1964.

44. BBC Summary of World Broadcasts, ME/1781/B/1.

45. Ibid.

had forced Dar-es-Salaam to take the embarrassing step of calling in the British army. However, the fact that the PLA provided the best model for the proposed Tanzanian army led inevitably to Chinese advice being sought.[46] Second, China proved to be more willing and able to provide Tanzania with the kind of arms and equipment it sought than any other power. Dar-es-Salaam had initially intended to obtain military aid from several different sources, including West Germany, in accordance with Nyerere's conception of nonalignment. However, West Germany stopped its military aid to Tanzania after the Tanzanian government's decision to accept an East German consulate-general in Dar-es-Salaam.[47] Nyerere had attempted to restore the relationship with West Germany from as early as April 1965, but the rigid Hallstein policy had prevented this.[48] Tanzania had then sought and obtained Canadian aid to replace West Germany's.[49] However, Canada's laws on military aid had prevented her from giving jet fighters and other types of combat equipment,[50] so that when Tanzania's aid agreement with Canada expired in 1969, Dar-es-Salaam decided not to renew it but to seek Chinese assistance instead.[51] This move paid off in the form of two squadrons of MIG-17 type interceptors and considerable Chinese assistance in the training of Tanzanian pilots.[52]

Tanzania took on a new significance for Peking when, in November 1964, Tanzania's Foreign Minister Kambona claimed that his government had concrete documentary evidence that the U.S. and Portugal "in collusion with certain brother African states" were preparing to attack Tanzania.[53] Although Washington vigorously denied the charges, relations between the two countries continued to deteriorate until, on 15 January 1965, the U.S. ambassador was given twenty-four hours' notice to quit Tanzania. Peking was clearly delighted to have found "proof" at last of its oft-stated thesis that the real enemy in Africa was the U.S. China's ambassador, Ho Ying,

46. Tanzanian military delegations visited China regularly from 1965 onwards. Information about the exact objectives of these missions is hard to come by, but it may be assumed that one purpose was simply that of observing the PLA in action.

47. *East African Standard*, 20 February 1965.

48. Niblock, "Tanzanian Foreign Policy," p. 94.

49. *East African Standard*, 20 March 1965.

50. Yu, *China and Tanzania*, p. 66.

51. *Los Angeles Times*, 16 June 1970.

52. *Daily Telegraph*, 13 July 1970.

53. *Keesing's Contemporary Archives*, vol. 15, p. 20756.

visited Nyerere to discuss "U.S. subversion" shortly after Kambona's accusation,[54] and the Chinese press lost no time in pointing to the moral of the story: "The course of striving for and defending national independence is also the course of waging intense struggles against U.S. imperialism. . . . [The Tanzanian affair] is also a great encouragement to the African peoples to enable them to see more clearly that U.S. imperialism is their most dangerous enemy."[55]

Little lasting damage to Tanzanian-U.S. relations was done by this incident.[56] However, Tanzania's foreign policy continued to win approval from Peking during 1965. In January Tanzania and North Korea agreed to establish diplomatic relations as well as to work together to assist liberation movements in Africa.[57] In March the Chinese press praised Tanzania for its decision to reject all West German aid following Bonn's cessation of military aid.[58] A gesture which must have been particularly pleasing to Peking was Tanzania's refusal in April to sign an appeal from seventeen nonaligned countries, including its neighbours Kenya, Uganda, and Zambia, calling for unconditional negotiations on Vietnam. Peking had denounced this appeal as "masterminded by the Tito clique."[59] Similarly Nyerere opposed British Premier Wilson's proposal at the Commonwealth Prime Ministers' Conference in June for a five-man Commonwealth peace mission to go to Vietnam.[60] Finally, Tanzania's rupture of relations with Britain in December over the Rhodesian UDI played a decisive role in bringing about a closer association between China and Tanzania, since it gave an added urgency to the Tan-Zam railway project.[61] In addition, Britain responded to Tanzania's breaking off relations by freezing a £6 million loan to Dar-es-Salaam, enabling China to step in with an additional aid offer.[62]

There is no evidence that Dar-es-Salaam made any of these foreign policy

54. NCNA, 17 November 1964.

55. NCNA, 18 November 1964. See also NCNA, 14 November 1964.

56. The U.S. agreed in the same year to finance a survey into the possibility of building a road between Tanzania and Zambia (*East African Standard*, 5 November 1965).

57. Dar-es-Salaam Radio, 14 January 1965.

58. NCNA, 11 March 1965.

59. *East African Standard*, 23 April 1965.

60. *East African Standard*, 19 June 1965.

61. Tanzania's rift with Britain was also applauded by Peking (NCNA, 18 December 1965).

62. Dar-es-Salaam Radio, 16 June 1966.

decisions as a result of prompting from Peking. In fact during 1965 Nyerere made a point of asserting his country's intention to resist great power blandishments and threats from any source. For example, when he visited China in February 1965 to sign a treaty of friendship, he said, "Neither the approval or disapproval of other countries will cause us to diverge from the path that we have chosen."[63] Similarly at a banquet for Chou En-lai, who visited Tanzania in June 1965, he remarked, "Neither our principles, our country, nor our freedom to determine our own future are for sale."[64] And, in a comment that might have been intended to apply to China as well as "imperialist" countries, he said, "We have . . . to guard the sovereignty and integrity of our United Republic against *any who wish to take advantage of our current need to get control over us.* . . . From no quarter shall we accept direction or neocolonialism" [emphasis added].[65]

On another occasion Nyerere replied to a speech by Chou En-lai, which had referred to the "bounden duty" of all "peace-loving peoples" to support Vietnam, by stating bluntly, "We the Tanzanians have said that our duty is twofold and no more. Our first duty is to build our country, and our second duty is to safeguard our country."[66] Nyerere refused to echo the Chinese leaders' denunciations of the United States on either of these occasions, remarking that the struggle against imperialism was not "a fight against any people, or any nation, but against an evil doctrine and evil practices."[67] Although the joint communiqué issued after Chou En-lai's visit criticised "foreign intervention" in Vietnam, this wording was far milder and more ambiguous than, for example, a similar passage in a China-Uganda joint communiqué a month later, which condemned "armed aggression" in Vietnam.[68]

Indeed, even after 1965 when Tanzania came to rely greatly on Chinese aid, Tanzania's independence in foreign policy matters did not appear to have been compromised. Nyerere on several occasions expressed his admiration for Yugoslavia's economic system and signed a friendship treaty with that country in 1969.[69] He visited the Soviet Union in 1969, at a time

63. NCNA, 21 February 1965.
64. *New York Times*, 5 June 1965.
65. NCNA, 4 June 1965.
66. NCNA, 5 June 1965.
67. NCNA, 8 June 1965.
68. The Sino-Tanzanian joint communiqué in NCNA, 8 June 1965; the Sino-Ugandan joint communiqué in NCNA, 16 July 1965.
69. *Sunday News* (Tanzania), 10 January 1971.

when Sino-Soviet frictions were at a high point,[70] and worked with both India and Yugoslavia in the nonaligned movement.[71] Where Dar-es-Salaam did adopt a stand in international affairs similar to that of Peking, this was in general because the personal convictions of Tanzania's leaders inclined them in that direction. Partial exceptions may have been Tanzania's refusal to sign the nuclear nonproliferation treaty[72] and its recognition of the Provisional Revolutionary Government of Vietnam in 1970.[73] Neither policy was incompatible with the values held by the Tanzanian elite, but Tanzania might not have taken a stand on these issues had not both been of vital concern to China. However, in neither case did Tanzania incur any costs by siding with China. As Nyerere himself described the Sino-Tanzanian relationship in 1968, "When we feel able to cooperate we do so; if either of us feels reluctant, then we move on to some other matter."[74]

Nevertheless, Tanzania's difficulties with the U.S., West Germany, and Britain undoubtedly gave an impetus to the development of Sino-Tanzanian relations. A new economic agreement between the two was signed in January 1965, involving Chinese assistance in the establishment of a state cooperative farm.[75] In February a trade delegation headed by Mr. Babu went to China to negotiate a long-term agreement on Chinese purchases of Tanzanian cotton.[76] In the same month Nyerere himself paid his first visit to China and returned having clearly been impressed by various aspects of Chinese society—notably its emphasis on frugality and mass involvement in nation-building.[77]

The most significant development in 1965 was, however, a reported offer from China to finance the Tan-Zam railway.[78] A curious sequence of events

70. *Standard* (Tanzania), 8 October 1969.

71. *Sunday News* (Tanzania), 10 January 1971.

72. A decision made much of during Nyerere's second visit to China in 1968 (NCNA, 18 June 1968).

73. *Standard* (Tanzania), 18 January 1970.

74. NCNA, 21 June 1968.

75. For details see *East African Standard*, 12 January 1965; Dar-es-Salaam Radio, 11 January 1965; and NCNA, 5 January 1965.

76. NCNA, 7 February 1965; *East African Standard*, 26 February 1965.

77. These were mentioned by Nyerere in two radio broadcasts: Dar-es-Salaam Radio, 24 and 25 February 1965, and in several speeches (for example, *East African Standard*, 9 March 1965 and 30 April 1965).

78. *East African Standard*, 2 July 1965.

followed the first report that China was interested in the railway scheme, which had been in abeyance since the World Bank declared it an uneconomic project in 1964.[79] First, officials in Dar-es-Salaam denied that China had made the offer, and Zambia's President Kaunda indicated his interest in the possibility of the railway being built by an international consortium. A week later Tanzanian officials approached London to see if it was interested in financing and carrying out a new survey into the economic feasibility of the railway. London's initial reaction was favourable, but a few days later Dar-es-Salaam informed London that what it really wanted was a full engineering study, not the feasibility study which London was considering. This caused some puzzlement as to why the original request had been made and almost immediately rescinded. The situation became even more confused three days later when a twelve-man Chinese team arrived in Tanzania to carry out an engineering survey. A possible interpretation of this confusion is that after China's initial offer, Kaunda together with certain Tanzanian ministers who had some doubts about drawing too close to China may have approached Britain with a view to obtaining an alternative source of finance. Peking, on hearing of this, might then have responded with an offer to commence work immediately on an engineering survey and made more definite its earlier offer to finance the whole project. In any case, what emerged clearly was China's strong interest in undertaking the Tan-Zam project.

China's involvement in Tanzania's economic development continued to develop after 1965 until it encompassed almost every aspect of Tanzanian society. Although the Tam-Zam railway, which was second in magnitude only to the Aswan and Volta dams,[80] overshadowed any other specific project, it was the all-pervasiveness of China's impact that was really striking.[81] Here I shall simply mention two projects thought to be of particular significance. The first was the establishment of a Tanzania-China joint shipping line in 1966, to involve the building in China of two vessels of 10,000 tons each.[82] Although miniscule by the standards of other major powers,

79. Account of the initiation of the Tan-Zam project from Nairobi Radio, 29 July 1965; *East African Standard,* 10, 20, and 21 August 1965; and Lusaka Radio, 24 August 1965.

80. *Wall Street Journal,* 29 September 1967.

81. G. T. Yu, *China and Tanzania,* pp. 51–61 and 67–72, has a full discussion of China's aid programme in Tanzania.

82. Dar-es-Salaam Radio, 7 July 1966.

this did represent for China a significant improvement in the capacity of its merchant navy, and one which could be built on in the future. Another venture with naval implications was China's undertaking in 1970 to build a naval base in Dar-es-Salaam.[83] An earlier British-Canadian investigation of the Tan-Zam rail project had stressed that the port of Dar-es-Salaam would need ten more deep water berths if it was to handle the greatly increased flow of goods that was anticipated from the opening of the railway. China's project, begun at the same time as the railway itself, appears to have been mainly intended to meet this requirement. However, here also Peking could anticipate some long-term benefits for its slowly expanding naval strength.

CHINA'S OBJECTIVES IN TANZANIA

One extreme view of the reasons for China's expenditure of so much money and even more scarce skilled labour in Tanzania may be dismissed at once. This derives from an alleged Red Guard pamphlet in 1967, in which it was said that Africa was "ripe for revolution" and that the Tan-Zam railway would need thousands of Chinese workers, who could expect to be rewarded with the "fruits of the African revolution," which their presence would hasten.[84] The real origin of this pamphlet is suggested by the fact that, more than two years earlier, Eastern European sources were spreading the rumour that China's long-term aim in Africa was to populate it with mass migration.[85]

Another opinion was expressed by Nyerere in 1972: " . . . relations with China have become particularly important, because of China's size and *its willingness to help our peaceful revolution* on the one hand and, on the other, our ability and willingness to help China break out from the isolation in which other nations were endeavouring to confine her" [emphasis added].[86] Similarly, during his third visit to China in 1974, Nyerere told his hosts, "I believe that you are helping Tanzania and the African liberation movements *as a contribution towards the cause of world revolution*" [emphasis added].[87] There is more to these two statements than might at first

83. *Standard* (Tanzania), 6 May 1970.
84. *East African Standard*, 18 September 1967.
85. *Australian*, 30 March 1965.
86. *African Review*, June 1972, p. 49.
87. *Peking Review*, 29 March 1974.

appear. What Nyerere was essentially arguing was that China had become committed to the *peaceful* transformation of Tanzanian society and that it saw this as part of a world revolutionary process. If Nyerere was correct, this would imply that China had come some considerable distance towards accepting the possibility of "peaceful transition" towards socialism, a concept that had hitherto been an anathema to Peking. I will argue here that, implicitly if not explicitly, this is precisely what Peking had come to accept by the 1970s, although before the Cultural Revolution its relationship with Tanzania was seen from the perspective of a more conventional Maoist conception of revolution. In other words, throughout the period under consideration, Peking saw its aid to Tanzania in terms of a long-range commitment to revolution. The only thing that changed during the period was Peking's understanding of what the African revolution entailed.

This is not to say that there were not also short- and medium-term benefits for China in its relationship with Tanzania. The advantages it could hope for in the naval field have already been mentioned. China could also expect ultimately to achieve various economic benefits. A Chinese diesel locomotive industry was established in the 1960s,[88] and it would have been somewhat churlish of Tanzania if it did not purchase its rolling stock requirements from China. Moreover the Tan-Zam railway was financed by a Chinese version of "lend-lease" in which "local costs"—principally the wages of the Chinese workers—were paid by China advancing credits in Chinese currency to Dar-es-Salaam, with the Chinese workers being paid the equivalent in Tanzanian currency.[89] Tanzania purchased Chinese goods with its credits from China, with the net effect being a substantial increase in Tanzania's imports from China. It is probable that this switch in Tanzania's trading patterns will be maintained now that the railway is completed. Finally, Tanzania's underpopulated southern regions, which contain substantial reserves of coal and iron, will be opened up by the railway,[90] and China might hope to share in the exploitation of these. Indeed, a recent grant of aid by China to Tanzania was a £31 million loan to develop these resources and build a 150-mile branch line for this purpose.[91]

Of more immediate importance to China was Tanzania's role as a showpiece of Chinese aid. China's foreign policy reverses in 1965–1970 had been greater in Africa than any other region, and its ability to demonstrate that

88. *Economist*, 13 April 1968.
89. *Washington Post*, 10 January 1970.
90 *Standard* (Tanzania), 6 March 1969.
91. *Asia Research Bulletin*, April 1974, p. 2632.

it could carry out large aid projects with the minimum of disruption of local life styles was a vital factor in its recovery in Africa.[92] However, it was not only the size of its projects that Peking wanted to publicise but the social and economic philosophy they reflected and the superiority of this over the alternatives from the West and the U.S.S.R. The Chinese workers were industrious to the point of spending their spare time "serving the people" in various ways, and this was a key point in Chinese propaganda.[93] The Chinese doctors and acupuncturists with the railway workers also spent their free time working in the villages, with major successes in healing usually attributed to the medicinal value of Mao's thought.[94] Another important part of China's message to Africa was the applicability of its low-cost, homemade techniques of production to developing countries, as opposed to the high-investment, advanced technology that characterised Western economics.[95] For example, the state farms that Peking helped to set up in Tanzania were modelled in part on Chinese communes, with each including a small factory making hand tools and animal-drawn farm implements.

Nonetheless, a long-term commitment to revolution has been an important and consistent facet of China's interaction with Tanzania. At first the significance for Peking of Tanganyika and especially Zanzibar derived from their support for revolutionary movements in the white-dominated states of southern Africa. One Chinese aid project, the building of a 150-kilowatt transmitter, was intended to provide propaganda facilities for the Frelimo and other guerrilla movements in Africa.[96] Similarly, the Tan-Zam rail project was said by Peking to have "great significance . . . in supporting the revolutionary struggle of the African peoples against imperialism and

92. W. A. C. Adie, "China Returns to Africa," *Current Scene*, August 1972, p. 8. Some disruption in local life styles was inevitable, however. For example, at first the Chinese survey team met with little cooperation from the apprehensive Tanzanian villagers, to a point where the Tanzanian Ministry of Transport was obliged to call on the villagers to be less suspicious and more helpful. *Sunday News* (Tanzania), 8 June 1969.

93. See, for example, "Chinese Technical Personnel Wholeheartedly Serve World's People," NCNA, 5 March 1968.

94. *Sunday News* (Tanzania), 3 August 1969.

95. See, for example, a *People's Daily* article reprinted in the *Standard* (Tanzania), 9 January 1971.

96. *East African Standard*, 25 July 1966.

colonialism."[97] This, presumably, was a reference to the possible utility of the railway for supplying guerrilla operations in Rhodesia.

While the importance of this aspect of Sino-Tanzanian relations did not diminish, a gradual and subtle change occurred in Peking's attitude to the African revolution and its perception of Tanzania during the late 1960s and early 1970s. The turning point was Nyerere's "Arusha Declaration" of 5 February 1967, in which he set out a blueprint for a Tanzanian society based on socialism and self-reliance.[98] In itself this was little different from many similar but still-born Third World declarations. However, Nyerere soon showed his intention to translate his words into deeds by such actions as the nationalisation of banks and foreign enterprises and the development of "Ujamaa" villages along the principles of village socialism that Nyerere also expounded in 1967.[99] Moreover, the Tanzanian conception of socialism evolved along increasingly radical lines, which included a new emphasis on "internationalism." For example, a TANU party document in 1971, setting out "guidelines on guarding, consolidating, and advancing" the Tanzanian revolution, asserted the principle of "cooperation with all friendly, socialist, revolutionary countries" in the U.N.[100] Peking had seldom, if ever, taken any notice of the "revolutionary" or "socialist" aspirations of non-Communist governments, in which practice it differed from the Soviet Union. However, in the case of Tanzania, it did take notice, and Chinese speeches and articles on Tanzania since the Arusha Declaration consistently and approvingly referred to Tanzania's "economic and national development following the lines of the Arusha Declaration."[101]

Of course, the reason for China's approval is the similarity of Nyerere's social ideas to those operating in China itself. This has caused many to suspect that Peking attained a position in Tanzania that amounts to dominance. In fact Tanzania's independence in domestic policies has been no less than in foreign policy. The origin of Nyerere's ideas on self-reliance and village socialism is not Peking but a period in 1962 when Nyerere resigned the premiership to devote time to working out a conception of the future Tanganyikan society.[102] During this time he read a book by a

97. NCNA, 22 April 1970.
98. *East African Standard*, 6 February 1967.
99. *East African Standard*, 7 July 1967.
100. *African Review*, April 1972, p. 4.
101. NCNA, 5 May 1972.
102. *East African Standard*, 23 January 1962.

French agronomist, Réné Dumont, entitled *False Start in Africa,* which urged the African states to stop looking to the West and industrialisation for the solution to their problems but instead to concentrate on village development.[103] Dumont's ideas confirmed Nyerere's own predilections, and the result of his reflections was essentially the concept of the communal ownership of land. This is not to say that Peking has not been influential—it clearly has—but merely it was not the chief inspirational source of Nyerere's social philosophy. Specific aspects of Tanzanian society have in fact been strongly influenced by the Chinese example, or indeed by Chinese instructors, as was the case of the Tanzanian militia which was established in 1971 in response to Idi Amin's bellicosity.[104]

Peking's evident approval of Tanzania's internal development policies was particularly striking since it originated during the ideological fundamentalism of the Cultural Revolution. Yet, implicit in China's support for the Arusha Declaration was an acceptance of the possibility of Tanzania's *evolution* towards socialism without the need for internal armed struggle or even a Marxist-Leninist party. None of these heretical views has yet been accepted as new orthodoxy by Peking. Nonetheless an indication that Peking's attitude to Tanzania might be tending in this direction was given in 1972, when Chi Peng-fei asserted that Sino-Tanzanian relations were a "fine example of international relations of a new type."[105]

The phrase "international relations of a new type" had hitherto been applied only to relations between socialist countries. Indeed, one article, dating from 1956, had argued,

> Can such new international relations, long desired by the whole world, be developed into the sole relations between all countries? Yes, they can. But it is a thing for the future, not now. For these new international relations can *only* exist between countries where the people hold the state power in their own hands and definitely make it their policy to pursue the socialist path opened by the Soviet Union [emphasis added].[106]

Hence the implication of Chi's remark was that Tanzania was already pursuing the "socialist path," which in turn suggests that Nyerere's com-

103. Interview with Nyerere in *Los Angeles Times,* 31 May 1967.
104. *Standard* (Tanzania), 22 February 1971.
105. NCNA, 20 August 1972.
106. Shih Lu, "The Five Principles in International Relations," *Hsueh Hsi,* 2 January 1956.

ment about China's willingness to help Tanzania's "peaceful revolution" might not have been far short of the truth.

If so, a major "adaptation" on the united front doctrine had taken place. China's aim in Tanzania remained revolutionary, but Peking seemed prepared not only to accept the hitherto unthinkable possibility of a "peaceful revolution" carried out under non-Marxist leadership but to assist in the carrying out of such a revolution. Indeed, it is difficult to see how any other interpretation can explain China's major economic commitment to a state which is not involved in conflicts with the U.S.A. or the Soviet Union (or with any other of China's adversaries), is not one of the most important or largest African states, and has no indigenous Communist party. Other factors, such as Tanzania's possible significance in the Indian Ocean, may have entered into Chinese calculations, as has already been suggested. However, none of these suffices to explain the size, extent, and character of China's involvement in Tanzania.

CONCLUSION

China's general perspective on Africa in the early 1960s seems quite clearly to have derived from the united front doctrine. Peking's basic assumptions about Africa—that it would inevitably develop along the lines of China's revolution, that it would come into collision with "imperialism," that this would give rise to Marxist-Leninist parties, and so on—all suggest a tendency to perceive and evaluate African affairs in the manner outlined in Propositions One to Six of the united front model. Similarly, China's actual policies in Africa suggest that they derived from a strategy that was in turn based on Peking's long-term view of the direction that events in Africa would take (Propositions Seven to Eight). Peking's contacts with leftist opposition forces, Chou En-lai's "special" five principles for Africa, and the timing of China's initiatives in Africa (with increased attention following the Suez crisis,[107] and the Algerian and Congo uprisings) all point to the importance of long-term revolutionary prospects in China's objectives in Africa. Similarly, the fact that the U.S. was not significantly involved in Africa suggests the relative unimportance of strategic and security factors and hence the irrelevance of the alliance model in this case.

107. Said by Chou En-lai to have been "a great revelation to us" (cited in Larkin, *China and Africa*, p. 25).

The initial impetus of China's policy towards Tanzania seems to have derived from Tanzania's support for armed guerrilla movements in Africa, which were seen by Peking as the major instrument for promoting in the long term Marxist-Leninist revolutions. It may be assumed that at this stage the Tanzanian leadership was regarded by Peking as simply another "vacillating" section of the "national bourgeoisie."[108] Certainly its reaction to Dar-es-Salaam's calling in the British army in 1964 suggests this. However, armed revolution in Tanzania itself was not one of Peking's priorities at the time, since far more promising prospects presented themselves in the Congo, Angola, Mozambique, and elsewhere. Hence, Peking probably viewed its relations with Dar-es-Salaam in united front terms on account of the "national bourgeois" nature of the Tanzanian leadership, but this means simply that Tanzania's leaders were regarded as bound to disappear—in the distant future.

Peking's eventual commitment to the "peaceful revolution" in Tanzania involved, as has been argued, a considerable "adaptation" of the united front doctrine. Indeed, despite Peking's clear revolutionary objective during this stage of its relationship with Tanzania (see Proposition 13, united front model), it is doubtful whether the relationship can even be termed a "united front." It lacks, for example, a "dual policy" element as well as any form of "united front from below" with Tanzanian leftist forces. In fact the new relationship defies easy classification. It may be termed a "united front from above," though not in the usual sense denoting common opposition to some *external* enemy, since the relationship actually involved a cooperative venture by two elites in Tanzania's *internal* development.

Since the Sino-Tanzanian relationship was not supported by the development of new, generally applicable Chinese doctrines on "peaceful transition," it is impossible to say whether it reflected a new line on the Third World as a whole or is a unique case. However, Chapter 3 has shown how Chinese statements on the Third World in the 1970s have frequently included verbal backing for "national development" or "economic progress." It may be that China's relative success in Tanzania has provided it with a model for its relations with other Third World states and that cooperation in "peaceful revolution" will become the normal pattern of China's activity in the Third World.

108. In 1961 Peking had privately expressed doubts about even as leftist a regime as that of Lumumba in the Congo (Cheng, *Chinese Red Army*, pp. 179–181).

Conclusion

Two tasks were set in this study: to ascertain the extent to which the united front doctrine has influenced China's foreign policy, and to consider whether China's participation in the international system has led to any "adaptation" of Peking's international united front formulations. A third major aspect is methodological—the attempt to develop a means for systematically examining the relation of ideology to foreign policy.

On the first point, the findings of this study may be summarised as follows. Although elements of the united front doctrine have been present in Chinese Communist appraisals of international affairs since before 1949, it was not until 1960 that an attempt was made to comprehensively translate the united front concept into a strategy for the conduct of China's international relations. During the period 1960–1965, the notion of a "broad international united front," with left, middle, and right components, was one of the guiding concepts of China's foreign policy. Peking seems to have believed that, in the course of time and through a process of education, criticism, and "consciousness raising," the members of the united front would become progressively more radical and assertive in their international stance and that this would create opportunities for Marxist-Leninist forces.

The effect of the united front doctrine on China's actual behaviour, as opposed to official formulations of policy, was fourfold. First, Peking's belief that it was able to forecast the general trend which events would inevitably follow, especially in the Third World, at times led to policies based on long-term projections. Second, Peking's appraisal of specific situations at times was based on preconceptions derived from the CCP's own revolutionary experience. Third, actual policies were often related to overall strategic requirements, and, fourth, Peking's tactics with individual countries and in international forums at times stemmed from a united front perception of world politics.

However, the impact of these four policy applications of the united front doctrine was not distributed evenly across the whole spectrum of China's international relations. China's general approach to Africa and its particular policies in Indonesia were strongly influenced by the doctrine, its policies towards Cambodia and Tanzania rather less so, and its relations with Pakistan not at all. There is no single explanation of these disparities, but rather a specific set of explanations in each case. In Africa, Peking's unfamiliarity with the situation seems to have been largely responsible for its attempt to make African affairs intelligible in terms of the CCP's own experience and to base its policies on unrealistic expectations based on that experience. A predisposition to perceive Africa through ideological spectacles was not, in other words, tempered by experience and knowledge of the African situation. In addition, China did not have, as in Pakistan and Cambodia, clearly definable strategic interests. In Indonesia, the same ideologically derived predisposition was reinforced by the very real and evident strength of the PKI. However, in this case China's policy was far more subtle and soundly based than in Africa, and it was more because of bad luck than misjudgment that its expectations were not realised. In Pakistan and, to a lesser extent, Cambodia the imperatives of China's security clearly overrode ideological considerations. In the case of Pakistan, Peking seems at first to have been reluctant to take the obvious but somewhat cynically expedient course of action after the eruption of its conflict with India, and this may have been in part because of ideologically based inhibitions. Nonetheless, *realpolitik* clearly asserted itself over these initial qualms. Tanzania was not one of China's priorities in Africa until setbacks elsewhere may have given Peking cause to ponder the wisdom of its united front approach there. Hence Tanzania was never the recipient of orthodox "specific united front" policies, and Peking had time to acquire a first-hand understanding of Tanzania on which to base its policies. It will be remembered that China's ambassador there held his position from 1962 to 1967.

That the united front did not really come into its own as a foreign policy strategy until 1960 was clearly related to the developing Sino-Soviet conflict. The cornerstone of China's foreign policy throughout most of the 1950s had been its alliance with the Soviet Union, and with this gone China both needed and was free to work out its own individual perspective on international affairs. In addition China's prestige and its struggle with the Soviet Union inside the Communist movement were bound up with its need to prove the relevance of China's revolutionary experience and doctrines.

Hence, although the rise to prominence of the united front doctrine in the early 1960s reflected a genuine conviction as to its validity, it also derived from power political calculations in the context of the Sino-Soviet dispute. Despite Peking's flexibility in its use of united front policies where clearly definable security interests were involved, it must be said that the united front approach, particularly its "dual policy" aspect, was partly responsible for many of the disasters which befell China's international relations in the 1960s. Nobody likes to be regarded as merely "transitional," and even the suspicion that Peking was attempting to hasten his "transition" would normally be enough to inject a major element of distrust into a Third World leader's perception of China. It was in part the problems that the united front approach engendered for China's state-to-state relations that led to its "adaptation," the other principal cause being the Sino-Soviet rift. This study has shown how tentative "adaptations" were made in 1963–1964 and then, on a much larger scale, in 1968–1971. Although the term "united front" and the belief in the inevitability of revolution remained, in practice the "adapted" version of the united front had as its main thrust the utilisation of all kinds of interstate rivalries and frictions and was thus primarily a "united front from above." To the extent that Peking has turned to conventional power politics in order to pursue its equally conventional conflict with the Soviet Union, to the same extent has Peking become "socialized" into the international system.

A principal impetus of this study was a sense of dissatisfaction with existing works on the relation of ideology to China's foreign policy. Most books and articles on China's foreign policy either dismiss ideology as a significant factor or draw up elaborate (and often excellent) frameworks of general principles under such headings as Mao's "global strategy" or "operational code" without following these with a detailed attempt to assess the *specific* impact of *specific* ideological principles on *specific* policies. To my knowledge, this study represents the first such attempt.

It was clear at an early stage in the research that there were good reasons why most writers were content to leave well alone the question of the precise effect of ideology on foreign policy. Ambiguities and circular reasoning seemed inseparable from such a venture. It was for this reason that the methodological approach of Chapter 2 was devised. By first asking what one could expect to observe in a united front policy, one would provide a detailed model against which China's actual conduct could be assessed. This approach made possible a fresh interpretation of China's policy in Indonesia and some insights into China's policy in Africa as well as the "general line" of China's foreign policy in 1960–1965 and the reasons why this was later "adapted." It was also possible to show that in a number of cases the united front doctrine was clearly *not* an influence. It must be admitted that the ambiguities and uncertainties surrounding the question of the role of ideology in foreign policy have by no means been completely dispelled. Nonetheless, even the limited and partial success of this study suggests that, in Talcott Parsons' words, "the beginnings of an escape from circularity" may be possible, and the approach used here may even offer the beginnings of a methodology for dealing with the problem.

Appendix

Interview with Chang Wen-Chin,
Assistant Foreign Minister, International
Club, Peking, 14 June 1973

This is a transcript from my own notes on an interview between Chang Wen-chin and a group from the Australian National University. Questions were put by W. A. C. Adie, A. Donnithorne, I. Wilson, and myself. Some days before the interview I had sent a number of written questions, set out as follows, to the Chinese Foreign Ministry. Mr. Chang chose to answer some of these in the course of a long reply to the first question put to him.

1. What do you consider to be the basic contradictions in the world today? Is one of these the principal contradiction?

2. A number of Chinese statements on foreign policy have said that a characteristic feature of the world situation today is "global upheaval." Could you explain in more detail precisely what is meant by this?

3. Questions on international united front.

    a. Which countries do you consider must be excluded from the united front?

    b. How would you define China's role in the front?

    c. What do you consider to be the purposes of such a front?

4. What is your opinion of the American idea of a five-power balance-of-power system?

5. What is your opinion of current proposals for the Southeast Asian region?

Q. I have been reading for the last few years many articles that have mentioned Chairman Mao's revolutionary diplomatic line. Some Western observers assert that the main thrust of the line is the containment of Russia. Could you comment on this?

A. I will speak very freely. First of all, how can we view the present situation? We can sum it up in one phrase—global upheaval. Many people think that the Chinese people love turmoil and want to create troubles everywhere in the world. It is already twenty-eight years since World War II. During this time minor wars have not ceased, but there have been no world wars. There have been many dialogues and some détente in the world situation. So the people hope this will continue and that there will be peace and no war. Some people do not properly understand China's war preparedness. We think it is natural for the people to want peace. Of course this is only the subjective wish of the people, but whether objectively the world is moving towards peace, and whether this will be lasting, we have some doubt. So we feel that superficially there has been some détente and wish this to continue, but the actual situation is that there has been no world war, but some parts of the world have been undergoing turbulence since World War II. For example, in Asia there was the Korean War and the war in Indochina. There have been three wars in the Middle East, three wars launched by India in the subcontinent, while in Africa the people's struggle for independence and against foreign subversion has never ceased. In Europe the situation has been tense all the time, although there is now some détente in Europe. Relations between China and the U.S.S.R. are rather tense. So our view is that there has been no world war since World War II, but small wars have never ceased.

The reason for this is that the superpowers desire to control the world. First Dulles tried to extinguish revolutionary war, and then came the Soviet Union which tried to seek hegemony with the U.S. In these years the U.S. overreached its arms and tried to control every place but met with failure. It has aroused opposition all over the world, especially in Indochina. The U.S. sent half a million troops and $100 billion, but in the end had to withdraw. Summing up the past two decades' experience, the U.S. drew the lesson that it would not do to overreach itself and that it had to limit its front. Drastic changes took place in the U.S. position—it dropped 10,000 feet. As Nixon put it, the U.S. never even dreamed of such changes twenty years ago. Now the Soviet Union has emerged and wants to step into its shoes. It is now contending for hegemony everywhere in the world. So in the past few years, the U.S. has been withdrawing from some places, but the Soviet Union has been stepping in. In the East it has practised expansionist policies; in the West it strives to maintain hegemony over Eastern Europe. Its arms have not only reached into continents, especially in the Middle East and the subcontinent, but into sea and air space. So this contention for hegemony had definitely aroused opposition. Wherever there is oppression there is resistance, wherever control . . . [Chang stopped, apparently assuming the quotation was familiar].

Nations want liberation, countries want independence, and the people want revolution. This is an irresistible objective law and a reflection of the nations' opposition to the two superpowers' policy of hegemony. This can be seen in the U.N., where membership has increased from 50 to 120, and which was first controlled by the U.S., then jointly, but now things have turned out so that this is no longer possible. We can also see in the U.N. that a great number of small- and medium-sized countries do not want to be controlled by the superpowers. This can also be seen in this fact: China was kept out of the U.N. Its place is now restored. At that time we did not think it would be so fast, nor did the U.S. think it would be so soon. Later it turned out that so many countries supported us that we had to go there, otherwise we would not live up to their expectations. Chiao Kuan-hua had only ten days to prepare. [The lesson is that] development is independent of one's own will. We saw the general trend but did not think that developments would be so fast.

As for China's policies, you must already be aware of them. We support the revolutionary struggle of the people of various countries, oppose the imperialist policies of war and aggression, and support peaceful coexistence on the basis of the five principles. In the present circumstances a lot of medium and small countries have arisen. Many have won independence—we support their struggle to maintain and consolidate their independence. Those not independent, we support their struggle for independence. There is a common desire not only for Third World countries but also European countries to oppose the superpowers' hegemony. Now the hegemonists and those countries in league with them constitute the main threat.

There are now only two countries in a position to practise hegemony. Nixon has said that there are five forces in the world. Of course in Europe the economic structure is powerful, but there is not yet political unity and in the military field they are dependent on the U.S. Japan is economically powerful, but this is an illusory power because it relies on raw materials from abroad. That is why we say that conditions are not yet ample for Japan and Europe to practise hegemony, whether they have the desire or not. As for China—of course it is an independent and sovereign country, but it is not so strong economically, and in the military field it only aims to defend itself. Also, its policies and the nature of its social system do not allow it to practise hegemony. Only the U.S. and the Soviet Union can practise hegemony in the present circumstances. Both have strong economic and military capabilities both in the conventional and nuclear fields, which they are still developing, and they have also established military bases abroad. As Kissinger put it, there are only two military powers. So if one makes a comparison between these two as to which is the greater threat, this should be viewed from different places and according to different circumstances—in Indochina and Latin America the struggle is mainly against the U.S. This is only natural as, since the Second World War, most parts of the world have been under U.S. control, and although it has shortened its line, some parts are still under U.S. control. But to take it as a whole and see it as a trend, because the U.S. has overreached itself, the Soviet Union takes this advantage to try to reach its arms into various parts of the world. So the U.S. is in a posture of defence, the U.S.S.R. in a posture of offence. So as a whole it has the greater desire for expansion. On the other hand the USSR is more deceitful, because it is waving the banners of so-called socialism, revolutionary war, peace, and collective security. The Soviet Union says it will support you, assist you, send you arms and weapons. Actually it sends its experts to control—weapons were given to Egypt, but they were not allowed to use them without Soviet consent and in certain cases their own personnel were in charge of the weapons. Unlike the U.S., the Soviet Union uses more deceitful means to carry out expansionism. Wherever there is an advantage it will seize it—for example, in Czechoslovakia, even though it was in its sphere of influence. Also in China, there was a treaty of alliance yet the Soviet Union provoked the boundary events and tried to control China. The other means at its disposal is to use the Communist party and self-styled leftists to carry out subversion and control. Also the so-called peace and friendship treaties—which are in fact military alliances to push ahead its aggression. Iraq, India, and Bangladesh are a case in point. So with regard to these hegemonies we consider the Soviet Union more dangerous because it is more deceitful and because quite a few people especially in the Third World cannot see through the Soviet Union. That is why we try to expose it.

With regard to the question of war. What is the reason for China's war preparedness. Superficially there is some détente, but we think that if you want peace, prepare against war. Only preparedness may force the hegemons to ponder a bit before launching war. Otherwise they may launch a surprise attack at any time. Of course in carrying out preparations against war, we do not mean that war will break out right now, but the danger always exists. The reason is that the nuclear forces of both superpowers are still on the rise. Though they talk about the nonuse of armed force or about collective security, these serve only as a camouflage. If vigilance is relaxed, this constitutes the greatest danger. Now the whole nation is carrying out the instruction of Chairman Mao—"dig tunnels deep, store grain, do not seek hegemony." It is easy to store grain everywhere—this is necessary to feed the population. Our grain supplies are increasing, although last year they decreased because of unfavourable weather conditions, but we still tried to build up reserves. Of course we still have to import grains—for example, from Australia. We will seek no hegemony because we consider that this will inevitably arouse opposition. If one seeks no hegemony, it is possible to have friendly cooperation with foreign countries.

Q. When I was in India last year, I was told that several officials were concerned about the growing Soviet influence there, and had recommended an approach to China, but had been informed that this had had no effect. Why?

A. Sino-Indian relations used to be very good in the 1950s, but later because of the exposure of India's expansionist policies we have had to maintain vigilance. The year before last the Indian government made some gestures to improve relations, and we gave these serious consideration, and took some steps to respond—for example, we indicated our willingness to exchange ambassadors, but just then the Indo-Pakistani war broke out. No matter what mistakes the Pakistani government made in East Bengal, we consider this their internal affair. Of course we do not consider the Pakistani policy to have been correct, but India should not have sent troops to dismember the country. That is why at the U.N. Twenty-Sixth General Assembly the issue of Indian aggression caused the greatest repercussions. At that time 104 countries were in favour of a resolution, which was also adopted by the Security Council, for a ceasefire and release of prisoners. India violated this and still keeps 80,000–90,000 Pakistani troops as prisoners. This we can't permit. Since China is in the U.N. and it cast a favourable vote, it will certainly continue to uphold its principles. We just uphold justice in this matter and have no selfish interest.

Q. It was reported in Western newspapers than an envoy sent by President Marcos of the Philippines to China was informed by Chou En-lai that

Lin Piao elements had been involved in the training of cadres for armed struggle in the Philippines. Would you comment on this, and have there been any other incidents?

A. First of all, it is true that the president of the Philippines did send representatives, but not true that we talked about Lin Piao elements. We consider that the affair of the government concerned. [With regard to armed struggle], we express sympathy and support to those opposed to colonial rule and provided moral support and also arms to the Palestinians and also some people from Africa, and for some independent countries we have also provided weapons to help build their defence—for example Pakistan, Vietnam, and Tanzania—but these requests were made by governments. We also send technical expertise to train people to use these weapons. During the Sukarno period we also supplied arms to him, but after the 1965 coup by the rightist junta they took over the weapons and used them against the people and we could not do anything about this.

Q. Could you inform us whether the struggle between two lines after 1969 involved foreign policy as well as domestic policy matters?

A. This was mainly bound up with domestic matters, but there was bound to be some reflection in the foreign policy field because foreign policy is a continuation of domestic policy. It is now very clear that Lin Piao was a careerist, and he certainly tried his best to explore ways of deceiving people. In essence he was a rightist, even though he pretended to be ultraleftist. You all know what happened to Lin. He boarded a plane which then crashed. So why did he try to flee north? Lin Piao pretended to be anti-imperialist, and he advocated down with everything, both at home and abroad, at a time when the revolutionary people were very enthusiastic. Lin tried to provoke tension with friendly countries in Asia, Africa, and Latin America, and he tried to sabotage relations with some European countries. But his role was limited, although there were some effects which were righted very soon. At the time things were not very clear; now they are. This was not simply a question of ideology. He wanted to create trouble everywhere, both at home and abroad. In the past few years a great development has been witnessed in foreign relations due to the implementation of Chairman Mao's line. This shows that the effect of Lin was not very big. Foreigners as well as ourselves can now see this.

Q. Many schemes have been advanced for regional cooperation. What are China's views of these schemes, and what sort of a useful role does China see itself playing?

A. There should be certain conditions before the desire for cooperation is realised. In Indochina there was war, but now an agreement has been concluded. Yesterday a new joint communiqué was signed. We think that this forms the preliminary basis for settlement. But we consider that peace in Vietnam is not stable. There is also the problem of Laos and the continuation of the war in Cambodia. The U.S. refuses to recognise and have direct talks with Sihanouk. Thailand was also involved in the war. In these circumstances it is very difficult to speak of regional cooperation in Southeast Asia. The first step must be a true end to the war. This will lead to a relaxation of tension. If the Southeast Asian countries want regional cooperation, this should be on the basis of independence and equality. Now the Southeast Asian states have raised this slogan. Our understanding is that no big power should interfere in their affairs so that their independence and sovereign rights can be respected. We are in favour of this approach. There is still a U.S. military presence in both Thailand and the Philippines. This is contrary to neutralisation. It is not an easy job for the U.S. to withdraw at once because the Soviet Union tries to involve itself there, so there must be a process [of withdrawal]. Of course we try to involve ourselves, but we are not very strong. W can say only empty words.

Q. Since Liberation there have been many Chinese statements on the formation of an international united front. Could you comment on the purposes of this, and on the role China proposes to play in a united front?

A. We feel that it is the common desire of medium and small countries to oppose hegemony. For this they must be united, so it is our hope to get all forces united. Wherever there is hegemony we will fight it. And we consider ourselves an equal member. We do not intend to become a leader because this is dangerous and we have limited strength. Even if we were strong we would not want to.

I'm sure you have all read the Sino-U.S. joint communiqué in which it was stated that neither should seek hegemony in the Pacific, and they also opposed other countries seeking hegemony. Of course many actions of the U.S. have not been in accordance with this principle, but it is a good thing that they should express the principle. There was a similar clause in the Sino-Japanese communiqué. But what merits attention is that the Soviet-U.S. communiqué did not have such a clause. So in the Pacific the U.S. and Japan have already stated this principle, but not the Soviet Union.

Q. How seriously is the threat of a Soviet attack taken at present? Do you have any thoughts as to when the Soviets might attack?

A. Relations are rather strained at the moment. There have been boundary talks over three years, but with no progress. At the same time they
have placed over one million troops on the border to exert pressure. You
must be aware that transport lines and geographical conditions in this area
are not so favourable [for us]. The Soviet Union has also launched a con-
certed propaganda campaign against China in order to help their internal
situation. As for the particular weight of this possibility and a particular
date, we can hardly assess this. Many friends have told the Chinese side
that if the Soviet Union attacks it will have lost its mind. The U.S. could not
win against Vietnam, and it will be the same here. The Soviet Union would
certainly meet with disaster. So we have the conviction that if the Soviet
troops are in China, even in concert with allies from other directions, we are
prepared. Once in China they will not be able to get out. So we must be
prepared because a war can easily break out if we miscalculate the situation.
We must not assume that the leaders of the Soviet Union necessarily have
common sense.

Q. Are you prepared to receive credit from abroad, and particularly
technical assistance? We have heard about large deposits of offshore oil
being discovered close to China. Will you be developing this in order to
give you export earnings with which to pay for your imports of
technology?

A. We do not want to incur debts. On the question of offshore oil we
have not made a very careful survey yet, nor have we the conditions for
developing it. Our order of precedence is agriculture-light industry-heavy
industry. We have a gradual approach to the development of offshore oil.
The oil will not become angry and run away.

Q. What are your views on the expansion of China's export and import
trade?

A. It is our intention to do this, but to have the intention alone is not
enough. We are trying and redoubling our efforts. The oil has caused us a
lot of trouble, with problems of transport and ports arising. We have a
foundation for exports, but this is not yet systematised.

Q. Will you be increasing tourism in order to earn foreign exchange?

A. We do not promote tourism to make money but it is important not to
lose too much. This is a losing operation in China, which is why we recently
put the prices up. Also we lack expertise.

Index